SETTLING
THE SCORE

795

WISCONSIN
studies in film

General Editors

David Bordwell
Donald Crafton
Vance Kepley, Jr.
Kristin Thompson, Supervising Editor

KATHRYN KALINAK

SETTLING
THE SCORE

MUSIC
and the Classical Hollywood
FILM

The University of Wisconsin Press

The University of Wisconsin Press
114 North Murray Street
Madison, Wisconsin 53715

3 Henrietta Street
London WC2E 8LU, England

Library of Congress Cataloging-in-Publication Data
Kalinak, Kathryn Marie, 1952–
Settling the score: music and the classical
Hollywood film / Kathryn Kalinak.
266 pp.   cm. — (Wisconsin studies in film)
Includes bibliographical references (p. 233) and index.
ISBN 0-299-13360-5 (cloth)   ISBN 0-299-13364-8 (paper)
1. Motion picture music—United States—History and criticism.
I. Title.   II. Series.
ML2075.K34   1992
781.5'42'0973—dc20   92-6853

For my parents,
Emil and Veronica Kalinak,
and my husband,
Ralph Bravaco

CONTENTS

ILLUSTRATIONS

ACKNOWLEDGMENTS

There are numerous people who deserve my thanks and to whom I would like to express my gratitude here.

Several people and institutions have made reference material available to me which was crucial to my task: Leith Adams of the Warner Brothers Archive and the staff of the Cinema-Television Library at USC; Steven Fry and the staff of the Music Library, Brigitte Kueppers and the staff of the Theatre Arts Library, and Victor Cardell of the Archive of American Popular Music, all at UCLA; Martin Silver and Christopher Husted of the Bernard Herrmann Archive at UCSB; the staff of the Margaret Herrick Library of the Academy of Motion Picture Arts and Sciences; Gillian Anderson of the Music Division of the Library of Congress; the late John Hall of the RKO Archives; and Cynthia Turner and the staff of the Music Department at Twentieth Century-Fox Studios.

I would especially like to thank the composers and their families who gave so graciously of their time: Mortimer Wilson, Jr.; Ernst W. Korngold and the late George Korngold; the late Mrs. Max Steiner; John Waxman; David Raksin; Ira Newborn; and David Campbell.

Many others helped to shape the book and encouraged me in the task of writing. Claudia Gorbman, Kristin Thompson, and Alan Williams read the manuscript in its entirety and offered insightful and useful criticisms which, quite simply, made the book better. Direction, suggestions, and review over the years came from Clyde Allen, Rudy Behlmer, Edward Branigan, Alexander Doty, Robert G. Goulet, Sandy Flitterman-Lewis, Anahid Kassabian, Miles Kreuger, Christopher MacGahan, Clifford McCarty, Martin Marks, Rocco Saragosa, Thomas Schleis, Diane Waldman, Charles Wolfe, my colleagues in the Film Studies program, Joan Dagle, Mark Estrin, and Claudia Springer, and my students in the film music courses I have had the pleasure to teach. Christopher Husted provided a meticulous critique of the *Ambersons* chapter and was a helpful and trusted resource for many musical matters in the book. I am grateful to Robert Carringer for prodding me in the direction of film music to begin with, for thoughtful advice at many points in this book's production, and for a detailed reading of the Welles-Herrmann material.

Rhode Island College provided me with several research grants, a summer stipend, a sabbatical leave, and teaching load reductions; its Graphic Services department with indispensible photographic work; and Linda Green in Interlibrary Loan with assistance that exceeded all expectation. David Bondelevitch produced the musical transcriptions. I thank him for his expertise (and patience) not only on the transcriptions but on many musical questions that arose during the course of the book's production. At the University of Wisconsin Press, thanks to David Bordwell and Kristin Thompson for their support and encouragement, and Raphael Kadushin for his commitment to the project.

Two chapters from this book have appeared elsewhere in slightly different form: "Max Steiner and the Classical Hollywood Film Score: An Analysis of *The Informer*" in *Film Music I*, edited by Clifford McCarty (New York: Garland, 1989), 123–42; and "The Text of Music: A Study of *The Magnificent Ambersons*" in *Cinema Journal* 27, 4 (Summer 1988): 45–63.

Special thanks go to two people: Claudia Gorbman, a generous and trusted colleague whose critique of the manuscript proved of inestimable value, and Fred Steiner, whose love of film music and commitment to its study inspired me to plod forward in my own task.

And finally, I wish to thank my husband, Ralph Bravaco: cheerleader, confidant, proofreader, hand-holder, and computer consultant—the wonderful guy to whom my heart belongs.

INTRODUCTION

The composer David Raksin is fond of telling this anecdote about the filming of *Lifeboat* (1944) and its director Alfred Hitchcock:

> One of [Hitchcock's] people said to me, "There's not going to be any music in our picture" and I said, "Why?" "Well, . . . Hitchcock says they're out on the open ocean. Where would the music come from?" So I said, "Go back and ask him where the camera comes from and I'll tell him where the music comes from!" [1]

Raksin's reaction is that of a composer. I wonder how many of us would respond in the same way. Film music is something we usually take for granted. It is that nebulous aspect of the soundtrack that originates somewhere outside the film's story space, a presence we register but don't always notice, a wash of sound to which we respond but whose meaning lies just beyond conscious recognition. Music constitutes a fundamental part of the filmic experience, yet, like Hitchcock, we often fail to acknowledge its importance to the way we perceive film.

Music's dispensability is evident even in higher education. Beginning film students quickly learn the vocabulary to describe a film's image track. The terminology of mise-en-scène, camera position and movement, focal distance, and editing is common currency in the textbooks and courses which introduce film in colleges and universities across the country. Within the last decade there has been a noticeable effort to regard the soundtrack with the same attention, and film students are being exposed in increasing numbers to the concepts and vocabulary necessary to describe the ways in which sound can be constructed. Yet music, one of the most basic components of the cinematic apparatus, is still relegated to marginal status. At present film music lacks even a consistent and precise vocabulary to describe it. Sadly, the vast majority of film students, undergraduate and graduate, will complete their degrees without ever formally studying one of the most powerful components in a filmic system.

The subject of this book is the film music we least notice and most often hear: the nondiegetic music which accompanies a narrative film. Cinema history encompasses a variety of practices which developed to settle the relationship between music and image. The most powerful of these became institutionalized in the Hollywood studio system during the first decade of sound production. In the tradition of David Bordwell, Kristin Thompson, and Janet Staiger's *The Classical Hollywood Cinema*, I use the terms "classical" and "Hollywood" to designate this narrative practice, a label which implies not only a historical designation but a nexus of style, ideology, technology, and economics which coalesced during a particular time and in a particular place.[2]

On its simplest level the classical Hollywood film score, or the classical score for short, can be defined as an institutional practice for the regulation of nondiegetic music in film. By nondiegetic here I mean the music which does not emanate from or occur within the world posited by the film. (It is the music heard by the spectators but not experienced by the characters.) Certainly there are other ways that music functions in a film (in the musical, for instance, music largely operates diegetically, recognized and heard by the characters as well as the spectators), and there are other film music practices which merit attention (the films of Sergei Eisenstein spring immediately to mind). But it is the classical film score, like the classical film itself, that defined a dominant practice. Both imitated and criticized, proclaimed and condemned, the classical Hollywood film score came to represent the norm and as such exerted a powerful influence over the musical accompaniment to films both inside and outside its tradition.

Any system of descriptive classification runs the risk of oversimplification, and labels such as "classical" and "Hollywood" can imply a monolithic and immutable practice. Not only was Hollywood itself a repository of diverse identities, nationalities, visions, and temperaments, but the films it produced were part of an ever-changing process which absorbed new technologies and adjusted to accommodate them. The classical score existed as part of this process. Rather than a prescriptive set of rules for accompaniment, it was a body of conventions which composers drew upon as a resource and a model. Although its practice was so pervasive as to necessitate some recognition of its conventions on the part of composers working in Hollywood (a score which totally ignored its precedent would not have been acceptable), it was not so unilateral as to exclude divergence and innovation (a score might deviate from facets of the model, forging new possibilities for other composers to imitate, adapt, or even ignore).

The body of musical conventions which constitute the core of the classical model derived from the privileging of narrative that characterized classical film itself. First and foremost, music served the story, and the classical score was generated from a set of conventions which insured unobstructed narrative exposition. These included the privileging of dialogue over music; a high degree of synchronization between music and action; the use of music to sustain continuity, particularly during moments when the narrative chain is most tenuous; and the use of music to control narrative connotation.

The following pages comprise an introduction to the study of the classical Hollywood film score as a historical practice. The book is divided into two sections: the first treats musical, theoretical, structural, and historical questions about film music in general and the classical score in particular, and the second offers extended analyses of representative texts. The first chapter serves as an introduction to the film score as music and is intended for those readers who consider themselves "nonmusical." Here I outline some of the problems the study of film music presents to the listener. By offering an analysis of a single cue from Bernard Herrmann's *Vertigo* (1958), I demonstrate how one might begin to think about a film score in musical terms. Since much of this first chapter deals with music on a very basic level, readers with musical training might wish to skip this chapter and resume with Chapter 2. Alternately, as the chapter is entirely self-contained, readers who don't feel confident about confronting music at the beginning can read it at a later stage, perhaps after the second chapter on theory and the third chapter on silent film. Chapter 1 also outlines the problems film music presents to the scholar and critic, defining issues of methodology and terminology that inform the rest of the book.

The second chapter addresses theoretical questions which underlie any discussion of film music and focuses on the visual bias in Western culture that has shaped, and continues to shape, the ways we think about film. By tracing this bias from the origins of acoustics to classical and contemporary film theory, I hope to expose the liabilities of visual priority in constructing a satisfying paradigm for film music's function. At the center of this chapter is an alternative model for the operation of the film score which argues for music's position as an interdependent component in a filmic system.

The third and fourth chapters situate the film score historically. Although it is generally accepted by critics and historians that the classical score derives from its silent predecessor, this perception masks a much more complicated relationship between them. The third chapter offers a structural model of the silent film score in America, analyzing points of confluence with and divergence from the sound film score, while the fourth chapter offers a structural model of the classical score. Using Erich Wolfgang Korngold's *Captain Blood* (1935), I isolate the functions of the classical model and demonstrate how they operate in a specific context.

The remainder of the book is devoted to the integration of theory and practice through individual analyses. Each of these examples has been chosen on the basis of its music, and each represents a different aspect of the classical score. Max Steiner's *The Informer* (1935) epitomizes a hyperbolic version of the classical model, a score which responds to every narrative opportunity with music. Bernard Herrmann's score for *The Magnificent Ambersons* (1942), on the other hand, represents a leaner, more minimalist version, which, although it strains the boundaries of the classical model, is ultimately situated within it. Although the classical score was firmly rooted in late romanticism, it was not impervious to other musical idioms as David Raksin's score for *Laura* (1944) reveals. Incorporating elements of jazz and other forms of popular music, Raksin demonstrates the adaptability of the classical model and its ability to absorb more contemporary musical languages. The last chapter addresses the place of the classical score in contemporary Hollywood. Here I trace the history of scoring practices over the last thirty years, an inquiry which reveals the flexibility of the classical score. Using John Williams' *The Empire Strikes Back* (1980), I analyze the ways in which the contemporary film score has adapted the classical model and the extent to which that model remains a powerful determinant on film scoring today.

The most important aim of this book, however, is diffused throughout its pages: to stir an appreciation of an oft-neglected component of film and to inspire an interest in its study. Film music, as David Raksin reminds us, "makes the difference . . . and there's no doubt about that. All you have to do to get the point of film music across to the skeptical is to make them sit through the picture *without the music*."[3] I hope that by the end of this book, no one would want to.

Part I

Film Music and the
Classical Hollywood Film Score

CHAPTER I

The Language of Music

A Brief Analysis of *Vertigo*

Film music is a stimulus that we hear but, by and large, fail to listen to, a simple distinction that continues to inform the way we experience music in film. As I will argue in Chapter 2, cultural biases that privilege the visual over the aural condition our perception of film music as peripheral to the visual image. The position of film music in the production process (added after the editing) reinforces notions that music is not a significant part of the apparatus that constructs filmic meaning. But there is another reason, and one that I would like to address here, for the prejudice against accepting music as an integral component in the filmic process. Quite simply, few film spectators listen critically.

The skills necessary for critical listening are perceived in our culture as present only in trained musicians. Yet the actual experience of many "nonmusical" readers belies this assumption. Can you recognize a melody (even if it's performed in different versions), whistle or hum a tune, sing "Happy Birthday," keep time to a musical beat, and detect mistakes in performance? These seemingly simple activities require a substantial body of experience with music and a complex set of assumptions about how it operates. I would like to offer a more global model of musical perception, defining music as a construct of the mind, a system whose basic properties are understood, either consciously or unconsciously, by the entire set of individuals in a given culture, not just a few.[1] A trained listener obviously will have more refined tools for experiencing music than a listener without such training, but this is not to say that music is comprehensible only to those who have formally studied it. As music theorist Ray Jackendoff argues, "Musical expertise is essentially a more refined and highly articulated version of an ability that we all share."[2]

My purpose in this introductory chapter is to externalize the most important components in the mental machinery that structures our understanding of music, to offer a context by which to listen as well as hear. This chapter is designed for a reader familiar with the analysis of film but unversed in the basic principles of music. The essay which follows is not a substitute for a musical education. It is a hands-on approach to the film score as music. Because the vocabulary of musical analysis may not be familiar, I define many terms as I use them. (Such terms are denoted by boldface.) I have, however, assumed a certain degree of familiarity with music and recommend that interested readers supply themselves with a dependable music dictionary to accompany their progress through the text.

Musical Language

Film music is above all music, and coming to terms with the filmic experience as a musical experience is the first step in understanding how a film's score wields power over us. I would like to offer a selective analysis of a cue from a classical Hollywood film score, Bernard Herrmann's main title for *Vertigo*, to demonstrate how one might begin to think about a film score in musical terms. (The **main title** refers to the music composed to accompany the opening credits.) Any printed text which attempts to replicate a process from which it is fundamentally different must confront the limitations of the printed word. The case of a text on film music is a pronounced example. There is no substitute for listening to music and I have specifically chosen a text which is widely available as music. I hope that readers will take the opportunity to listen to it. Although I have tried to include musical notation here and throughout the text to stimulate the experience of listening, such notation is not meant to substitute for it.

Music is a coherent experience, and because it is a system of expression possessing internal logic, it has frequently been compared to language. While a linguistic analogy is fraught with difficulty, it does, at least on a preliminary level, help to reveal something fundamental about how music works. Like language and other systems of human communication, music consists of a group of basic units, a vocabulary, if you will, and a set of rules for arranging these units into recognizable and meaningful structures, a grammar. The pitches themselves constitute

the vocabulary of the system and harmony the grammar for organizing them. Like language, music is also a culturally specific system. The
Western world, especially from the eighteenth century through the
twentieth, has organized music around a single note, called the **tonic**,
which serves as a focal point for its structure. "All other pitches are
heard in relation to this pitch and it is normally the pitch on which
a piece must end."[3] **Tonal music** or **tonality**, the system of music
derived from this principle, constitutes *one* possible way of organizing
music. It will, however, be the system of music explored here as it is
the system which forms the basis of the classical film score.

In tonal music, the pitches or notes may be combined horizontally,
that is, in succession, or vertically, that is, in simultaneity.[4] The most
familiar strategy for organizing notes horizontally is **melody**, which can
be defined as an extended series of notes played in an order which is
memorable and recognizable as a discrete unit (hummable, if you will).
One of the most distinguishing characteristics of tonal music since about
the middle of the eighteenth century is the extent to which melody is
privileged as a form of organization. Its presence prioritizes our listening, subordinating some elements to others and giving us a focal point
in the musical texture.

How does melody, as an organizing construct, figure in the main title
of *Vertigo*? It largely doesn't. One of the most identifying characteristics
of *Vertigo*'s score, indeed of most of the Herrmann Hitchcock oeuvre,
is the absence of hummable melody. (Try whistling the shower scene
from *Psycho* [1960] or the main title from *North by Northwest* [1959].)
Herrmann begins *Vertigo* with a musical figure associated in the film with
vertigo itself, alternately descending and ascending arpeggiated chords
played in contrary motion in the bass and treble voices. This may sound
rather technical and somewhat daunting but a quick look at Figure 1.1
may make this description clearer. Notice how in the top part of the
composition, the **treble** voice, the musical notation moves down and
then up, while in the bottom part, the **bass** voice, the musical notation moves up and then down; in other words, they move in opposite
directions or in **contrary motion**. The chords here are described as
arpeggiated because in both the treble and bass voices the notes of
the chord are played in succession (or horizontally) instead of simulta-

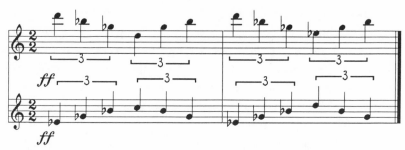

Figure 1.1.
Measures 1–2, *Vertigo*

neously (or vertically). Ultimately, this figure resists definition as melodic (I, for one, have trouble even humming it) in three ways: the contrary directions it incorporates defeat a sense of linearity inherent in the concept of melody; both parts are equally important musically (which one is the "melody," the treble voice or the bass voice?); and the arpeggiated chords themselves are unstable and shifting harmonic constructions.[5] Herrmann's main title for *Vertigo*, as we shall see, is unnerving in the context of tonal music. One of the reasons for the discomfort of the opening is the absence of a conventional melody, which denies the listener the familiar point of access.

Harmony is an equally important component of musical language and one which figures importantly in the *Vertigo* example. **Harmony** can be defined as a system for coordinating the simultaneous use of notes. (Generally, three or more notes sounded simultaneously are known as a **chord**.) Tonal harmony privileges those combinations of notes described as **consonant**, which do not require resolution, over those combinations described as **dissonant**, which do require resolution. Consonance and dissonance underlie tonal music's patterns of tension and resolution enacted through chordal structures that deviate from and ultimately return to the most stable and consonant of all chords in the harmonic system, the **tonic chord**, or a chord built on the tonic note. In tonal music the desire to return to the tonic chord for a sense of completion is so great that to deny it at the end of a piece of music is to constitute an intense disruption. An example of a score that exploits this desire is Michel Legrand's music for Jean-Luc Godard's *Vivre sa vie* (1962). Though tonal, the score fails to offer the tonic chord in each of the dozen times musical accompaniment occurs in the film.[6] Expectation concerning a resolution becomes so strong that at the end of the film, when the tonic chord is missing even from the music which accompanies the closing credits, a common reaction among listeners is to turn to the projector, wondering if a mechanical breakdown or faulty print is the cause of this deliberate act of musical irresolution.

Vertigo is a score which exploits harmony for disturbing effect. Its opening, as we have seen, is formed by arpeggiated chords. I'd like to return to Figure 1.1 and be musically specific for just a moment. These are seventh chords, which include and draw attention to the seventh and least stable note of the scale. Contributing to the dis-ease created by the seventh chords are the intervals constructed by the intersection of the bass and treble voices. An **interval** may be defined as the relationship between any two given notes, measured according to the number of notes that span the distance between them. In this example from Vertigo the opening notes in the bass and treble voices form an extremely grating interval, the major seventh, and the point at which the arpeggiated chords come closest together forms a major second, another dissonant interval. The specifics of the preceding analysis are far less important to remember than the main point: Herrmann has created a harmony to disturb tonality. Royal S. Brown has compellingly argued that the scores Herrmann composed for Hitchcock are distinguished by exactly this kind of "harmonic ambiguity whereby the musical language familiar to Western listeners serves as a point of departure." The extent of this ambiguity is almost immediately discernible to the ear. "Norms are thrown off center and expectations are held in suspense for much longer periods of time than the listening ear and feeling viscera are accustomed to."[7] There is something quite unsettling about listening to Vertigo, and at least part of that something is its harmonic structure.

Musical Affect

The main title for Vertigo is disconcerting in a number of ways, musically speaking. I have been analyzing its basic structure as music, the way it avoids melody as a construct of organization and the way it bends the syntactical "grammar" of harmony. Music, however, means on a number of levels, and like other systems of human communication it is capable of producing meaning outside of itself. Expressivity is not intrinsic or essential to music: yet as any listener can attest music may and often does arouse an emotional or intellectual response. What is the source of music's expressivity, its ability to produce extramusical meaning in its listeners? In a pioneering study published in 1956 musicologist Leonard B. Meyer encapsulates the problem in equating music too closely with a language system.

> Not only does music use no linguistic signs but, on one level at least, it operates as a closed system, that is, it employs no signs or symbols referring to the non-musical world of objects, concepts, and human desires. Thus the meanings which it imparts differ in important ways from those conveyed by literature, painting, biology, or physics. Unlike a closed, nonreferential mathematical system, music is said to communicate emotional and aesthetic meanings as well as purely intellectual ones.[8]

The question of how music can stand for concrete and identifiable phenomena when its method of signification is neither direct nor inherent is one not yet fully theorized. The mechanism by which music encodes meaning has been an object of study in a variety of disciplines including musicology, physiology, anthropology, sociology, cognitivism, psychoacoustics, and psychoanalysis. One of the most popular of these arguments is the one articulated by Deryck Cooke in 1959 which posits the existence of precise relationships between intervals and emotions. For instance, the major third connotes "joy," while the minor third, "stoic acceptance, tragedy."[9] More recently, cognitivists have theorized musical affect as the result of a response to musical structure. Arguing along lines laid out by Meyer, Ray Jackendoff suggests that musical affect is "a function of being satisfied or surprised by the realization or violation of one's expectations."[10] Jackendoff's argument is predicated upon the premise that perception is largely unconscious and that in some sense we are "*always* hearing the piece [of music] for the first time."[11]

Regardless of its source, music's ability to produce specific effects is undeniable. One of the most demonstrable of the ways in which music can have a definite, verifiable, and predictable effect is through its physiological impact, that is, through certain involuntary responses caused by its stimulation of the human nervous system. The most important of these stimulants—rhythm, dynamics, tempo, and choice of pitch—provide the basis of physiological response.

The power of rhythm has frequently been traced to primitive origins, music "borrowing" from human physiological processes—heartbeat, pulse, breathing—their rhythmic construction. **Rhythm** organizes music in terms of time. The basic unit of rhythm is the **beat**, a discernible pulse which marks out the passage of time. Since the Renaissance, rhythm has been characterized by regular patterns of beats, usually composed of groups of twos or threes. The term **meter** refers to the way these units are used to organize the music, providing a kind of sonic grid against which a composer writes. Western art music is characterized by a high degree of regularity in terms of both rhythm, that is, the patterns themselves, and meter, that is, their organization. Regular rhythms, perhaps because of their physiological legacy, and certainly because of the way they have been conventionalized, can be lulling and even hypnotic because of the familiarity created through their repetition. Irregular or unpredictable rhythms attract our attention by confounding our expectations and, depending on the violence of the deviation, can unsettle us physiologically through increased stimulation of the nervous system.

In *Vertigo* Herrmann confuses a clear perception of rhythm. The metrical organization of the main title is a **duple** meter, or one in which there are two beats to the measure. Conventionally, such a meter would cause the primary accent to fall on the first beat of each measure, creating a rhythm of alternating accented and unaccented beats (something like a trochee in English metrical verse). And, in fact, for most of the main title, the first beat carries the accent. At certain points, however, Herrmann displaces this point of emphasis for disturbing effect. In measures 12 to 15, for instance, he begins a restatement of the arpeggiated chord in the flutes on the second beat of the measure, instead of the first, which disturbs the pattern. Notice the presence of a **rest**, the musical notation for silence, ====-=== at the beginning of the first measure in both Figure 1.2 and Figure 1.3. Herrmann emphasizes this

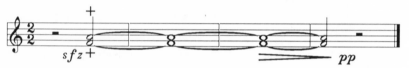

Figure 1.2.   Copyright 1958 Famous Music Corporation
Measures 12–15, *Vertigo*

Figure 1.3.   Copyright 1958 Famous Music Corporation.
Measures 12–15, *Vertigo*.
The " + " directs the player to muffle the sound, usually by placing the hand in the bell of the instrument.

displacement through the use of the **sforzando** (sfz), a sudden, loud attack on a note or chord, on the second beat in the horns (Fig. 1.3). Besides avoiding identifiable melody and flirting with tonal ambiguity, the opening moments of the score exploit the effects of an unpredictable rhythmic change which contributes to the agitation many listeners feel in hearing this cue.

The most obvious way in which music or any type of sound can elicit a direct response is through its **dynamics**, or level of sound. Volume reaches the nervous system with distinct impact, increasing or decreasing its stimulation in direct proportion to its level. Extremes in sound are the most noticeable dynamic because of their pronounced divorce from the natural sound level of everyday life. Extremely loud music can actually hurt the listener, while extremely soft music tends to drop out of the range of human perception. **Crescendos** and **decrescendos**, or the increase and decrease in the volume of sound, respectively, help to modulate the stimulation and can be used to heighten or diminish it. Quick and unexpected changes in dynamics intensify this process.

Herrmann's main title clearly demonstrates the effect of volume. By juxtaposing **fortissimo** (very loud) and **pianissimo** (very soft) both successively and simultaneously, Herrmann creates discernible effects in us. Listen for the change in dynamics at the beginning of the main title. Measures 1–8, for instance, contain six measures (1–6) of sustained *fortissimo* (denoted ff) followed by only two measures (7–8) to decrease the sound level to *pianissimo* (denoted pp). Although this passage contains a *decrescendo* to help modulate this change, the asymmetry, if you will, of the sound dynamics keeps us off guard musically.

Tempo modulates the speed with which a piece of music is performed. Quick tempi tend to intensify stimulation of the nervous system; slow tempi tend to dissipate it. Diverging from a characteristic pace can also cause a physiological response. The **accelerando** and **ritardando**, a speeding up and slowing down of the musical pace, respectively, help to control such response, heightening, sustaining, or diminishing it.

In the main title of *Vertigo* the tempo is basically regular (Herrmann marks it "*Moderato Assai*" in his score), but it does incorporate a sudden change in its second half which has the effect of doubling the tempo. Near the end of the main title (at measure 53 to be exact) the arpeggiated chord is heard twice as fast as its previous occurrences. Herrmann has accomplished this effect by cutting each note value in half. Where the motif had initially taken a full measure to perform in the violin part (Figure 1.4A), it can now be performed twice in the same amount of time by the harps (Figure 1.4B).

Even choice of pitch can elicit response. Herrmann frequently manipulated pitch to create anxiety. The shower scene in *Psycho*, for instance, is scored for violins; the players execute upward *glissandi* culminating in the highest note in the pitch system. In the scene which precedes it, notes of extremely high pitch erupt out of the musical tapestry often an octave or more above the musical line which precedes or follows them. In the main title of *Vertigo* a six-note rising and falling figure is played high in the violins' register. It is set off against the extremely low pitch of the tubas, not only exploiting the effect of pitch

Figure 1.4.A   Copyright 1958 Famous Music Corporation
Measures 51–52, violin part, *Vertigo*

Figure 1.4.B   Copyright 1958 Famous Music Corporation
Measures 53–54, harp part, *Vertigo*

but combining it with the dis-ease created by splitting the listener's attention between widely divergent musical registers.

Musical Conventions

One of the best ways to understand the power of music is to study the conventions by which musical affect circulates through a culture. A musical convention harnesses musical affect to specific and concrete meaning through the power of association. Musical conventions which become ingrained and universal in a culture function as a type of collective experience, activating particular and predictable responses. In tonal music, for example, an **habanera** rhythm ▓▓▓ is a musical convention which summons up thoughts of Spain. Harmonic structures such as open fourths and fifths are used to represent ancient Greece and Rome. Quartal harmony, based on the interval of the fourth, suggests the Orient. To an overwhelming extent, the classical score relied upon such conventions. Composers, working under the pressure of time, used familiar conventions to establish geographic place and historical time, and to summon up specific emotional responses predictably and quickly. The fact that musical conventions are often arbitrary seems of little consequence. The *habanera* rhythm associated with Spain is actually of Cuban origin (via a French composer); the open fourths and fifths associated with the classical age are modern conjecture; quartal harmony is not used exclusively in music of the Orient. But for all their lack of authenticity, conventions are nonetheless powerful.

The classical Hollywood film score relied largely on the resources of the standard symphony orchestra with unusual instruments added for particular effects. Thus at its disposal was a veritable arsenal which could be tapped to activate specific associations. The string family, for instance, because of its proximity in range and tone to the human voice, is thought to be the most expressive group of instruments in the orchestra. For this reason strings are often used to express emotion. In particular, the violin is characterized by its ability to "sing" because its **timbre** or tonal quality is close to that of the human voice. In the opening sequence of *God Is My Co-Pilot* (1945), for example, Franz Waxman uses violins to add emotional resonance explaining, "[for a] deeply religious, emotional tone . . . I used massed violins playing in a high register to convey the feeling." [12] Herrmann, on the other hand, in *Psycho*, exploits these associations for ironic effect: the entire score of this chilling thriller, one of Hitchcock's grisliest films, is composed for a string orchestra.

Horns, with their martial heritage, are another obvious example. Because of their link to pageantry, the military, and the hunt, horns are often used to suggest heroism. Says Henry Mancini, "The most effective and downright thrilling sound is that of all of the [brasses] playing an ensemble passage." [13] Erich Wolfgang Korngold, who was known for his use of brass instruments, exploits a complement of horns for the rousing main title of *Captain Blood*. John Williams relies on horns in the epic *Star Wars* trilogy to suggest the heroic nature of this futuristic saga. Even a contemporary score like *RoboCop*'s (1987) exploits the conventional associations of the horns, using different combinations of brass instruments to accompany the death-defying deeds of the robocop.

Rhythm, like instrumentation, can also provoke specific responses. Dance rhythms, in particular, can be very evocative. Thus, when Herrmann in *The Magnificent Ambersons* characterizes the Ambersons with a waltz, he is employing a familiar convention to project the sense of grace and gentility that the family symbolizes. When Waxman bases the theme music for Norma Desmond in *Sunset Boulevard* (1950) on a tango, he is characterizing her as steamy, sultry, Latin, and in 1950, conspicuously out of date. Carlotta's theme in *Vertigo* exploits the fiery and passionate associations of the *habanera* rhythm, transferring to the icy exterior of Kim Novak's fragile Madeleine the sensuality of her psychic ancestor, Carlotta. Musical conventions are profuse and can even be intercepted by a personal response, but to overlook their effect is to ignore the power of collective association in human perception. Film music, when it taps this source, is appealing to a strong response that can impact spectators whether they are consciously aware of it or not.

A crucial site for the acquisition of a culture's musical conventions is the cinematic auditorium itself where musical effects are combined with visual imagery to reinforce them. In fact, for spectators who are basically unversed in art music, films are the major site for the transmission of a culture's musical conventions. The association of **tremolo** strings (the sustaining of a single note through rapid repetition) with suspense, for instance, is a response acquired, in all likelihood, not from an acquaintance with the musical idiom of the nineteenth century, where it is earlier exemplified, but from film scores which exploit it. One of the most interesting aspects of Herrmann's score for *Vertigo* is the way it avoids the most obvious musical convention for suspense, *tremolo* strings, and exploits subtler techniques for the creation of tension such as harmonic instability, shifting and unpredictable rhythm, tempo, and dynamics, and absence of conventional melody.

Music and Image

Our experience of music in film is shaped by both its constitution as music and its function as an aural accompaniment to visual images. Film music shares with music composed for performance in the concert hall its basic underlying structure as music as well as its power of expressivity. But film music is part of a dual discourse which incorporates both an aural and a visual component. The first step in an analysis of film music is to hear it as music; then it becomes necessary to analyze it as a part of a larger construct, that is, to analyze film music in conjunction with the image and sound track it accompanies. Issues involved in the relationship between music and image and the theory that underlies it are treated in more depth in the following chapter. Let me here simply point to the nature of that relationship and its consequences for the *Vertigo* example.

Film music obviously does not exist in a vacuum. It shares with the image track (and other elements of the soundtrack) the ability to shape perception. Film music's power is derived largely from its ability to tap specific musical conventions that circulate throughout the culture. But that power is always dependent on a coexistence with the visual image, a relationship bounded by the limits of credibility itself. Imagine a perfectly innocuous setting, an eighteenth-century drawing room where two lovers are reunited after numerous narrative complications. But instead of a soaring melody played by an offscreen orchestra, we hear *tremolo* strings and dissonant chords. Our tendency as spectators would be to perceive that music as meaningful, specifically to read the scene as suspenseful. We might even expect some kind of narrative complication or even a visual shock because of the music. If these expectations are thwarted, most spectators would feel manipulated, even cheated. Craig Safan, a contemporary film composer, explains it in these terms: "You excite an audience in a certain way and if you betray them they won't want to see your movie. And musically, you can betray your audience. You have to be very careful about that."[14] Music and image collaborate in the filmic process. The farther music and image drift from a kind of mutual dependency, the more potential there is for the disruption or even destruction of the cinematic illusion.

The music for the main title of *Vertigo* plays out against a series of brightly colored geometric spirals which spin against a black background. Hitchcock films often give Herrmann's main title free rein by overtly drawing attention to the music through abstract visual constructions. (*Psycho* and *North by Northwest* are two other examples.) In *Vertigo* the correspondence between the circularity of these images and the film's title is obvious, but it is equally important to note the relationship between these images and Herrmann's music. *Vertigo*'s opening consists of alternately descending and ascending arpeggiated chords played in contrary motion in the bass and treble voices. At this point I would like to define it as a **motif**, a distinctive musical passage that is repeated (and varied) throughout a musical text. This motif progresses in time without establishing a clear direction (neither up nor down) or, as discussed earlier, a clear harmony (hovering dangerously close to an abnegation of tonality). It is an almost uninterrupted undulation from beginning to end. This quality of the music is, interestingly enough, reflected graphically in its very notation. It is Herrmann's mesmerizing evocation of dizziness. Spinning in time with the spiraling geometric forms, the motif reinforces and is in turn reinforced by the vertigo suggested by the images.

Musical Texts

Before I conclude this chapter, I would like to add a brief section on the nature of documentary evidence in the study of film music and the problems the discipline faces working with a variety of widely scattered, sometimes inconsistent, frequently inaccessible, and often missing primary material. A basic enterprise of criticism involves determining and authenticating sources: excluding variants, authenticating versions, even attributing authorship. The criticism of film music faces a formidable barrier. As the opening essay in a recent anthology on film music argues, "There exists in the world today a huge body of contemporary music for which there is virtually no bibliographic control, very limited or nonexistent access, and only the most minimal attempts at preservation." [15] More critically, an acceptable or even consistent nomenclature for the evidence at hand has yet to be adopted. The final section of this chapter identifies the types of evidence that exist in the field and defines the terminology I use.

The film score exists in its primary form as the musical portion of a film. As such it is experienced in time as a component of a larger textual system. Secondary forms of the film score exist as both recordings and manuscripts. (At this point in time I do not know of any Hollywood film score that exists, in its entirety, in published form.) The most accessible recording is the commercially released phonograph record, tape, or disc containing selections from a film's score. These recordings are known by the somewhat misleading label of **soundtracks**. Although interesting for the opportunity they afford to hear a film's music without competition from dialogue or sound effects, soundtracks are of minimal value to the researcher. Their authenticity is questionable. The music heard on soundtracks may be arranged expressly for commercial purposes. Soundtracks may even contain material not heard in the film. The original **music tracks** which preserve, on a variety of formats, the actual studio recording sessions provide a more reliable record. Unfortunately, music tracks are uncatalogued, frequently missing, often of poor quality, and largely inaccessible.

The film score also exists as a manuscript in the form of musical notation on a piece of paper. Unlike film critics who have at their disposal an agreed upon terminology for transcription of visual elements, film music critics are dependent upon a system of musical transcription which by its very nature is variable.[16] Thus for critics of film music a manuscript version of the score is crucial. Many manuscripts remain in the hands of the studios and at present are unreliably catalogued and difficult to access. The few directories of musical holdings in libraries and archives are useful but limited.[17] To compound problems, institutional catalogues of film music archives are sketchy and sometimes even inaccurate. The researcher is often reduced to a scholarly equivalent of hunt and peck, with frustrating results. The union catalogue proposed by the Society for the Preservation of Film Music is a sorely needed and eagerly awaited addition to the discipline.

In Hollywood, film scores exist in a variety of manuscript forms. A **sketch** is a rudimentary rendering of musical intention, sometimes consisting of melody and simple annotations for orchestration, sometimes more elaborate. Because of the restrictions imposed on composers by time, the sketch would frequently be passed on to other members of the music department for completion. The sketches of someone like Max Steiner, because of his close working relationships with his orchestrators and the extraordinary demands made on his services by the studio, often are rough. (See page 74 for a page from his sketch for *King Kong*.)

The **full score**, often simply referred to as the score, is the fully orchestrated version that is heard in the film. (See page 18 for a page from Herrmann's full score for *Vertigo*.) In Hollywood, the full score

From Bernard Herrmann's autograph score for *Vertigo*. Since Herrmann orchestrated his own music, the autograph copy is also a full score. Although Herrmann generally avoids *tremolo* strings in the main title, he does use them in the opening measures. *Tremolo* is denoted by the slash marks on the note stems in the violin part.

was frequently the product of more than one agent, a combination of composer, orchestrator or orchestrators, copyist or copyists, and possibly an arranger or arrangers. Breaking down the full score into its instrumental components (violin, flute, cello, etc.) yields **parts**, the music recopied for individual instruments in the ensemble. Sometimes all copies of the full score have been lost or destroyed, and the music for a film will exist only in parts. Such is the case with Edmund Meisel's score for *The Battleship Potemkin* (1925). Although a complete version has not been found, orchestral parts were discovered, and from these a full score could be reconstructed.[18]

The **piano conductor part**, also known as the **conductor part**, and sometimes the **short score**, is yet another version of a film score. This term refers to a reduced version of the full score, often used for conducting the recording session. (See pages 180–81 for a page from the piano conductor part of David Raksin's *Laura*.) Finally a score in any of its variants can also be an **autograph**, a copy written in the composer's own hand. (This is also known as a **holograph**.) An autograph copy can be as simple as a sketch or as complete as a full score depending on the individual circumstances of a score's creation.

The text which follows incorporates a variety of the evidentiary forms enumerated here. Whenever possible I have included as part of the analytic process all the source material known and available to me including sketches, full scores, conductor parts, and autograph copies, as well as production records, oral histories, and personal interviews. Reference citations include location and condition of all sources in the hope that others will find their way to this material.

CHAPTER 2

A Theory of Film Music

What is music's power in film, and what is the relationship between its power and that of the image? How does music function in the processes that construct film? What is its relationship, for instance, to narrative? What makes film music so compelling? What are the pleasures that listening to it offers, and what is the source of these pleasures? In short, how can we begin to account for the hows and whys of film music? This book offers a historical and structural study of one particular type of film music, the classical Hollywood film score. Yet it would be an incomplete study at best that neglected the theoretical assumptions underlying its approach and disregarded the deeper issues that motivate these assumptions. This chapter then is designed to confront the fundamental issues in film music, the hows and whys, if you will. As such it has a dual purpose: first, to find and articulate a satisfying theoretical paradigm for the operation of film music, and second, to seek strategies for coming to terms with music's unique hold over us as spectators of the visual image.

A historical survey of both classical and contemporary theories of the soundtrack, especially those which treat film music, reveals the extent to which the visual bias of the culture is reproduced in the ways we think about film. From the most commonplace clichés (seeing is believing) to the syntax and vocabulary of our language, seeing is a more precise and varied experience than hearing. The eye's sensory apparatus functions with the immediacy of the light rays which it uses to identify the stimulus. The ear functions with the acuity of prolonged stimulation; its perception is based on sensitivity to the motion of sound waves which require duration. But the distinction between them has continually been distilled into the superiority of the eye over the ear as a perceptual mechanism.

As I hope to demonstrate, classical film theory reproduces this bias, prioritizing the visual at the expense of the aural, and rendering problematic an uncritical adoption of its central and highly influential paradigm for the relationship between sound and image: the transcendent power of the image and the dependence of the soundtrack. The authority of this paradigm is nowhere more evident than in classical theory's position on film music. Assumptions about the relationship of the visual and the aural were extrapolated to the musical portion of the soundtrack, constituting a virulent model for thinking and writing about film music that continues to be used even today. Such a model, however, both reflects and masks certain ideological assumptions about the ways we see and hear, assumptions which infuse the history of sonic investigation.

The origins of acoustics demonstrate an ideology of visual and aural perception mapped onto the body, an inscription manifested initially in the writings of the ancient Greeks and sustained in scientific discourse until the advent of modern acoustics in the nineteenth century. Ancient theories of cognition clearly differentiated between the ear and the eye. The ear was a receiving site in sound transmission which functioned as a conduit to the actual place of cognition, the soul. As Plato explained: "We may in general assume sound to be a blow which passes through the ears, and is transmitted by means of the air, the brains, and the blood, to the soul, and that hearing is the vibration of this blow, which begins in the head and ends in the region of the liver [the seat of desire]."[1] The ear was often represented in terms of its emptiness. Alcmaeon described it as an "empty space" which resonates sound to the soul. Democritus termed it "a cavity"; Aristotle, a "void."[2] Empedocles used the analogy of "the 'bell' of a trumpet, ringing with sounds like those it receives."[3] According to Anaxagoras the vibrations were then conducted from the ear through the bones, which were themselves hollow.

In contrast, the object to which the eye was most often compared was the sponge. The eye was absorptive and porous, containing matter (variously, combinations of air, water, and fire) capable of rudimentary processing of sensory input. To the Greeks, the eye contained a rudimentary cognitive apparatus which facilitated the processing of knowledge about the outer world; the ear did not. This difference was inscribed with value: visual perception was not only faster than aural perception but more reliable. Heraclitus echoes the thought of both

Plato and Aristotle when he claims: "Eyes are more accurate witnesses than are ears."[4]

On the other hand, because the passage of sound was unencumbered by any intervening mechanisms, the ear was represented as having direct and unmediated access to the soul where emotional response originated. Hearing, more than any other sense, activated emotion. Aristotle maintained that "hearing alone among the objects of sense . . . affects the emotional temperament of the hearer."[5] Theophrastus put it more simply: "Hearing is the sense that most deeply stirs our emotions."[6] Music, which was free of what Aristotle termed "the meaning" attached to speech, and heightened by gifts from the Muses—harmony and rhythm—was thought to be the purest form of sound, and thus the most potent elicitor of emotional response. Thus, already in place in the ancient world was a paradigm for understanding sensory perception which connected the eye to the ordering structure of consciousness and posited the ear as free from such mediation.

Major challenges to the ancient model of cognition awaited the age of the experiment (generally, after the Renaissance, about the sixteenth century). The Middle or so-called Dark Ages had little to add to the classical model. Of course the Dark Ages are dark only when seen through the prism of Western ethnocentrism. The Arabic world largely sustained discourse on acoustics, not only preserving and translating but also refining Greek treatises on sound. It is interesting to note in the convergence of the Arabic and Greek thought the same model for aural transmission and a similar physiological representation for the reception of music. Theologian al-Ghazzali in the twelfth century writes: "There is no way to the extracting of their [hearts'] hidden things save by . . . listening to music and singing, and there is no entrance to the heart save by the antechamber of the ears."[7]

A revealing variable in antiquity's discourse on acoustics is the source of the mechanism which initiates the perceptual process. The definition of natural science in antiquity differs considerably from the modern conception of scientific inquiry. Rather than a foundation of information universally agreed upon, to which new information consonant with it is added, ancient science simultaneously embraced a variety of theories, some of them conflicting. The validity of a position depended on the rhetorical skill with which it was argued. There is a compelling consistency in the discourse on acoustics with regard to perception once a stimulus entered the body. But there is disagreement over the forces which initiated this mechanism. At issue is the nature of perception itself, and debate centered around whether it was initiated at a point exterior to the body or whether it issued from the interior of the body. In fact, perception was often represented as a flow of arrows sometimes inward and sometimes outward from the body to the object of perception. With the reconstitution of the self during the Renaissance this variable would be transfixed with a specific direction—outward. Note the way that the invention of perspective by fifteenth-century architect and artist Filippo Brunelleschi is described by a contemporary historian: Brunelleschi "envisaged himself as a kind of camera. He assumed that objects are perceived by means of a pyramid or cone of visual rays extending from the eye out into the world." [8]

It was in the fertile ground of the nineteenth century's scientific revolution that acoustical research blossomed. Georg Ohm's theory of audition was published in 1843, followed by the work of Hermann Helmholtz, Edward Gurney, and John William Strutt, Lord Rayleigh, among others. The limitation of subjective observation which had fettered acoustics since its inception was transcended by a combination of the experimental method and the development of calculus. By the end of the nineteenth century a fundamental theory of audition was in place, the basis of acoustical research to this day. Yet there remains around the edges of the written discourse (introductions, chapter summaries, and conclusions) the residue of the ancient model.

Specifically, nineteenth-century acoustical research sustained a model of sensory perception which connected the eye more closely to the mediating structure of consciousness than it did the ear. In the introduction to *On the Sensations of Tone*, for instance, Helmholtz claims that visual art appeals to the intellect because the physical stimuli it provides must be translated into images. On the other hand, aural art, and in particular music, "stands in a much closer connection with pure sensation than any of the other arts" because it is directly apprehended "without any intervening act of the intellect." [9]

Edward Gurney in *The Power of Sound*, published in 1862, begins his

study with similar considerations: exploration of the aesthetic consequences attached to differences in the perceptual mechanisms of the
eye and the ear. The perception of form (which Gurney asserts is necessary to the appreciation of Beauty) is dependent upon "a combining
and coordinating faculty on . . . elementary sense-impressions." In the
eye, such "supervention of the higher faculties" takes place "*habitually,*"
while in the ear this supervention or "discrimination" takes place only
"exceptionally." [10] For Gurney vision passes through "a combining and
coordinating faculty," the mediating force of consciousness; the ear's
perceptions may or may not. Part of Gurney's aesthetic project then
becomes the investigation of a sonic analogue for visual beauty which
is, not surprisingly, music.

The scientific discourse of the nineteenth century, in fact, casts into
relief the ideological subtext driving acoustical investigation: the value
of objectivity over subjectivity. The mediating force of consciousness in
the act of vision serves to objectify the information processed through
it, while the act of hearing is more suspect because of its stronger connection to subjectivity. Gurney, for instance, argues that "the things we
see gain a quite unique character of objectivity and permanence." [11] The
connection between music and subjectivity became part of the intellectual currency of nineteenth-century romanticism. Perhaps its most
virulent expression can be found in the writings of Richard Wagner
who asserted that music was accorded the power to express emotion
"quite independent of the restraint of logical laws of thought." [12] In fact,
one of the most distinguishing characteristics of the history of acoustics
is the prevalence of the collateral beliefs that consciousness mediates
vision more directly than it mediates hearing and that such mediation
functions to objectify the information it processes.

This historical legacy formed the foundation of classical film theory.
The language that classical theorists used to describe the operation of
the soundtrack coalesced around two key terms that reveal implicit
assumptions of visual ascendancy and aural subordination. Sound was
divided according to its function in relation to the image: either parallel or in counterpoint to the visual image. Such nomenclature assumes
that meaning is contained in the visual image and that sound can only
reinforce or alter what is already there. Classical film theory found the

terminology and a rationale for this model in Soviet formalism, primarily the writings of Sergei Eisenstein and V. I. Pudovkin. Frequently quoted in this context is the "Statement on Sound Film," one of the earliest theoretical texts to use the concept of counterpoint: "ONLY A CONTRA-PUNTAL USE of sound in relation to the visual montage piece will afford a new potentiality of montage development and perfection." [13] These concepts take on a controlling presence in classical film theory, providing both the terminology and the methodology for its analysis of the soundtrack.

Classical theory's position on film music mirrors its discourse on the soundtrack. Concerned largely with methods for assessing the appropriateness of specific music for particular images, classical theory turned again to parallelism and counterpoint. Rudolf Arnheim, for instance, appeals to the example of the art song as proof that unity in art is the result of parallelism: "music and speech can be combined only when a parallelism between two complete and segregated components—a poem and a melody—is provided." [14] This is why music "completes" the silent film so effectively: "it vigorously transmits the feelings and moods and also the inherent rhythm of movements [in] the visual performance." [15]

Béla Balázs similarly relies on the concepts of parallelism and counterpoint to describe the functions of film music.

> Thus the sound film in its most recent development no longer seeks to illustrate passions seen in the pictures, but to give them a parallel, [and] different musical expression. The visible reflection in the picture and the audible manifestation in the music of the same human experience thus run parallel without being dependent upon each other.[16]

Like Arnheim, Balázs is seeking a vocabulary for the musical dimension of film. But his use of two key terms, parallelism and counterpoint, reveals their basic inadequacy as descriptors of the soundtrack. In the quotation above, for instance, the very meaning of parallelism shifts from one sentence to another.

Siegfried Kracauer in his classification of the uses of sound posits the concepts of parallelism and counterpoint as points on either end of a continuum. Kracauer's attempt to subject music to the same model is fraught with the visual bias incorporated by Arnheim and Balázs. Kracauer sets parallelism, defined as "music [which] restates, in a language of its own, certain moods, tendencies, or meanings of the pictures it accompanies" in opposition to counterpoint with its "alien motifs—alien to what the images themselves convey."[17] "In the case of parallelism the film maker is bound to have the music duplicate what the pictures impart, while in the case of counterpoint he is at liberty to assign to it all possible functions and tasks."[18] For Kracauer, as for Arnheim and Balázs, a film's meaning, ultimately, is contained in "what the pictures impart."

Popular writing on the subject is infused with this model, particularly the spate of texts on film music published in the seventies and early eighties.[19] Techniques of film scoring have been subjected to a system of classification in which they either parallel or counterpoint the visual image. Parallelism, generally dismissed as merely duplicative, has become a watershed for all scoring practices which match visual and aural information. (The most obvious type of parallelism is **Mickey Mousing** which matches the beat of the music to physical action in the image.) Counterpoint, on the other hand, has been used to describe music which does not duplicate visual information. Music which foreshadows, undercuts, provides irony, or comments upon situation or character has been termed contrapuntal.

Even contemporary film theory, which has abandoned the concepts of parallelism and counterpoint, is subject to the culture's visual bias. Unlike classical film theory, contemporary film theory has addressed itself to issues of ideology, revealing that the image is not a duplication of the experiential world but a representation of it, structured by a complex set of relationships between the cinematic apparatus and the spectator and between the spectator and the image. Yet contemporary theory is still under the sway of an ideology which privileges the visual when it comes to the soundtrack, where there remains a tendency to perceive sound as an unmediated discourse. As Tom Levin points out, contemporary theory shares the "*short-sightedness*" of the culture at large. Citing Stanley Cavell, Christian Metz, and Jean-Louis Baudry, among others, Levin argues that in "the ideological critique of the cinematic apparatus the focus was once again on the visual at the expense of the acoustic, neglecting as a result, to submit the reproduction of sound to the scrutiny afforded the technology of the visible." What Levin calls for is just such an enterprise, "a critique of the acoustic apparatus." [20]

Levin's critique has yet to be fully realized within contemporary film theory although its terrain was mapped out decades ago by Theodor W. Adorno. In *Introduction to the Sociology of Music* and in his collaboration with composer Hanns Eisler *Composing for the Films*, Adorno examines the filters which mediate aural perception, the physiological as well as the sociological mechanisms through which the ear processes raw stimuli.[21] Adorno and Eisler offer a critique of the visual bias inherent in postindustrialized society. Reversing the terms of the nineteenth century's equation of sight with objectivity and sound with subjectivity, Adorno and Eisler argue that visual bias in advanced capitalism is the result of the way society constructs reality through material goods. The eye "has become accustomed to conceiving reality as made up of separate things, commodities, objects." [22] It is trained to be selective and active and is associated with valued concepts in the postindustrial world: the objective, the definite, and the verifiable. Hearing, on the other hand, does not establish the same relation to the material world. "The phenomena it transmits are not the phenomena of things. . . . Hearing neither establishes a transparent relation to the world of things . . . nor can it be controlled from the standpoint of this work. . . ." [23] As a result, the ear finds it more difficult to perceive separate objects, and thus it is not as crucial to the perpetuation of postindustrialized society's value system as the eye. Because the ear is indefinite and passive, it is better able to resist the rationalization of commodity culture and can embody a regression toward a nonobjective perception. Adorno, however, with characteristic pessimism, points out that hearing fails to fulfill its radical potential. Hearing, "lagging, as it were, behind the production process, furthers the delusion that the world itself is not yet wholly rationalized, that it still has room for the uncontrolled—for an irrationality that has no consequences for the demands of civilization and is therefore sanctioned by them." [24]

Only in the last decade or so have contemporary critics concerned themselves with the ideological issues that interested Eisler and Adorno, and only recently have they begun Levin's critique of the acoustic apparatus in earnest. Kristin Thompson, for instance, questions the viability of classical film theory's approach to the soundtrack as a theoretical *and* a historical model. Turning to the position on sound promulgated by Eisenstein, Pudovkin, and Alexandrov in "A Statement on Sound," Thompson challenges the dualistic model extrapolated from Soviet sound theory and suggests that the concept of polarity is not necessarily helpful or even accurate in understanding it. Counterpoint as it is used in the "Statement" is a nebulous term. In fact, Thompson points out, its definition does not even appear in the document. Her analysis of Eisenstein's other writings of the period suggests that he did not define counterpoint as a "radical and constant disjunction between sound and image," nor did he oppose parallelism per se.[25] What Eisenstein reacted to most strongly was the pervasive predominance of synchronized dialogue in sound film. Thompson argues that Eisenstein greatly admired Walt Disney's "excellent" animated cartoons because of their music. "In these for example, a graceful movement of the foot is accompanied by appropriate music, which is, as it were, the audible expression of the mechanical action."[26] To Eisenstein the concepts of parallelism and counterpoint were not necessarily antithetical, nor was one superior to the other. Even Mickey Mousing was not immediately dismissed by Eisenstein especially when it was used nonnaturalistically.

In 1975 Irwin Bazelon in his study *Knowing the Score* also questions the terminology of classical theory. Developing Eisler and Adorno's earlier critique of parallelism and counterpoint ("A photographed kiss cannot actually be synchronized with an eight-bar phrase"), Bazelon argues that "the audio components of rhythm, melody, harmony, orchestration, form, and style are only superficially related to visual components—that is, speed of movement, directional motion, scene, or tangible object, environment, and image."[27] Bazelon argues that any correspondence between music and image is "at best ambiguous," complicated by the fact that musical structure can be strictly codified (here he suggests an analogy to mathematics) while the visual image cannot be expressed in such terms.[28] Echoing Adorno and Eisler, Bazelon reverses the traditional formula that equates the ear with emotion and irrationality and the eye with logic and rationality. His comparison of music and mathematics offers a radical critique of the concepts which have shaped the analysis of film music, but, like Eisler and Adorno, he fails to escape into a new paradigm.

The problems inherent in film theory's approach to the film score are succinctly summed up by Claudia Gorbman writing in the 1980 edition of *Yale French Studies.*

> The restricted number of possible film/music relationships as discussed by most scholars seems curiously primitive, limited largely to the concepts of *parallelism* and *counterpoint*. Either the music "resembles" or it "contradicts" the action or mood of what appears on the screen. . . . Is there no other way to qualify film music which does not lie between these opposites but outside them? [29]

It is, of course, the crucial question for contemporary critics of film music: how to theorize the musical score without falling into the traps of an earlier model. Gorbman suggests the concept of "mutual implication" in which music and image function in a "*combinatoire* of expression." [30] Such a reconceptualization offers a solid framework for building a new paradigm.

Classical theory depends upon the assumption that meaning is contained in the visual image and that music either reinforces or alters what is already there. Certainly our experience confirms the impression that music can affect an image. Any owner of a Walkman or car radio for that matter can attest to music's power in affecting the visual field. (The urban phenomenon of protecting oneself against the threat of the cityscape through listening to music is one specific example.) I merely have to put Herrmann's score for *Vertigo* or better yet *Psycho* on my car cassette player to transform a lush New England landscape into menacing surroundings. But it is also true that music is affected by the visual field. It takes only a few moments for the familiarity of the New England terrain to reassert itself as I listen to *Psycho*. It is this projection of affect from the aural realm onto the visual field and its almost simultaneous readjustment which constitutes the primary perceptual mechanism constructed by the culture for the relation of aural and visual stimuli. The power of this model derives from a potent historical legacy which represents sound and especially music as a direct conduit to emotional response and sight as the rational check on such intuitive processes.

Film music depends upon this same mechanism which binds the visual and the aural into interdependence. This is to say that while certainly music affects the image, it is likewise the case that the image affects the music. In fact, the relationship between them is so interdependent that when one cannot be "squared" with the other, credibility itself is threatened, however momentarily, and the suspension of disbelief necessary to maintaining a fiction becomes potentially disruptible. Take an example from *The Informer*, for instance, in which the protagonist, Gypo Nolan, gazes at a British wanted poster for Frankie McPhillip, an Irish rebel. The intercut close-up of Gypo's face is ambiguous (he stares straight ahead and rubs his chin): is he emoting hatred for Frankie or for his British oppressors? Or is he simply absentmindedly staring? Steiner scores the close-up with a sinister version of "Rule! Britannia," and music anchors the possible readings of Gypo's face in one that defines his sympathies as anti-British. Here image and music are mutually credible, that is, the reading of the shot suggested by the music is consonant with the possible readings contained in the image. One can imagine the confusion, however, that hearing a piece of nondiegetic music totally incongruous with the image, say, Bing Crosby singing "White Christmas," would create.

A conceptual model in which music and image share power in shaping perception has a number of important implications for the study of film music as well as the study of film itself. Among them is the necessity of confronting a reliance upon terminology that perpetuates, wittingly and sometimes unwittingly, an earlier paradigm. While it is relatively easy to discard the concepts of parallelism and counterpoint, it is much more difficult to abandon terminology that sustains attendant assumptions about the transcendence of the image and the dependence of the music in relation to it. Language that suggests music reinforces, emphasizes, contradicts, or alters the image falls into this trap.

Interdependence, however, has consequences beyond the terminological and necessitates rethinking the function of music not only in terms of its relation to the image but in terms of other filmic processes. One such process is the construction of narrative, and the same assumptions about the transcendence of the image must be confronted here as well. Narrative is not constructed by visual means alone. By this I mean that music works as part of the process that transmits narrative information to the spectator, that it functions as a narrative agent.

Mood, emotion, characterization, point of view, even the action itself are constructed in film in a complex visual and aural interaction in which music is an important component. Thus when *tremolo* strings are heard, the music is not *reinforcing* the suspense of the scene; it is a part of the process that creates it. Indeed, one might argue that without the music, the suspense might not be as compelling or in certain cases perhaps even exist! (Would the ocean seem menacing without the shark theme in *Jaws*?) Certainly the creation of themes does more than *reinforce* characterization. As I hope to show in Chapter 5, Gypo's theme in *The Informer* is an important part of the process by which Gypo's character is established. In fact, its rhythmic construction and instrumentation are important components in establishing sympathy for Gypo. Similarly, John Williams' theme for Darth Vader, with its disconcerting ambivalence between major and minor, is part of the reason Vader is both so threatening and so recuperable. (He actually turns out to be none other than Luke Skywalker's father!)

Each of the analyses which comprise Chapters 4 through 8 offers specific readings of individual texts informed by a model that emphasizes the interdependence of music and image and assumes music to be an interactive agent in the narrative process. I stress, however, that such a paradigm is only a starting point for coming to terms with film music; it addresses the "how," if you will, of music's operation in a filmic text. Why film music works, the sources of both its powers and its pleasures, must also be addressed if we hope to fully understand music's unique hold over us as spectators. An investigation of these issues leads in two directions: toward culture where film music is produced and toward consciousness where film music is perceived. What is the relationship between film music and culture? What is film music's relationship to our very consciousness? In 1947 Eisler and Adorno argued that to understand film music it is necessary first to understand music. This might seem a startlingly simple observation, but the premise behind it, that film music derives its power from its constitution as music, is a critical starting point in the investigation of what music brings to the filmic experience.

The premise that music is a product of culture owes much to the groundwork laid by the Frankfurt School and especially to the work of Adorno which demystified the production of art under advanced capitalism. Attacking cherished notions of creativity and the individual's transcendence over social and cultural contexts, the Frankfurt School asserted that art is a mediated discourse, pervaded by cultural ideology in both product and perception. Music, like any art form, is a social object, specifically a discourse of listening structured by a complex set of relations between music and listener. For Adorno, however, music has a unique position among the arts. Because it seems less mediated and more direct than other arts, music actually has more power to deceive. Music offers the illusion of individual creativity, a possibility of self-expression, which masks the intellectually and emotionally alienating effects of life under advanced capitalism. Music lulls its listeners into an acceptance of the status quo, preventing them, as Adorno says, from "reflecting on themselves and their world," [31] pacifying critical and therefore dangerous impulses in the culture.

Such ideological analysis has yet to be embraced by traditional musicologists who posit music's autonomous function and assume its transcendence over social and cultural contexts. As a result, most of the ideological critique of music continues to be produced outside the discipline. A striking case is the work of economist Jacques Attali, whose text *Noise: The Political Economy of Music* situates music in terms of its political function. For Attali, as for Adorno, music is never innocent. "More than colors and forms, it is sounds and their arrangements that fashion societies." [32] Music is a tool for social hegemony, encapsulating a hierarchy of organized sound that both reflects and sustains the structure of the political order. Unlike Adorno, however (but like Eisler), Attali believes in the subversive power of music and in the possibility of change through the liberation of music's anarchic power.

There is even work to suggest that musicology itself is now the object of ideological criticism. In a recent collection of essays, *Music and Society: The Politics of Composition, Performance and Reception,* editors Richard Leppert and Susan McClary question "the notion that music shapes itself in accordance with self-contained, abstract principles that are unrelated to the outside social world." [33] The essays that follow represent a variety of responses to this issue. Not surprisingly most of them are written by scholars outside the tradition of musicology, from such diverse fields as art history, sociology, and literary studies. (McClary is one of only three musicologists who contributed to the volume.) Perhaps the most virulent strain of contemporary ideological analysis, however, can be found in the British cultural studies critics who analyze how rock and other forms of music become articulated under industrialized capitalism.[34]

But it is Adorno again, this time in collaboration with composer Hanns Eisler, who applies the conclusions generated by his study of autonomous music to film music, who begins, in effect, an ideological investigation of film music's operation. In *Composing for the Films*, Adorno and Eisler offer a historical explanation for musical accompaniment, arguing that it is music's ideological function that caused it to become institutionalized as a practice. Films both produce and reproduce the needs of their spectators, but the material basis of that process, the cinematic apparatus itself, threatens the success of its operation and becomes masked through a number of strategies which render its mediated form invisible. Film music is one of the primary mechanisms of this process. Like autonomous music, film music distracts; it turns the spectator's attention away from the technological basis of film, functioning as "a cement, which holds together elements that otherwise would oppose each other unrelated—the mechanical product and the spectators."[35] Film music binds the spectator into the fictive reality through its promulgation of identificatory affect between audience and screen. It is not without import that Eisler and Adorno refer to film music as a drug.

Film depends upon music to achieve the illusion of reality, and the standardization of film music during the silent period institutionalized this ideological function. Eisler and Adorno point out that in the early days of silent cinema, musical accompaniment was spontaneous and improvisatory. As a result, musical accompaniment was often inappropriate and even anarchistic. Cinema lacked a machine for determining musical response, that is, it lacked institutionalized conventions. What became standardized with film's shift from a cottage industry to big business was a practice that expelled the threat of impulse by strictly codifying musical accompaniment. Eisler and Adorno refer to this process as the "catalogue and pigeon-hole treatment," which standardized musical effects and left little room for individual input.[36] Eisler and Adorno's historical depiction of early film music as haphazard has recently been called into question. The period in which music functioned spontaneously and anarchically is now thought to be far shorter than Eisler and Adorno describe. (Musicologist Martin Marks has uncovered cue sheets and original scores from as early as 1895.)[37] Although the time frame Eisler and Adorno constructed is now suspect, their model for the process that produced musical conventions provides a convincing mechanism for explaining the speedy standardization that attended the development of musical accompaniment.

Yet there are questions that Eisler and Adorno leave unanswered, questions which suggest that an ideological critique of film music is not yet fully articulated. What are the possibilities of subversion through music, for instance, particularly textual subversion through musical accompaniment? Eisler and Adorno argue that music can radically critique and even undercut a film's dominant ideology. In fact, as part of *Composing for the Films*, Eisler and Adorno offer an alternative film music practice which they hoped would expose cinema's material contradictions and sever the spectator's hypnotic absorption into the film. This practice, however, is more problematic than they admit. Eisler worked briefly as a composer in Hollywood, and his work, though interesting, often sounds just like the classical scores he was trying to avoid. While Eisler's inability, by and large, to put theory into practice does not invalidate his critique, it does reveal serious questions about the nature of film and its relation to music that *Composing for the Films* does not address. Gorbman, for instance, wonders what would happen if Eisler were to score *Mildred Pierce*: "An Eisler score, designed to unmask contradictions throughout *Mildred Pierce*, would surely just sound wrong to an audience thoroughly steeped in—and paying for—identification of the kind Adorno and Eisler rail against."[38] It is entirely possible that an audience wouldn't even notice a difference. The ability of music to rupture a text is an issue that currently divides Marxist critics. What are the terms by which this might be worked out? Is such disruption unique to a *filmic* text? Are there distinguishing circumstances in the filmic process that allow music's power to be released?

The work begun by Adorno and Eisler has been taken up, in English, in two recent texts: Claudia Gorbman's *Unheard Melodies: Narrative Film Music* and Carol Flinn's dissertation, "Film Music and Hollywood's Promise of Utopia in Film Noir and the Woman's Film," both of which situate film music ideologically. Gorbman's text, the first serious theoretical study of film music in English since Eisler and Adorno's, expands on the central analogy in their work between music and film music. Her comparison between easy-listening music and the nondiegetic film score extends the terms of Eisler and Adorno's analysis and reinforces their conclusions. Whether it is heard in an elevator, or at a film screening, music is defined by its ideological function: to alleviate potential distraction and displeasure. Along these lines it is interesting to consider Attali's reminder that Muzak initially promoted itself as "the security system of the seventies."[39]

The terms of Gorbman's comparison are compelling. Both easy-listening music and film music operate as part of a larger field of reference, whether it is a shopping mall, the dentist's office, or narrative film. Both forms of music are regulated by a controlling context which determines its presence or absence, the interruption of a store's background music to make announcements, for instance, or the diminished volume of scoring under a film's dialogue. Neither easy-listening nor film music is created to draw attention to itself, and neither demands the listener's undivided attention. Most important, both easy-listening and film music accompany and, in fact, drive away unpleasantness. Music encourages us to consume whether products or images and makes consuming effortless. Easy listening soothes the anxiety of the dentist's office and the guilt over spending, "its purpose to lull the individual into being an *untroublesome social subject.*"[40] Film music also holds displeasure at bay, warding off the tension of film's ghostly images and "uncertain signification," as well as distracting the spectator from a recognition of cinema's material and technological basis. Thus film music operates in a way similar to easy-listening music. It functions, in short, ideologically, "to lull the spectator into being an *untroublesome* (less critical, less wary) *viewing subject.*"[41]

Carol Flinn's work also incorporates the theoretical perspective of the Frankfurt School. Like Eisler and Adorno, Flinn posits the function of film music as a cement that unifies the film as an aesthetic object and binds the spectator into the fictive reality. To explore the mechanisms by which this process is put into effect, however, Flinn turns to Ernest Bloch and the discourse of utopia: the connection between music and an idealized, utopian past. Music becomes a "souvenir" of a more perfect, less alienating, more integrated (precapitalistic) world.[42] Applying these connections to classical narrative film, Flinn posits that music offers the filmic text its sense of completion, an illusion of unity or integrity that the cinematic apparatus is unable to produce without it. Music in the classical film creates this effect by playing upon "idealized, lost conditions" and activating a nostalgia for an integrated, primitive, and utopian past.[43]

Ideological criticism positions music in the cultural register, analyzing how music works to sustain hegemony: autonomous music to pacify dangerous anarchic impulses in the culture, and film music to mask the technological basis of film and support its illusion of reality. An equally important aspect of film music's power derives from its relationship to consciousness. How music works in the psychic register and how psychoanalytic processes create a social subject necessary to the function of ideology are crucial questions in the investigation of film music's power. In particular, psychoanalysis offers insights into music's role in the development of subjectivity that hold promise for understanding how the filmic spectator is engaged as a subject through music. Recent work by French psychoanalytic critics such as Didier Anzieu, Dominique Avron, Guy Rosolato, and Francis Hofstein have begun to explore this terrain.[44] Unfortunately, many key texts in this vein have yet to be translated into English, creating something of a blindspot in scholarly exchange of these issues.

Psychoanalysis situates the development of subjectivity within the acoustic realm. A defining construct within this discourse is the image of infantile space as an aural cavity. Anzieu describes it as a "sonorous envelope of the self": Rosolato as a "sonorous womb, a murmurous house"; Gérard Blanchard as a "sonorous space."[45] Even in the womb the infant's experience is composed of sound: the involuntary sound produced by the mother's body, such as breathing, heartbeat, and pulse, as well as voluntary sound, primarily vocal emission. (Psychoanalysts frequently point to the ability of the newborn to recognize its mother's voice.) A point of commonality among the sounds of the womb is their constitution through musical elements: rhythm (repeated, predictable patterns of sonic impulse), pitch (high versus low sounds), and dynamics (volume). The mother's voice both incorporates and heightens these same musical elements. In fact, Rosolato posits the prebirth experience as the original site of the connection between music and the maternal.

After birth, the infant continues to exist in what Julia Kristeva describes as the "chora," the prelinguistic, pre-oedipal receptacle of the imaginary.[46] This presubjective stage is sustained by the mother's voice, which carries with it the trace of the original fusion with her body. Psychoanalytic writing frequently theorizes this period of development in terms of music. Hofstein, for instance, describes the maternal voice in these terms: "At the same time that she nurtures, the mother speaks, a charged speech imprinted with rhythm, pitch, timbre, tempo, [and] intensity. . . ."[47] Rosolato's work most directly connects the maternal voice to music, forging a critical link for theorists of film. "One might suggest that it [the maternal voice] is the first model of auditory pleasure and that music finds its roots and its nostalgia in an originary atmosphere, what might be called a sonorous womb, a murmuring house—or *music of the spheres*."[48]

It is here that we can begin to understand the origin of the pleasure of listening to music, a pleasure constituted by a desire for the imaginary (and lost) fusion with the mother. Again the work of Rosolato is particularly important in understanding how harmony restores the lost maternal object.

> The deployment of harmony and polyphony can perhaps be understood as a succession of tension and release, of unity and divergence of parts which arrange themselves into chords which are then resolved into their simplest unity. It is thus the dramatization of these separated and reunited bodies that harmony supports.[49]

There yet remains the difficult task of applying the complex psychoanalytic discourse on the development of subjectivity to film music itself. In English this work has just begun.[50] Flinn's work derives from the psychoanalytic position that music's pleasure emanates from the memory of plenitude, an imaginary fusion with the mother's body, connecting film music's powerful hold over the spectator to its ability to activate this psychic register. From this point Flinn turns to the discourse that constructs this model. In a 1986 article in *Screen*, she argues that the "feminine metaphor of music" is constructed from a patriarchal framework. The psychoanalytic position which theorizes music as a lost maternal object is highly problematic for feminists since it assumes a connection between regression and the female body.[51]

Gorbman's text grapples with the difficulties of coming to terms with exactly how the psychoanalytic model can be applied to film music. A key question in this enterprise is how film music might actively engage unconscious response, how it might recall psychic traces. Gorbman posits that it is film music's position in the structure of narrative film as much as its content that activates such unconscious memories. Film music "plays in a film 'secondarily' to the register of language, of narrative"; it lurks in cinema's perceptual background creating a kind of semihypnotic trance, lowering the "threshold of belief" and "bypassing the usual censors of the preconscious."[52] Placing music in the context of Baudry's subject-effect, Gorbman argues that because music more or less short-circuits consciousness it facilitates the process by which the spectator slips into the film. In such a state there is a "greater disposition for the subject to accept the film's pseudo-perceptions as his/her own," that is, to become its subject.[53] Thus film music fuses the spectator to a more integrated, whole, and omniscient presence, the film itself becoming a plenitude reminiscent of the pre-oedipal imaginary.

In the process of generating from psychoanalytic work on music a theory of film music, both Gorbman and Flinn have produced illuminating perspectives on the operation of the musical score. Such new terrain, however, is not yet fully explored, and the application of psychoanalysis raises many questions that have yet to be answered. What is the connection, for instance, between tonal harmony and the lost maternal object? Although recent theoretical work has examined the resonance of Rosolato's connection between music and the maternal for the voice in cinema, there is much to be done in examining the consequences of this connection for music.[54] How can psychoanalytic theory and Rosolato's work in particular account for the triumph of romanticism over other forms of music, particularly atonal composition, in the classical Hollywood film score? Carol Flinn's questions about the antifeminist bias in psychoanalytic theory constitute another rich site of investigation, especially for feminists working out a place for female subjectivity and theorizing female spectatorship.

The most important requisite, however, for continued investigation into film music lies outside the growing discipline which has developed to study it. For a variety of reasons, film music theory has been segregated from film theory. Cultural biases have played a large part in this segregation as has the perception that film music is an addition to rather than an integral part of a film. These biases are compounded by a lack of standardized methodology and terminology for film music as well as the lack of attention to music in film education (and it might be added, in our educational system in general). As a result contemporary film theory developed without much attention to the function of the musical score. Questions of how music affects the process of spectatorship, the creation of a spectator, and the perception of the film itself are not yet fully answered because such investigation, historically, has not been part of the concerns of film theory. It is time to take up the work of film music: to recognize its centrality in the filmic experience and to make it fully a part of the ways in which we think about film.

CHAPTER 3

The Silent Film Score
A Structural Model

The classical Hollywood film score did not spontaneously appear with the coming of sound; it inherited a legacy of musical accompaniment which evolved during the era of silent film. The accumulated experience and expertise of accompanists in this period generated an identifiable set of practices readily and easily available to the first musical directors of the sound era. In fact, the initial impulse of the industry was to transplant these practices to the sound product intact. Certain characteristics of silent film accompaniment were absorbed into sound film, but, ultimately, film scoring in Hollywood was transformed by the mechanical reproduction of sound. Although the silent film score has generally been accepted as a prototype of the classical Hollywood film score, it represents a different practice. To be specific, the basis of the silent film score, the principles of continuous playing and selective reproduction of diegetic sound, was rejected in the sound era in favor of a model based on the principles of intermittent music and faithful reproduction of diegetic sound. What happened to the practice of silent film accompaniment reveals the extent to which sound technology and its impact on narrative construction fundamentally changed the relationship between music and image.

Music and Silent Film: A Functional Approach

An exploration of the functions of film music leads inevitably back to silent film, to the inception of film itself, and to the practice of live musical accompaniment to the visual image. A relationship between moving images and music seems inherent in the very concept of the motion picture. Thomas Edison initially envisioned moving pictures as a marketing strategy for his newly invented phonograph. As early as 1887, W. K. L. Dickson was experimenting with mechanized synchronization at the

Edison labs "which should do for the eye what the phonograph does for the ear." [1] The Edison kinetoscopes proved a testing ground for mechanically reproduced accompaniment; some provided music which was recorded on cylinders and synchronized to a perforated film strip. The Edison laboratory was not alone in joining music to image. In December 1895, when the Lumière brothers presented their first public screening in Paris, they used piano accompaniment and later an organ in the London showing of the same program a year later.

Silent film became, at once, a synthetic art form. Like Greek drama, Elizabethan theater, opera, nineteenth-century melodrama, and the theatrical spectacle, frequently cited as cinematic precursors, silent film combined sensory stimulation of the eyes and ears. Music was readily available in the early homes of cinema: the musical halls, vaudeville, burlesques, and carnivals where musicians would play for the films as they would for other parts of the evening's entertainment. The standard pragmatic explanation for the amalgamation of film and music is functional: music covered the noise of the projector. Restless audiences, unconditioned in movie etiquette, would talk and eat during showings. Even courting was not an unlikely activity in the darkened anonymity of the auditorium. But the noisy projector (and audience) was soon quieted, and the synthesis of film and music persisted. To understand what initiated and sustained the practice of musical accompaniment to the visual image from a relatively early period in the development of the medium through its continuation in sound cinema, it is necessary to look beyond a pragmatic answer.

The image is a representation not a presentation of reality, and even in its earliest manifestations film belied the position of a mirror held to life. From the slightly oblique camera angle in the Lumière brothers' *Arrivée d'un train à la Ciotat* (1895) to the vanishing objects of Georges Méliès' magical narratives, film was at once in the business of creating a world of its own. Cinema was barely in its infancy when self-conscious recognition of the cinematic process surfaced in films such as *The Great Train Robbery* (1903), *The Story the Biograph Told* (1904), and *Uncle Josh at the Moving Picture Show* (1902). In this last film a country bumpkin confuses film with reality, eventually falling through and destroying the screen to attain the elusive image. Early filmmakers recognized and even

The Edison Kinetoscope with phonograph attachment, circa 1894. The Edison laboratory's earliest attempt to synchronize image and music offered the spectator musical recordings, via stethoscope-like earphones, in accompaniment to the images. Edison marketed films accompanied by music again in 1912 with the Kinetophone, a combination phonograph and projector for theaters, and the Home Projecting Kinetoscope for the home. Neither proved commercially viable.

promoted this confusion, a concept sadistically exploited in the first/ last shot of *The Great Train Robbery*. Here a bandit aims and fires a pistol point blank at the camera (and thus at the audience). Yet film, especially silent film, presents a number of impediments to an easy transversal between the experiential and the diegetic worlds. Film music provides a bridge.

One of the problems in negotiating the spectator's suspension of disbelief emanates from the actual mechanical process which calls the image into being. The illusion of movement in film is created by a succession of stills jerked through the gate of the projector at twenty-four frames per second. At this speed our eyes cannot distinguish the images as separate, thus creating the illusion of continuous movement. But this phenomenon carries with it a certain threat. Film is an art form which exists as process, the precariousness of which can be attested to by anyone experiencing the breakdown of a projector. The resonating thud of disappointment when the image is arbitrarily seized from us by faulty equipment or operators looms over every frame that is projected.

It is this threat that musical accompaniment to silent film addresses so squarely. Music covers over the mechanical and thus precarious production of moving images with the organic and thus more trustworthy production of music. (Music in the sound film, of course, is as mechanically reproduced as the image—it is not organic at all. But even the musical score of a sound film, and I might add recorded music in general, is still perceived as materially unaffected by mechanical mediation. Consider the recent "Is it live or is it Memorex?") Silent film, which faced a greater threat to a perpetuation of the illusion of movement than sound film (equipment and operator problems, nonstandardized projection speeds, poor quality and flammability of film stock), balanced its greater threat of disruption with a greater proportion of music. In fact, as I will demonstrate later in the chapter, silent film depended upon musical accompaniment played out in a relatively unbroken chain of continuous expression.

In general, silent film demanded more of its musical accompaniment than sound film. With its synchronized soundtrack containing dialogue and sound effects, sound film was not as reliant upon music to establish the credibility of the image. With the exception of early and largely failed experiments in live narration, silent film did depend upon music to create an aural dimension perceived necessary to constructing the image as real. Accompanists exploited music's ability to imitate sounds (water, wind, bangs, and crashes) and to suggest both the quality of the human voice and the intonation of speech. But music's utility to silent film also derived from its physical presence in the theater, a phenomenon widely noted in literature of the period. Note the copy from this advertisement for the Barton Orchestral organ. "Out of the misty depths of the silversheet, shaking the shadows from them, come the people of the screen stories. They come dancing—running—fighting or with soul-weary steps—and music, *real* music, should always be with them." Silent film accompaniment, after all, was produced by live musicians whose presence lent credibility to the images themselves. The sight of live performers actually producing music transferred to the silent images a sense of here and now, a quality that the Bartola Musical Instrument Company described in its advertisements as "next to human," a visual assurance that images on the screen are "real."

The constitution of the image itself presents further impediments to the leap of faith necessary to accept the filmic world as real. Film is a two-dimensional representation of a three-dimensional world. Its very flatness impedes its credibility. Music, however, has harmony, texture, and instrumental color, all of which lend it the quality of fullness. The actual production of sound in the auditorium reinforces this perception. The image is projected onto a flat surface not far from the back wall of the theater. Only the beam of light which projects that image enters the actual viewing space of the spectator, the theatrical auditorium. Music, however, like any sound, is carried as waves *through* the viewing space. This "front to back" quality of the music (music is perceived as emanating from the front of the auditorium and traveling to the back) creates a sense of depth for the spectator, and through a kind of transference or slippage between sound and image, the depth created by the sound is transferred to the flat surface of the image.

Silent film's two-dimensionality, its dependence on black-and-white film stock, and especially its silence led Hanns Eisler and Theodor W. Adorno to an interesting theory on the value of musical accompaniment. They argue that because of these characteristics silent film has an uncanny, dreamlike quality. Its representations are ghostly, an uncomfortable reminder of human mortality, and carry with them a kind of psychological shock. Music exorcises these negative effects, smoothing over the gap between the experiential world and the world of the film.

> Music was introduced as a kind of antidote against the picture. The need was felt to spare the spectator the unpleasantness involved in seeing effigies of living, acting, and even speaking persons, who were at the same time silent. The fact that they are living and non-living at the same time is what constitutes their ghostly character, and music was introduced not to supply them with the life they lacked—but to exorcise fear or help the spectator absorb the shock.[2]

Music's consequence, however, extends beyond its function as a kind of aesthetic and psychic bridge. Historically, music constitutes a primary component in the development and definition of the relationship between the spectator and the screen, fulfilling a crucial, indeed primary, function during the period when early cinema was beginning to develop. I define early cinema here as that period of film from the late nineteenth century to the development of continuity editing in the first decade of the twentieth. But before continuity editing and the integrated use of close-ups helped to control spectator response, music established shared experience among spectators. Through its exploitation of musical conventions, accompaniment created a conduit for meaning refining and honing an image track which had yet to develop the techniques for manipulating the spectator into predictable and consistent response.

It is this function of music as explicator of response that sound film was to adopt as a model for its own practice. As pointed out earlier, sound film differed from silent film in the intermittence of its musical accompaniment. When the possibility of synchronized speech and sound effects released sound film from its reliance upon continuous musical accompaniment, it initially rejected music entirely. But the life span of the all-talking picture was brief, the need that music filled quickly reasserting itself. Sound film reintegrated musical accompaniment, refining music's more encompassing functions in silent film to suit its own particular need.

It is that need which has fascinated critics of film music. One of the

The Console illustrated here is the beautiful Barton Organ installed in the Fair Park Auditorium, Dallas, Texas.

The Golden Voice Barton
Brings Silver to Your Box Office

What brings the crowd back next night? What fills those last remaining seats — *your profit seats?* The Picture? Yes — and NO! Somewhere — hidden in the orchestra pit, or in full view — there is a man or woman who makes your shows infinitely better. He or she — the organist — sways your audience to the moods of the presentation. Has your organist the equipment to move your audience? Consider if he or she sends them away forever — or to come back again? To handi-

cap your organist is a mighty big risk. To give your organist full co-operation is to install a "Barton." The Barton Orchestral Organ is bringing capacity crowds to many leading theaters of the country. It can do likewise for yours. The Barton has an exceptionally wide and varied range. Its interpretations are conceded to be "next to human." Its completeness, its flexibility make the Barton truly an organ with an appeal — a box office appeal.

> Of course, the New Wisconsin—being an advanced theater chose the Barton as well as did the Joliet theater, Joliet, Ill., and Retlaw theater, Fond du Lac, Wis. All these are C. W. and Geo. L. Rapp designed theaters.
>
> Let us send you full particulars about the Barton without obligation. Merely give us the size of your theater

IT'S A Barton ORCHESTRAL ORGAN

BARTOLA MUSICAL INSTRUMENT CO.,
313-316 Mallers Bldg.   Chicago.

Advertising copy for the Barton Orchestral Organ. This advertisement highlights several motifs in the literature of silent film accompaniment: music as the "voice" of the silent image; the importance of the human component in musical accompaniment; and music's ability to bring a humanness to the black-and-white, two-dimensional silent images.

first and most enduring explanations for the amalgamation of film and music is music's ability to provide unity. As early as 1936 Kurt London articulated the idea that music unifies the variegated impressions of the image into a whole, into a logical succession of thought and action. Because film is composed of short spans or intervals of time, irregular in duration, structure, and content, music is needed to provide a formal structure, a unity that moves in measured time and predictable form. London argues, "Variety in the film images and uniformity in the music."[3] Siegfried Kracauer argues along similar lines, citing music's most crucial function as its ability to provide continuity for a phenomenon which by its nature is discontinuous.[4] Music historian Frederick Sternfeld notes that the "scope" of the camera, that is, its ability to move from near to far, to capture distance as well as intimacy, and to expand time by exploring detail, thwarts filmic narrative. Music, which has a regular and cohesive structure, balances the visual component, which can be disjunctive in its ability to manipulate time and confusing in its ability to shift perspective.[5]

Underlying music's function as a unifying agent is its constitution as rhythm. The position that music is an "art that exists in time"[6] is a principle that surfaces in several studies of film music. According to this argument, musical accompaniment is critical to an art form that lacks a clear system for marking its own chronological progression. Noël Burch notes that music "provides a time scale against which the 'rhythms' of the decoupage become far more concrete," and Jean Mitry identifies "fundamental rhythmic structure" as that phenomenon "which gives the cinematic development what it lacks: the notion of temporality."[7] Through rhythm, music's ordered articulation of time is transferred to film itself. Rhythm, an inaudible metronome which regulates the deployment of images disparate in time and place, contributes to their seeming inevitability.

As early as 1936, Kurt London argued that human perception does not accept movement as artistic unless it is accompanied by regular, predictable, and audible rhythms. "The reason which is aesthetically and psychologically most essential to explain the need of music as an accompaniment of the silent film, is without doubt *the rhythm of the film as an art of movement*."[8] The cinema is constantly attempting to embody that rhythm. From the metered cutting of its editing to the patterns of its mise-en-scène, cinema is constantly offering the semblance of ordered time. The tick of this clock is nowhere more audible than in the soundtrack itself. It emerges from the intonation, timbre, and cadences of human speech. But it finds its most pronounced expression in musical accompaniment. Music's metronomic function imprints reel time with real time, marking out an ordered progression for the dispersal of images.

Music served a crucial function in the silent film auditorium, traversing the bridge between a two-dimensional, black-and-white, silent image and the spectator, covering over film's material basis as a mechanical process with the organic production of music. What was the particular structure that music took in relation to the silent film? How did musical accompaniment develop as a form? What are the constraints, both economic and aesthetic, that helped to shape it and what is the historical process by which music for silent film became conventionalized?

Music and Silent Film: A Structural Approach

It has become axiomatic in studies of film music to assert that the very earliest musical accompaniment was largely improvisatory and bore only a coincidental relationship to the images. Recent work by Martin Marks argues that at least some early musical accompaniment was not haphazard at all, and offers convincing evidence that even in the 1890s there existed original musical scores.[9] Attempts to standardize musical accompaniment from within the industry coincide with the development of continuity editing during the period 1909–1912. In one important way this standardization succeeded. The scope of musical accompaniment in the silent period varied from the solo performance of a pianist or organist to motion picture orchestras with as many as a hundred players. The nature of the performance ranged from total improvization to careful compilation and/or composition. But all accompaniment shared a common aim: to absorb the spectator into the fictive reality. Silent film practice generated a model to meet this need based on three basic components: the principle of continuous accompaniment, correspondence between music and the implied content of the image, and unification of musical selections through the structural principle of the leitmotif.

The highest priority in this model was continuous accompaniment, from "before or with the screening of the picture" to "the last moment and a little beyond it." [10] That music was to be provided in an unbroken stream was stressed repeatedly in manuals, trade papers, and reviews, and reflected in cue sheets and orchestral scores of the era. Reconstructing the musical practice of the silent era is largely dependent upon the evidence available through such documentation; recordings were not made of actual performances. It is important to remember, however, that these sources delineate an ideal practice, and that its faithful execution was always dependent upon the individual accompanist's ability and cooperation as well as the size of the house. The deluxe theaters in big cities could afford large staffs, top players, and even rehearsal time. The highest standard of playing could be heard in these auditoriums. Smaller houses without such resources operated under a different standard. Although literature of the period abounds in examples of problematic accompaniment (Kracauer's experience with the drunken pianist springs immediately to mind), there was a standard promulgated within the industry, and dispersed through manuals, trade publications, and theater organ schools. [11] Audience expectation also helped to control continued and outrageous departures from the accepted norm.

One of the most influential manuals, George Beynon's *Musical Presentation of Motion Pictures*, articulates the approach to continuous musical accompaniment that dominated publications on silent film music: "Allowing the picture to be screened in silence is an unforgivable offense that calls for the severest censure. No picture should begin in silence under any conditions." [12] The score for *Ben-Hur* (1925), for instance, is cued to begin with the lowering of the lights and the raising of the curtain. The musicians were also instructed to continue playing until the lights came up and the patrons began to exit. [13] Although well-chosen moments of silence were tolerated and even encouraged, being "productive of a splendid effect," [14] the length that such silence was permissible was rigidly prescribed from the ambiguous "momentary," to the clarity of *Moving Picture World*'s dictum that "10 seconds" was the maximum allowable.[15] Techniques for covering lapses in continuity occasioned by practical considerations (changing music, turning pages, etc.), known as "holes" in the trade, were shared in advice columns and manuals.[16] Changes between selections should be bridged with modulations; if this proved impossible, breaks should be positioned during intertitles. "In such cases," accompanists were instructed "to play the last few measures of the last selection and the first few of the new one softly, so as not to intrude the break upon the ears of the audience."[17]

The principle of continuous playing by and large prevented the accompanist from being very responsive to editing. A major challenge was the "flash-back," an early term for parallel editing or crosscutting. Narrative development which reorganized time and space in defiance of the laws of empirical reality taxed the accompanist's ability to simultaneously provide a continuous musical accompaniment and make it appropriate for alternating scenes of disparate narrative content. The principle of continuous music had become such a determining force that the standard advice for "flash-backs" became "*not* to *disrupt* the continuity of the music while the flash-back lasts, but to *change* the *intensity* by playing the music, characteristic of the main action, in a dynamic degree of loudness or softness which befits the secondary action."[18] "Flash-backs" remained "a continuous source of trouble" to many accompanists however: "We can only hope that they will be eliminated in the course of time."[19]

Pianos and organs were even produced to help insure a continuous stream of music. During this era a number of manufacturers such as Seeburg Piano and Marquette Piano of Chicago, Berry-Wood Piano of Kansas City, and Wurlitzer of North Tonawanda, New York, marketed mechanical and electrical "player" pianos and organs to cost-conscious theater owners. The ad for Marquette's Cremona Theatre Orchestra-Organ boasted: "Any girl or man, after simple instructions, can operate the Cremona with most enchanting results." Unique in their double head construction, these player pianos and organs could hold two rolls simultaneously. This allowed the operator to cue up one roll while another was playing, thus assuring continuous music.

An important device in facilitating continuity was the **cue sheet**, a list of musical selections synchronized to the individual sequences in a film. As early as 1909 Edison Pictures attempted to standardize accompaniment to their films by distributing lists of musical cues broken down by scene and often annotated with performance suggestions. The idea was copied by other studios, columnists in trade publications such as Clarence E. Sinn in *Motion Picture World* and M. M. Hansford in the *Dramatic Mirror*, and enterprising individuals such as Max Winkler, Erno Rapee, Ernst Luz, and Joseph Zivelli. Cue sheets were the most complex musical apparatus yet created for the accompaniment of silent film. The most sophisticated of them, thematic music cue sheets, included actual transcription of pieces from the concert hall or film music repertoire visually cued and timed to the appropriate scene. Universal's thematic cue sheets were designed to establish "a more definite locale of the production, a more perfect sequence of modulations from one selection to another, a more careful working out of the dynamics and effects, and in fact to take the place of a complete music score." [20]

The orchestral score, consisting of musical selections fully transcribed and copied for members of an orchestra, was a natural extension of the cue sheet. Scores consisting of completely original composition were comparatively rare in the silent era although a number of prestigious composers, mostly abroad, experimented with the form. In 1908 Camille Saint-Saëns composed the accompaniment for *L'Assassinat du duc de Guise*. Among the most famous of the art composers who wrote original silent film scores were Edmund Meisel (*Battleship Potemkin* [1925] and *October* [1928]); Arthur Honegger (*Napoleon* [1927]); Darius Milhaud (*L'Inhumaine* [1925]); Dmitri Shostakovich (*The New Babylon* [1929]); Paul Hindemith (*Krazy Kat at the Circus* [1927]); Jacques Ibert (*The Italian Straw Hat* [1927]); Erik Satie (*Entr'acte* [1924]); and in America, Mortimer Wilson (*The Thief of Bagdad* [1924], *Don Q, Son of Zorro* [1925], and *The Black Pirate* [1926]). Most scores, however, were compilations of previously composed material with original composition limited to bridge passages and possibly a distinctive theme. And at least some critics preferred it that way: "When the music of the world is at the disposal of an arranger and the libraries are rich in musical numbers, written by renowned composers, suitable for accompanying such a delightfully fantastic picture, why worry any one man to write a

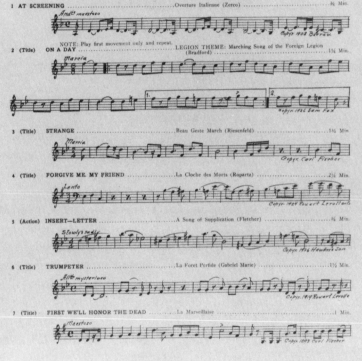

From James C. Bradford's cue sheet for *Beau Geste*. There was also an orchestral score for *Beau Geste* compiled by Hugo Riesenfeld. With the exception of the "Beau Geste March" by Riesenfeld, the cue sheet and orchestral score are completely different. It was a common practice to distribute cue sheets for a film which had an orchestral score since many houses did not have an orchestra. The more economical cue sheets could be adapted for any number of accompanists, including a single performer on the piano or organ.

new 'note for every gesture'?"[21] The first American orchestral score is generally acknowledged as *The Birth of a Nation* (1915) by D. W. Griffith and Joseph Carl Breil. Little more than an elaborate cue sheet utilizing well-known classics such as Wagner's "Ride of the Valkyrie" and Grieg's "In the Hall of the Mountain King," it did contain some originally composed music, including the famous "Love Theme." Other compiled scores representing the development of the form in Hollywood include *Intolerance* (1916), *Way Down East* (1920), *Greed* (1925), *Ben-Hur, Beau Geste* (1926), *The Iron Horse* (1924), and *The Big Parade* (1925).

Orchestral scores, however, presented problems in production and distribution which limited their use. The cost of commissioning a score far exceeded the cost of economical cue sheets. Not all movie houses had an orchestra; the logistics of arranging and publishing parts for the various combinations of instruments that existed in pits throughout the country confined the performance of orchestral scores to major houses in large cities. Conductors, who had gained status through their control of the choice of musical accompaniment, were resistant to relinquishing their power to published music. In spite of these limitations orchestral scores were a mark of distinction, and the public came to expect them in big-budget, prestige productions. These scores also leave the most detailed and accurate record of musical practices in the silent era, generating models that were discussed and analyzed in trade papers and accompanist's manuals, important sources which influenced the day-to-day performance of cinema accompanists throughout the country.

Like cue sheets, scores indicated timings and visual cues for the conductor. Mortimer Wilson's score for *Don Q, Son of Zorro* includes the original timings of scene breakdowns which would have enabled the conductor to fit the music to the appropriate scene. Notations such as "follow with next" at the end of selections as well as "all this continuous" and "join on next" indicate Wilson's intent to compose a seamless aural accompaniment.[22] Likewise, a typical score annotation in Victor Schertzinger's score for *Robin Hood* (1922) reads: "Long tympani roll till change of scene."[23]

The antagonism with which accompanists greeted departures from chronological narrative development as well as the accompanying attempts to rectify such perceived inconsistencies with music points to

The Roxy Theatre and its orchestra. One of the most elaborate of the dream palaces of the twenties, the Roxy boasted an orchestra of over a hundred players.

the primacy of narrative continuity in silent film practice. Critics and accompanists assumed the image's inability to sustain this continuity without the presence of music, and, as a result, music and image developed a reciprocal relationship in terms of narrative. At those moments when the images' ability to sustain continuity is perceived as the most tenuous (transitions between scenes, sequences of parallel editing, filmic openings and closings), the music is uninterrupted, eliding fissures by offering its own continuity in place of the images'. When the images are most able to sustain disruption (intertitles which largely reinforce narrative content and climactic moments of unambiguous narrative intent), music is allowed the prerogative of responding to practical exigencies (page turning, etc.) or dramatic concerns (adding emphasis in the form of pauses).

Continuous music insured narrative integrity and safeguarded the absorption of the spectator into the fictive world. This power was carefully regulated by practices which attempted to render in music the perceived content, both narrative and emotive, of the image. Characterized by the contemporaneous terms "correspondence," "illustration," and "fitness," the practice of coordinating music and image was guided by the perceived appropriateness of the music to the image.

Little deviation from the principle of correspondence was tolerated. Successful accompaniment was predicated upon the spectator's continued absorption into the narrative experience, and the prerogative which fell to the individual accompanist was limited to the amount of disparity spectators would tolerate between image and music. Thus there was a clear system of checks and balances in place at every performance. Narrative gaps created by a disjunction of music and image were greeted with laughter, or worse yet for the hapless accompanist, verbal derision. As if this weren't enough, practices not founded in correspondence were openly attacked in print in the early teens. By the twenties such practices had been largely expelled from the formalized conventions articulated by the film music establishment. Musical punning was singled out as particularly inexcusable: "it kills the photographer's art" and was "not only worthless, but offensive." [24] Ironically, contemporary screenings of silent films which employ live musical accompaniment for historical verisimilitude frequently fall into this trap. At a recent screening of *Getting Evidence* (1906), for instance, I heard the theme from *Chariots of Fire* (1981) as accompaniment to a shot of characters running in the surf on a beach.

Also deemed unacceptable was a reliance upon literary description in a song's title to make the connection to the image instead of using the descriptive powers in the music itself. *Moving Picture News, Moving Picture World*, cue sheet pioneer Max Winkler, and others attacked the practice of using popular tunes whose titles may seem appropriate but whose musical structure or character was inappropriate. Winkler's example concerns the film *War Brides* (1916) in which Nazimova stars as a pregnant and destitute peasant who kills herself when entreaties to her former lover fail. "The pianist had so far done all right. But I scarcely believed my ears when, just as Nazimova exhaled her last breath, to the heart-breaking sobs of her family he began to play the old, frivolous favorite, "You Made Me What I Am Today." [25]

While the principle of appropriateness was rigidly prescribed, its practice was much more loosely defined. A key issue in the process of fitting music to image was the degree to which music should reproduce or imitate references to diegetic sound.[26] The priority placed on continuous musical accompaniment made it difficult and sometimes impossible for accompanists to respond to every diegetic sound. The most obvious diegetic reference was the direct sound cue or sound effect. Although most pianists, organists, ensembles, and cinema orchestras had at their disposal a vast array of apparatuses for producing sound effects, the reproduction of diegetic sound in the silent film theater was highly selective. With seventy-six cues and literally dozens of opportunities for gunshots, horses' hooves, banging, clanking, and other assorted mayhem, the cue sheet for the action-adventure picture *Beau Geste* suggests only four occasions appropriate for reproducing direct diegetic references to sound. Many cue sheets contain no cued effects at all, and the industry was cautious, even discouraging, about their use. Advises Clarence Sinn: "I don't believe it's best to call attention to [diegetic sound] at all." Echoes *Motion Picture World*: "discrimination should be the saving grace of the man with the effects."[27]

The same selectivity was advocated for reproduction of diegetic music. While manuals and trade columns encouraged the reproduction of such references, it was not always an easy task to render on-screen references to music (occasioned by the presence of musicians or the most problematic of all, dancers), especially when editing disrupted the progression of time necessary for direct synchronization. Thus like diegetic references to sound, diegetic references to music were only selectively and intermittently reproduced by the accompanist in the theatrical auditorium. *Beau Geste*'s cue sheet includes four direct musical cues for a trumpeter, or an organist with the appropriate stops pulled to imitate the sound of a trumpet, to render diegetic references either with "Taps" or with the march of the French Foreign Legion. But the film includes nine diegetic appearances of a trumpeter playing.

Another problem was the laxity with which musical scenes were captured on film. As early as 1913 Ernst Luz complained: "scenes [with diegetic music] are gotten over with in so careless a manner that the musician, unless he allows them to pass as nil, he must of necessity feel greatly discouraged in his endeavors."[28] Often actors portraying musicians mimed their performances with little or no attention to authenticity. In *Beau Geste* the actor rendering the final reiteration of

From the piano conductor part for Mortimer Wilson's *The Black Pirate*. It was a common practice in the silent era for the conductor to use such a reduction of the full score on the podium. The notations in the music describe visual action simultaneously occurring in the film. Note, however, the lack of precision in synchronizing specific visual gestures to the music.

"Taps" in close-up has not matched his breathing to the necessities of actual performance, making the task of the live accompanist almost impossible. Directions for synchronizing such references are typically imprecise. A cue for a diegetic reference in *The Auction Block* (1917) notes the on-screen appearance of an orchestra for 1⅛ minutes but gives no specific instructions to the accompanist on how or even whether to attempt synchronization. Typically this was left to the discretion of the accompanist and noted "ad lib."

Not only was the reproduction of diegetic sound reference limited in the silent film auditorium, but the vast mimetic capability of theater organs was utilized in much the same way—only selectively. The best known of these organs, the Mighty Wurlitzer, was manufactured specifically for use in cinema auditoriums, adding so-called theatrical stops to simulate common noises such as doorbells, footsteps, and wind. Enterprising accompanists could add their own unique effects such as a bark or a sneeze. An orchestra, of course, had at its disposal the combined resources of as many as a hundred players. Lang and West in their manual *Musical Accompaniment of Moving Pictures* offer such technical advice as how to simulate wind and rain ("light string tone in fast chromatic scales in 3rds, 6ths, and 4ths"), bird calls, animal noises and other natural phenomena.[29] Yet music's mimetic capacity is encouraged in only a cautious way and its use largely segregated in slapstick.

In addition to the hesitancy within the industry in promoting music's mimetic capacity, there was a reticence in encouraging synchronization between the tempo of the action and the tempo of the music. In fact, the very term synchronization had been coopted by the literature of accompaniment to refer to the much more important practice of achieving a continuous musical accompaniment by timing musical selections to footage counts. Synchronization to a silent film accompanist meant not matching music to action but rather calculating the correct length of music to fill the entire film. Music and image should exist "in perfect synchrony. By this we mean that if a dominant scene has a footage of one hundred and fifty feet, the appropriate selections should run exactly two minutes and fifteen seconds."[30] Not surprisingly, those people who chose and compiled music for orchestral accompaniment were known as synchronizers.

Part of this cautionary position was the result of problems in achieving even approximate synchronization between pit and screen. The lack of standardization in tempo markings, the individual temperament and experience of the players, the condition of the celluloid itself, and even the amount of electrical current supplying the projector could wreak havoc in the process of matching music to image. Leo Forbstein, who began his career as a musical director during the silent era, used a speedometer on the conductor's stand to mark projection speed. The solo accompanist, who could compensate for some of these variables, could attain a higher degree of correspondence than the cinema orchestra, but in general direct attempts to synchronize diegetic action to music through rhythm or tempo were infrequently and very cautiously encouraged.

The cue sheet for *Beau Geste*, for instance, comprises seventy-six cues but contains only one in which the accompanist was asked to directly synchronize visual action: "catch shot and fall." [31] While George Beynon in his manual for cinema accompanists notes that "care must be taken, when the marching soldiers appear, the music is kept in perfect time with their step," [32] a typical cue sheet was rarely more specific in its directive to match screen action to music than this Hansford cue: "play a few measures of Coronation March through business of marching." [33] Beynon warned the cinema conductor that

> it required considerable deftness of timing and a close following of the picture to make the required synchronous effect. Moreover if the orchestra arrived at the big chord before the climax had been reached in the picture, there was a semblance of burlesque that completely spoiled the feature. [34]

In place of diegetic reproduction or direct synchronization as the master plan of the silent film score was the more loosely defined concept of mutual correspondence, in which the structural properties of music (its tempo, rhythm, or harmonics) or its associative powers were loosely matched to the implied narrative content. The most reliable indicator of such correspondence was visual reference. That which could be represented most directly on the screen, such as geographic location

and time period, or discerned with a quick glance, such as the tempo
of the action, triggered the most immediate and identifiable musical responses. Thus an image of a pagoda engendered Oriental music (usually
a bass of open fourths or fifths); an eighteenth-century ball suggested a
minuet. Likewise, a scene of quick action, a chase for instance, merited
an *agitato* or some variety of "hurry music," while a scene with deliberately slow action, a funeral procession, elicited an *adagio* or even a *largo*.
Manuals stressed alertness to the screen ("*the player's eyes should be
on the screen as constantly as possible*")[35] and attention to the obvious.
Rapee's encyclopedia even offers "neutral music" designed for situations
"where *there is neither action,* nor atmosphere, nor elements of human
temperament present in any noteworthy degree."[36]

In lieu of direct reference accompanists were expected to call on
their own acumen and experience in discerning a scene's content and
were urged to become students of human psychology in order to more
quickly and accurately render a musical illustration of the image's content. Of primary importance was the quick recognition of such intan-
gibles as mood and emotion and their simultaneous translation into
music. Lang and West offer this advice:

> Human nature, in spite of its complication, can be reduced to a rather
> limited field of observation, so far as the "movies" are concerned. . . .
> Such fundamental emotions, and their related affections, should be care-
> fully studied by the player; he should be able readily to recognize them,
> and he should seek to express them in turn by means of music.[37]

Accompanists were not left solely to their own devices, however.
Influential in establishing the conventions of mutual correspondence
were the numerous musical encyclopedias widely disseminated within
the industry such as J. S. Zamecnik's *The Sam Fox Moving Picture Music*,
Giuseppi Becci's *Kinobibliothek*, and Erno Rapee's *Encyclopedia of Music
for Pictures* and *Motion Picture Moods*. These volumes contained hun-
dreds of examples of musical selections, both transcriptions from the
classic repertoire and originally composed music, divided into categories
representing intricately described narrative situations and the emotions
they engender. Accompanists could find a narrative situation or visual

reference in the table of contents and turn to the pages which offered various musical options deemed appropriate for its accompaniment. Volume I of *The Sam Fox* series, for instance, offers three separate types of music for battles—"In the Military Camp," "Off to Battle," and "The Battle"—and four types of music for the chase—"Hurry Music," "Hurry Music (for struggles)," "Hurry Music (for duels)," and "Hurry Music (for mob or fire scenes)." The *Encyclopedia of Music for Pictures* lists music appropriate for scenes from Abyssinia to Zanzibar. Deluxe houses collected extensive libraries compiled along the same lines. Loew's theater chain had fifty thousand volumes; the Roxy thirty thousand.[38] Such libraries, together with the more modest musical encyclopedias, helped to regulate the process by which the accompanist selected music for the screen.

The basis of the conventional practice established in these texts was a body of collective musical associations largely derived from nineteenth-century Western European art music. Manuals, advice columns, cue sheets, and compiled scores exploited the classical repertoire for proven examples of music fitted to narrative situation. Opera and program music provided a wealth of material, and the works of composers such as Rossini, Puccini, Verdi, Liszt, von Suppé, Richard Strauss, Tchaikovsky, Grieg, and von Weber constituted the backbone of musical encyclopedias and libraries. Besides its perceived appropriateness to dramatic situations, and its price (since most classical music was in the public domain, its use was free of charge), the classical repertoire offered the accompanist "unique opportunities for the education of the masses."[39] With almost missionary zeal, manuals, advice columns, and cue sheets advocated the use of the classics to pave "the way for the man in the street to come into an appreciation of good music."[40] Though a common complaint was the unsympathetic theater owner who insisted on popular music, accompanists did their best to circumvent musical restrictions and traded techniques with each other for slipping classical music past unsuspecting management.

But it was Wagnerian opera with its continuous musical expression, its linkage of music to drama, and its use of the leitmotif to unify its structure which provided the most direct model for the silent film accompanist.[41] Richard Wagner's theoretical writings explicate an operatic

Treacherous Knave

(Villain Theme, Ruffians, Smugglers, Conspiracy)

Piano

J. S. ZAMECNIK

From *The Sam Fox Moving Picture Music*, Volume IV. This is a typical example of music composed expressly for silent film accompaniment. Descriptive titles such as this one helped the accompanist match music to image.

model, a *Gesamtkunstwerk* (total art work), opposed to the historical practice of prioritizing music at the expense of the drama. Wagner attacked what he perceived as opera's slavish reliance upon music and its lack of regard for the text. "An ideal perfection of the opera, such as so many men of genius had dreamed of, could in the first instance only be attained by means of a total change in the character of *the poet's* participation in the work."[42] Wagner, at least in theory, tied music to dramatic function. "Let us therefore explain to the musician that every situation of his expression (even to that which is least important) in which the poetical intention is not contained, and which is not necessarily conditioned by that intention for its realisation, is superfluous, disturbing and bad."[43]

Wagner's insistence on music composed in relation to the drama offered a model to the silent film musician, and although few accompanists seriously thought that film music could claim a share of the audience's attention equal to that of the images, the relationship Wagnerian opera established between music and spectacle was perceived as a model to emulate. As early as 1911, W. Stephen Bush in *Moving Picture World* asserted, "Every man or woman in charge of music of a moving picture theatre is, consciously or unconsciously, a disciple of Richard Wagner," and promoted the filming of Wagner's operas (accompanied by his scores) as the apex of picture making.[44] Erno Rapee would later assert: "it was Richard Wagner who established the fundamental principles of the music drama of today and it is his work which typifies to the greatest extent and in the minutest detail the accompanying of action with music."[45]

Given the affinity so often cited between Wagnerian opera and silent film, it is hardly surprising that Wagner's concept of the leitmotif became the musical glue which joined the disparate musical selections comprising the silent film score. The **leitmotif** or leading theme is a musical phrase, either as complex as a melody or as simple as a few notes, which, through repetition, becomes identified with a character, situation, or idea. The notion that the silent film score should be a structurally integral discourse with a unity separate from that imposed by the narrative is derived from Wagner's model in which leitmotifs served to unify lengthy and often convoluted material. The concept of unified form (as opposed to a series of random selections) was integral to the development of the silent film score, and the adoption of the principle of the leitmotif coincides historically with the industry's earliest efforts at standardization.

Some of the earliest surviving cue sheets utilize the principle of the leitmotif. An Edison cue sheet for its 1909 production of *Frankenstein* borrows a motif from von Weber's *Der Freischütz* to signal the presence of the monster. With the first music columns in trade papers came advice about using the leitmotif as well as cue sheets which put this theory into practice. By 1910, the association of a musical theme with individual character was so basic to the silent film score that Bert Vipond could call it "a natural law which must on no account be broken."[46] In fact, the use of the leitmotif became so formulaic that Lang and West in their manual could assert: "This theme should be announced in the introduction, it should be emphasized at the first appearance of the person with whom it is linked, and it should receive its ultimate glorification, by means of tonal volume, etc., in the finale of the film."[47] Because of the nature of silent film accompaniment, leitmotifs tended to be lengthy during this era, and it was not uncommon for a substantial piece of music to function as a musical identification. This practice would change radically during the sound period when mechanical reproduction made shorter leitmotifs not only viable but preferable.

Film music in the silent cinema offered a model of musical practice which conceived of music as integral to the experience of filmgoing. While the actual accompaniment to any given film was tempered by the ability of the player and a performance could differ in content as well as in quality from one auditorium to another and even from one screening to another, guidelines for accompaniment formally articulated in manuals, encyclopedias, cue sheets, and trade columns were promulgated within the industry and shared among practitioners. What spectators/auditors in the cinematic auditorium did experience in common was a continuous musical accompaniment bearing only an intermittent and selective relationship of diegetic fidelity to the image, structured as an integral entity by the principle of the leitmotif, and executed in a loose correspondence rather than direct synchronization to narrative action. By the end of the silent period, musical accompaniment to the motion picture, which began as a seemingly appropriate and novel gesture, had developed into a practice indispensable to the cinematic experience.

That facet of the relationship between music and image, its indispensability, would survive the chaos occasioned by the success of mechanical reproduction of synchronized sound. But other characteristics of the model would not. Film music in the silent cinema proves not so much a forerunner of the classical Hollywood film score as an alternative practice, a set of conventions developed in response to particular needs. The classical score appropriated from the silent model its insistence on narrative integrity through an amalgamation of music and image and its translation of musical experience into collective associations which could be harnessed in service to that narrative. But it fundamentally altered the relationship which the silent film score established between the spectator and the screen. What characterizes the sound model is a movement away from the diegetic nonspecificity and continuous musical correspondence of the typically compiled silent film score to uncompromising diegetic fidelity and selective musical accompaniment.

CHAPTER 4

The Classical Hollywood Film Score

Captain Blood: A Working Model

The mechanical reproduction of the musical score with Warner Brothers' *Don Juan* (1926) ignited a revolution in cinematic practice whose battleground was the soundtrack. Music was a crucial factor in that battle, and the early sound years are characterized by attempts to define both its place and its function in the new medium. As the silent film score had responded to a unique set of circumstances with a set of conventions to standardize its practice, the sound film score responded to the intersection of changing technology, aesthetics, and economics with the same impulse: to generate a set of conventions to formalize its practice.

Technological limitations posed a formidable barrier to the continuous stream of music which had characterized silent film. Initially single tracks recorded all ambient sound simultaneously with the recording of the image. With postproduction dubbing an almost impossible task, a combination of music and sound, particularly music and dialogue, had to be mixed directly on the set, posing sometimes insurmountable problems. The mechanical reproduction of synchronized sound also shifted aesthetic priorities, moving film closer to the realism Hollywood sought to capture on celluloid. A nondiegetic musical score was almost immediately at odds with an ideology that saw sound as an opportunity to strengthen the impression of reality. Finally, with the change from silent to sound production, the financial burden of musical accompaniment shifted from the theater owner, who bought cue sheets or original scores, maintained a film music library, and paid musicians and conductors, to the studios. While costs for the production of mood music on the set was a typical item in a silent film's budget, studios were now expected to cover added costs, an unwelcome constraint during the first cost-intensive years of sound production. Film music needed a form compatible with these demands, and the early sound years were characterized not so much by a steady progression toward the practice which coalesced into the classical Hollywood film score as by the simultaneous existence of a variety of practices which responded in different ways to the demands of technology, aesthetics, and economics.

Transplanting the silent film score more or less intact to the sound film was the initial strategy adopted by the industry. In fact, standardizing and improving musical accompaniment was one of the most compelling reasons for Warners' plunge into Vitaphone production. No less than the New York Philharmonic recorded the score for *Don Juan*. Warner Brothers, forging ahead with *The Jazz Singer* (1927), continued to transfer conventions of the silent film score to the sound product. Al Jolson's fortuitous ad-libbing unleashed the power of synchronized dialogue, and Warners revised its plan, putting its resources into the possibilities of "talking" pictures and largely abandoning its initial commitment to standardizing silent film accompaniment. Other studios, however, vainly trying to preserve silent production either as the normative practice or as a viable alternative (and recuperate substantial investments in films either awaiting distribution or in production as silents), continued the practices of silent film music. Influential composers/compilers of silent film music, such as J. S. Zamecnik, Hugo Riesenfeld, and the team of David Mendoza and William Axt, finding themselves musical directors for the new sound films, reproduced the model familiar to them in films like *Sunrise* (1927), *The Wedding March* (1928), and *The Wind* (1928). Even as late as 1932, Max Steiner transplanted the continuous score to the sound film in *Bird of Paradise*.[1]

The most common practice in the period, however, restricted music to diegetic use, where its presence was occasioned by dialogue cues ("Just listen to that music") or visual reference (the appearance of on-screen musicians, for instance, or the presence of radios or phonographs). This meant that, in many films, there was no musical accompaniment at all.

A large body of films actually mixed practices. *The Jazz Singer* juxtaposed two diametrically opposed musical practices: one allowing for nondiegetic and continuous music, the other expurgating it. Those portions of the film shot as silent footage are accompanied by continuous nondiegetic music structured around the principle of the leitmotif (the love theme, for instance, from Tchaikovsky's *Romeo and Juliet* to represent Jack Robbins' feelings for his parents) and loosely corresponding to the visual images (a quotation from the popular song "East Side, West Wide," for instance, to accompany the opening street scenes on New York's Lower East Side). The brief synchronized sound portions of the film, however, include only that music diegetically justifiable on the image track. During the famous dialogue sequence between Jack and his mother, the only music to be heard is that produced by Jack as he vamps a few chords at the piano.[2] Other films were equally inconsistent. An early Clara Bow talkie, *The Wild Party* (1929), uses nondiegetic music during the opening and closing credits, and in some but not all of the film's sporadic intertitles. Musicals seemed less reticent about nondiegetic accompaniment, perhaps because music was a part of the film in some form already. In *The Love Parade* (1929), for instance, diegetic music in the production numbers spills over as nondiegetic music for ensuing scenes.

Thus film music initially responded to the upheaval presaged by technology without generating a definitive model. Some films used music as it had been used in the silent film, as a continuous musical stream in loose correspondence with the image. Other films used music only diegetically, a practice which yielded both the filmed stage plays which contained no music at all, and the all-talking, all-singing, all-dancing musical, which encompassed the diegetic production of its own score. Some films, most notably musicals, actually used short nondiegetic cues, usually to cover transitions. Others mixed practices using continuous nondiegetic accompaniment in some sequences and strict diegetic fidelity in others. Lacking conventions for treating music, the industry often turned to what was expedient. Ironically, the one constant throughout this period is the persistence of live musical performance in the form of concert prologues, vaudeville acts, and the sing-alongs which would not be expurgated from movie theaters for decades. The classical Hollywood film score awaited the technological progress which offered the possibility of sound mixing (dependent upon the shift to sound-on-film systems) and the attendant changes in aesthetics and economics which stabilized the viewing experience.

By the early thirties these technological developments had arrived. The most important of them occurred in 1929: postsynchronization, multiple track recording, and prerecording and playback. King Vidor's experiments with postsynchronization in *Hallelujah!* allowed him to shoot some sequences silent and add sound in postproduction. Rouben Mamoulian's use of double track recording in *Applause* introduced the possibility of mixing sound from separate tracks. The prerecording of a musical number from Harry Beaumont's *The Broadway Melody* and its playback on the set further liberated filmmakers from the limitations of early sound technology. With these developments came viable sound-proofing for the camera which freed it from the confines of the glass booth. Improved techniques of miking, including the use of directional microphones and booms which allowed selective recording of sound, and the introduction of four tracks in 1932, negotiated the technological impasse which impeded the simultaneous presence of music, sound effects, and dialogue.

Similarly changing were aesthetic constraints on the presence of non-diegetic music in dramatic films, which began going to absurd lengths to redefine such music as diegetic. Max Steiner recalls such an example. "Many strange devices were used to introduce the music. For instance, a love scene might take place in the woods and in order to justify the music thought necessary to accompany it, a wandering violinist would be brought in for no reason at all." [3] Such convoluted narrative paths suggest the extent to which music's power to reinforce narrative content and arouse emotional response was never wholly abandoned.

Even those films which placed the highest priority on realism succumbed to the power of music to heighten dramatic effect. In *Thunderbolt* (1929), Josef von Sternberg's gritty example of social realism, a small musical ensemble of prisoners mysteriously materializes on death row where they practice in a conveniently empty jail cell. The piano they use is serendipitously present—another inmate happens coincidentally to be an accomplished player. During a particularly dramatic moment in the film, the last hours of an innocent man awaiting execution, the musicians coincidentally (?) decide to practice, providing offscreen but diegetic music which underscores the action (incredibly, excerpts from von Suppé's *Poet and Peasant* overture). The film, however, is not without a certain degree of self-consciousness about its use of music: the death row prisoners complain that they keep losing their tenors.

By the early thirties it was clear that sound films had replaced silent films as the normative practice. The vast creative energy which had been harnessed to solve the problems of the mechanical reproduction of sound resulted in several technological improvements that paved the way for the simultaneous use of dialogue and music. It was in this climate that producer William LeBaron asked composer Max Steiner to "write just a few lousy things" for his epic western Cimarron, scheduled to open in four weeks.[4]

The score for Cimarron (1931) is actually quite meager, roughly half a dozen musical cues totaling less than ten minutes. Most of the cues are diegetically produced with the music's source included in the frame. Even the sequence with the most extended accompaniment contains narrative justification for the presence of music. A formal luncheon celebrating Sabra Cravat's election to Congress is underscored by what sounds like typical party music. The sequence begins with a close-up of an invitation and continues through the dissolve to the elegant hotel where the festivities are in progress. Although no musicians appear on screen at any point, narrative justification for the syrupy underscoring to Sabra's melancholic memories is included. In one brief shot, a man in formal dress (a conductor?) signals somewhere offscreen and music begins. But in the final shot, there is no diegetic justification for the orchestral music which swells the soundtrack transcending the film's diegetic boundary and spilling over into the final credits.

The importance of Steiner's score for Cimarron, however, rests not only upon its transgression of the industry's priority on diegetic realism in a dramatic context (it was not the first or only film to do so), but also upon a recognition within the industry of Steiner's departure from the accepted norm. Steiner encapsulates this process in his own inimitable style.

> The picture opened. The next morning, the papers came out and reported that the picture was excellent. And what about the music—it said that it was the greatest music that ever was written. Their [the producers'] faces dropped, and I got a raise of fifty dollars.[5]

Steiner's claim is a bit hyperbolic, but newspapers did single out the score, an unusual practice for the time, with feature articles on Steiner and his music for Cimarron.[6] Hollywood now had yet another practice for the musical accompaniment to sound films, distinguished by a selective use of nondiegetic music for dramatic emphasis. But rather than adding another model to the alternatives available in the sound era, the scoring principles contained in *Cimarron* laid the groundwork for a definitive practice which would evolve into the classical Hollywood film score.

The position of this new musical model was solidified with the success of, among other films, *King Kong* (1933). The film's producers, instinctively sensing the vulnerability of the special effects, sought Steiner's help in authenticating them, hoping that music would "save" the film. Merian C. Cooper was particularly worried about the credibility of Kong. Recalls Steiner:

> But when it was finished the producers were skeptical about what kind of public reception they could expect. They thought that the gorilla looked unreal and that the animation was rather primitive. They told me that they were worried about it, but that they had spent so much money making the film there was nothing left over for the music score. . . .[7]

When Steiner got the go-ahead from Cooper he composed a massive score. In fact, once protagonist Carl Denham and crew reach Kong's home on Skull Island, the film is almost continuously scored. (Roughly seventy-five of the film's hundred minutes are accompanied by music.) Not surprisingly, with the exception of the battle with the dinosaur, all of Kong's appearances are accompanied, as are those of his gigantic enemies on Skull Island. As Cooper sensed, Kong's monstrous presence strained the limits of Hollywood's standard of realism. The presence of music signaled the entry into the fantastic realm, facilitating the leap of faith necessary to accept Kong as real. The score became a crucial element in films of this genre where music inherited the responsibility of creating the credible from the incredible.

Yet even in *King Kong* the priority on realism can still be felt in the film's opening musical cues. As in *Cimarron* the score initially depends on music that can be narratively justified, however tenuously. The first cue, excluding the main title, works to fuse the nondiegetic and diegetic and obscure the boundary between them. As Denham's ship approaches Skull Island, musical accompaniment can be heard, primarily a series of harp arpeggios with string accompaniment. As the boat nears the island, drumbeats become faintly audible; it is not clear whether they are diegetic or not. Suddenly Jack Driscoll announces, "That's not breakers, that's drums." Like Steiner's proverbial wandering violinist, Driscoll both naturalizes and authorizes the presence of music, the diegetic reference to music masking the presence of the nondiegetic harp arpeggios.

The Academy of Motion Picture Arts and Sciences added the originally composed film score as an award category in 1934. (Steiner won his first Oscar the next year for *The Informer*.) By the mid-thirties musical accompaniment which depended on original composition and incorporated the selective nondiegetic use of music became the dominant practice, replacing older traditions (Chaplin's use of continuous music in his early sound films, for instance) and alternative practices (Warner Brothers' cycle of social realism films which omitted music entirely). What would become known as the classical model was almost immediately absorbed into Hollywood practice, its production both reflecting and reinforcing the structure of the studio system.

Studio production was not new in the sound period. Silent filmmakers depended upon the collective resources of a studio to produce, promote, and distribute their films. What the sound period did was institutionalize a mode of production which contractually bound the individual agents who create a film to the studio. The classical score developed during a period which saw the solidification of the producer's power. A composer, like other craftspeople employed by the studio, experienced a relationship to any given film that was specific, transitory, and subject to the authority of the studio.

A determining characteristic of the studio model was its efficiency, keeping the assembly line of production moving with a highly diversified division of labor. Personnel were assigned tasks specific to their talents and capabilities and were expected to execute them with skill and speed. The process by which music became part of a film was broken down into its various parts and divided up among personnel trained to complete these assignments quickly. Composers, usually with a music editor, sometimes with other production personnel, spotted the film, that is, identified likely places for musical accompaniment. Composers were then expected to compose, sketching out their ideas on anywhere between two and eight staves of music. These sketches were passed on to an orchestrator or orchestrators, who chose particular instruments to voice specific lines. The terms "orchestrator" and "arranger" were used fairly interchangeably in Hollywood, although technically an arranger orchestrated a preexistent piece of music (like "Dixie" in *Gone With the Wind*.) On "B" films, with abbreviated production schedules, this process was often subdivided even further with teams of composers and/or orchestrators dividing up the work.[8] Copyists transcribed the finished score into parts for the orchestra. The conductor conducted the recording session which synchronized score to film. This division of labor was built for speed and efficiency. In practice, however, the distinctions between the various components of the process were not always clear.

The division between composition and orchestration was the most frequently blurred. Although most composers did not orchestrate their own scores, it is a misconception to assume that they did not exert a determining influence in this regard. In fact orchestration was a sore point among those composers in Hollywood (and there were many) who were clearly capable of orchestrating their work, but were prevented from doing so by a system which used them for their compositional talents. Bernard Herrmann simply demanded that he be given the time to orchestrate his own scores. A contemporary example of a composer who orchestrates his own material is Georges Delerue. Other composers compensated for what they considered a liability in the system by detailing their sketches to such an extent that the orchestration would be obvious. The sketches of composers such as David Raksin and John Williams are so complete that the orchestrator need do little more than copy out what is outlined in them. Even Max Steiner, who was not known for his detailed sketches, delineated instrumentation as his sketch for *King Kong* demonstrates. On his sketches for *The Informer* he is even more specific, writing to Bernard Kaun: "Bernard: Brass *not* on melody, but underneath (symphonic style). Also please put chimes in for end title."[9] Since Steiner had established a relationship with Kaun he could be confident that his notation would be implemented. As he himself said, "The orchestrator just takes what he is given to do and if he has any ideas of his own, he had better not show them."[10]

Other composers established a relationship with an orchestrator who

From Max Steiner's sketch for *King Kong*. Specific instructions for orchestration appear in measures 2, 3, 5, and 9.

would become so familiar with the composer's orchestral style that he could reproduce it instinctively. Hugo Friedhofer, a composer who began his career in Hollywood as an orchestrator for Steiner and Erich Wolfgang Korngold, worked on seventeen of Korngold's eighteen original film scores. Friedhofer claims that he knew what Korngold wanted,

even if it was not notated in the score. "Well, it was a very close association. He always liked to look at the score. We'd discuss the sketches
very thoroughly. He had a fantastic way of playing the piano with an
orchestral style so you could almost sense what he was hearing in the
orchestra." [11] A contemporary example of an established relationship
between a composer and an orchestrator is the one between John
Williams and Herbert Spencer.

Many composers, however, insisted on conducting. While it was the
common practice for a studio's musical director to conduct a score,
especially on "B" pictures, it remained the prerogative of the composer
on the big-budget, prestige productions. Korngold, Steiner, Alfred
Newman, and Herrmann usually wielded the baton for the scores they
composed.

The Hollywood production model also dictated the time frame in
which composers were expected to work. Scoring started after a film
was in rough cut, and had to be completed in the time it took to finish
a print for distribution. Typically this period would extend from four to
six weeks, but a more accurate indicator of the actual time a composer
was allotted is a continuum. One end represents the shortest amount
of time humanly possible for the composition of a score. Max Steiner
claimed he lived without sleep for the eight days it took him to compose
and conduct *The Lost Patrol* (1934). The other end represents the maximum amount of time over the roughly six-week limit that a composer
could negotiate. Erich Wolfgang Korngold's contract for Warners, for
instance, allowed him longer than the usual six weeks to complete a
score. In addition, it was not uncommon for one composer to work on
several productions simultaneously or for several composers to work
on one production simultaneously. These conditions did not promote
allegiance to a single film, but rather fostered primary allegiance to the
studio.

The classical Hollywood film score proliferated in the thirties but in
an interdependence with the growing power of the studio. The hierarchy which positioned management over labor permeated every facet
of a film's production from its visual style to its music. In the case of the
score, the music department often became the intermediary between
studio and composer. A few composers, like Max Steiner at RKO and

Alfred Newman first at United Artists and then at Twentieth Century-Fox, were also heads of music departments themselves and had easier access to and more clout with studio chiefs as a result. Ultimately, however, this structure of accountability affected the composer's responsibility for the score and gave the studio more direct control over how a score would be fashioned. David O. Selznick's famous memos often contained intricate instructions on the music. Hal B. Wallis' music notes for *Captain Blood* ran five single-spaced pages. Some studios even instituted the policy that all title music be written in a major key. (Irving Thalberg once wrote a memo on main titles requesting MGM composers to "kindly refrain in the future from using minor chords.") [12]

This intervention marks a major difference between the classical film score and its silent predecessor. The mediating devices which regulated the conventions of the silent film score (manuals, columns in trade papers, musical encyclopedias, and cue sheets) were, for the most part, produced independently of the studio whose authority had only an indirect and limited impact on the music. It was over the silent film's orchestral scores that studios wielded the kind of power that they exercised in the sound film. But even here the studio was not invulnerable. Theater organist Gaylord Carter recalls a battle with Paramount over the score for *The Student Prince* (1927) in which the studio capitulated to pressure by accompanists to use Sigmund Romberg's music instead of the studio's score. [13]

Control over music was most directly felt in the influence wielded by studio production chiefs and line producers. Some, like Selznick and Wallis, had strong backgrounds or at least good instincts about music. Others knew little or nothing about it. Anecdotes concerning musical ignorance on the part of producers are legendary. The punchline is always the same: the composer must initiate the producer into the realities of music. There is the producer who wanted to "Frenchify" the score with French horns; the producer who wanted the score to duplicate the chordal harmony of the zither in *The Third Man* on a solo flute; the producer who wanted "his" score to sound like the music of Johannes Brahms and suggested flying Brahms to Hollywood to conduct it; the producer who wanted a Russian sound and, when the soundtrack was mistakenly played backward for him, was delighted to have gotten

Lose the music under the KING JAMES sequence, where he sends the slaves to Jamaica, and bring the music up a little when it comes in now, just when KING JAMES speaks the last speech is where the music should start.... where it starts on that lift... but bring it up a little higher in the duping.

Also, lift it way up on that long shot of the boat and right up to where the man says "AHOY! PORT ROYAL!". The music should lift up there on these silent shots.

Up a little in the sound, both times where BISHOP slaps BLOOD.

OLIVIA DeHAVILAND'S laugh, after she says "How annoyed PETER BLOOD would be if he knew I was going to do him another favor"...... the last part of her laugh, after the fade-out, there's a piece that comes through; just kill it.

Take out the line on the exit of BLOOD and THE GOVERNOR from the NUTALL trial, where he says "Let's go and find Mrs. Steed and tell her about it". Just before he speaks that line, we'll cut to the exterior and let it run two or three feet before BLOOD comes out.

After the two men exit from the room, cut outside and instead of cutting to a long shot with BLOOD coming out, cut to the carriage driving up, and then go to BLOOD coming out at the door.

Take out the three cuts in the scene with HONESTY NUTALL on trial; one cut of NUTALL and a cut of BLOOD and a cut of THE GOVERNOR.

Held down on the girl's "Hello" when she sees BLOOD in the garden.

Don't reverse the cuts on the carriage and BLOOD. Leave it just the way it is at the beginning of the reel.

Hold the music down under the dialogue in the bunk house.... As soon as BLOOD begins to talk hold the dialogue way down. Hold the music way down under the dialogue. You'll have to drop the dialogue way down, too.

Take the music out under the scene with BAYNES at his bedside, and start it up again when the guards come toward the place.

Take out the one little piece of music between the girl and the boy when the girl is on horse-back, before FLY NN gets on to go and take care of the GOVERNOR.

Lose the scoring in back of the voices as the CAPTAIN BLOOD'S row boat pulls up along side the Cinco Legas. We just hear the singing until the men rush down stairs, then pick up that music.

Lose the second shot miniature of the big boat bombarding the small ones.

(Continued)

From Hal B. Wallis' production notes on *Captain Blood*. Note his intricate instructions on the placement of the musical accompaniment.

it. Maurice Jarre recalls a recording session in which he was ordered to give a certain part to the clarinet. His response, that the clarinet was already playing the part, met with total silence. Later, when the oboe played, Jarre was told, "That's it. That's the clarinet." [14]

More far-reaching, however, than the lack of musical knowledge on the part of Hollywood's powerful producers was the conservative position with regard to music that they fostered. Hollywood was comfortable with what was familiar: scores based on the classical repertoire of the nineteenth century. Twentieth-century music, particularly atonality, as well as other experimental styles which abandoned the transcendence of melody and familiar tonal harmony, were suspect. Although most of the composers of the classical film score had embraced a romantic model, some composers working in Hollywood were thoroughly conversant with modern compositional techniques and anxious to try them. But reticence toward experimentation impeded the introduction of these elements into the classical score. David Raksin tells the story of his experience with a producer who wanted an unusual musical score, "something different, really powerful—like *Wozzeck*." Raksin's response was one of ecstasy.

> To hear the magic name of Alban Berg's operatic masterpiece invoked by the man with whom I would be working was to be invited to be free! To hear it correctly pronounced was to doubt the evidence of my own ears: here was a nonmusician who was not only aware that *Wozzeck* existed, but actually thought of his film as one to which so highly expressive a musical style might be appropriate. It was too good to be true.

Later at Raksin's home, the producer asked, " 'What's that crap you're playing?' 'That crap,' replied Raksin, 'is *Wozzeck*.' " [15]

The Classical Hollywood Film Score

In much the same way that the internal structure of the Hollywood studio system affected the production of the classical film score, the ideology of that system affected its form. Classical narrative depends upon the spectator's absorption into the filmic world. The signs of cinematic production which mark the film as a created artifact (artificial lighting, editing, camera movement, etc.) are erased, rendered as invisible as possible. The nondiegetic presence of music threatened this model, and composers faced the paradoxical perception that good film music is "inaudible." Composers objected to this perception (quipped Steiner, "If they don't hear it, what the hell good is it?"),[16] but the classical score developed around this very paradox. Its form was based upon a set of conventions for the composition and placement of nondiegetic music which prioritized narrative exposition. These conventions included the use of music to sustain structural unity; music to illustrate narrative content, both implicit and explicit, including a high degree of direct synchronization between music and narrative action; and the privileging of dialogue over other elements of the soundtrack. The medium of the classical Hollywood film score was largely symphonic; its idiom romantic; and its formal unity typically derived from the principle of the leitmotif.[17]

As I've argued in the Introduction, the classical Hollywood film score can best be understood not as a rigid structural or stylistic manifesto but rather as a set of conventions formulated to sustain and heighten the fictive reality of the classical narrative film. A score can be termed classical because of its high degree of adherence to these practices. This is not to say that all scores composed in Hollywood fit this model or that the model didn't change in response to innovation and experimentation. A conventional practice for scoring films, however, did develop during the first decade of sound production. By the mid-thirties its principles found acceptance and proliferated. Composers who negotiated successful careers in Hollywood relied upon the principles which garnered Academy Awards and prestigious assignments for its practitioners.

One of the most influential of those practitioners was Erich Wolfgang Korngold whose first original score for Warner Brothers' *Captain Blood* (1935) was regarded, along with the work of Max Steiner and Alfred Newman, as the apex of musical achievement in Hollywood during the crucial first decade of sound production. Scores like *Captain Blood* set the trend for originally composed, full-length, symphonic scores modeled on a nineteenth-century musical idiom. The remainder of this chapter will be devoted to this score, to an analysis of selected cues which demonstrate key techniques and practices that characterize the Hollywood model.

The classical Hollywood score differed from its silent predecessor in two important ways. First, it reproduced every diegetic reference to music in the film, unlike the silent score which reproduced such references only selectively. Second, the classical score provided intermittent musical accompaniment rather than a continuous stream of music. A contemporary textbook on composing for film and television puts it this way: "A constant flow of music gets in the way." [18] In fact, the classical Hollywood film score actually reversed the crucial relationship in silent film between continuity and selectivity. In silent film continuous music took precedence over diegetic fidelity. The reproduction of diegetic reference to music was intermittent, left to the prerogative of individual accompanists. In sound film it was diegetic fidelity that took precedence over continuous music. Musical accompaniment was intermittent, its placement determined by the individual composer.

Music and Structural Unity

One of the most important ways in which music became conventionalized in the classical model was through shared perceptions about when music should be heard. Formal concerns provided immediate and identifiable points of entry for musical accompaniment. The silent film score both compensated for the silence of the theatrical auditorium and sustained narrative continuity. The sound film score was freed from the necessity of seamlessness, but inherited from the silent film its function as arbiter of narrative continuity. It is not surprising, then, that composers of the classical score gravitated toward moments when continuity is most tenuous, to points of structural linkages on which the narrative chain depends: transitions between sequences, flash-forwards and flashbacks, parallel editing, dream sequences, and montage. Virgil Thomson articulates the problem from a composer's point of view: "The cinema is naturally a discontinuous medium. . . . [Music] should envelop and sustain a narrative, the cinematographic recounting of which is after all only a series of very short incidents seen from different angles." [19] In the classical system of narration the reconstruction of time and the re-definition of space were controlled through lighting, camera placement and movement, and techniques of continuity editing. An overlooked element in this process is music which helps render the presence of these other elements in the classical narrative system invisible.

Marlin Skiles's text on composing for film and television cautions the would-be composer that "he will be faced with having to literally fill the gap with some music. . . . without its application, scenes such as these could have a disastrous effect on the overall story." [20] This structural reciprocity between narrative continuity and the musical score can be seen in the practice of the bridge, a musical transition which elided gaps occasioned by spatial and temporal disjunctions. Music compensates for potentially disruptive shifts in the form of continuous playing and frequently through reliance upon extended melody or established musical forms. This reciprocity governed the use of musical accompaniment in situations ranging from those as simple as the straight cut to those as complex as the montage. An example which falls between these extremes is a transition in *Captain Blood* precipitated by the shift from Jacobean England, where Dr. Peter Blood (Errol Flynn) has been convicted of treason, to the British colonies in the Caribbean, where he is sent as a slave. It is precisely this kind of narrative moment which engendered musical accompaniment.

The transition is effected in a sequence of twelve shots facilitated by editing techniques which establish the passage of time, such as the lap dissolve, and a superimposed text which establishes the shift in geographic location. Music negotiates this spatiotemporal ellipsis in a number of ways. In this case Korngold uses a standard ABA form built around two motifs associated with Peter Blood: the exposition of theme A (heard here in the minor), followed by a contrasting theme B, and a return to the original theme A. (See Fig. 4.2.) [21] To provide maximum continuity, music begins *before* the shift in time and place, immediately following the delivery of King James's speech decreeing that rebels awaiting execution be sent to the colonies as slave labor. The first theme or A section, played initially in a standard symphonic setting with the violins carrying the melody, enters at a low volume which is noticeably increased during the lap dissolve to the next shot, a ship at sea with a superimposed text explaining its destination. The musical cue continues uninterrupted through the succeeding lap dissolve to a close-up of one of the prisoners aboard ship. Here the Blood motif is repeated in an instrumental variation (horns with accompanying woodwinds and strings). A sequence in the ship's hold follows with a contrasting melody, the B section, played in the low registers of the strings and woodwinds. At the lap dissolve which covers the ellipsis in time and shift in geography, the A theme returns in its initial orchestral setting. A dialogue cue confirms the progress of the ship ("Ahoy, on deck. I've sighted Port Royal"). As the establishing shot of the port replaces the ship on the screen, the score offers the exotic motif representing the city. Rather than break the melodic integrity of the cue, Korngold inserts this new material into a pause in the Blood motif. The disjunction between the establishing shot of Port Royal and the following shot of Blood on board ship is negotiated by several techniques: a dissolve to a reverse eyeline match from Blood's point of view, a repeated word from the previous dialogue cue ("It's a truly royal clemency we're granted, my friends"), and the repetition of the Blood motif in a developmental variation. The sequence concludes with close-ups of Blood's impassioned speech about injustice and a return to the closing phrase of his motif. The reliance upon an established form, the use of continuous music, and the dependence on extended melody rather than short phrases creates the effect of unity reinforcing the narrative at a potentially disruptive moment.

The montage made even greater demands on the music. Quick cuts seldom matched, superimpositions of sometimes three or four images including overlays of text and graphics, and the absence of dialogue, diegetic sound, or both, taxed the conventions of narrative construction, particularly the representation of time. Music lent its rhythmic temporality to such sequences, regulating the flow of images. While it was not necessary or even desirable in the classical narrative system to accompany every transition with music (there were a number of factors which went into this determination including length, narrative content, and proximity of other musical cues), it was almost impossible to allow a montage to exist without accompaniment.[22]

In *Captain Blood* one such montage compresses the exploits of Peter

Blood's pirate career. The structural function of the bridge, to provide continuity in moments of spatial-temporal disjunction, is extended here to cover a fifty-eight-second sequence with multiple superimpositions of image and text. The montage is preceded by a long shot of Blood as he commits himself to a life of piracy on the high seas. Music, which sneaks in under the men's rousing cry of approval, again precedes the actual beginning of the montage, eliding the boundary between the unobtrusive, invisible style of narrative exposition and the technical artifice of the montage. One element fundamental to that artifice is the manipulation of the soundtrack. This often takes the form, as it does here, of a suspension of diegetic sound. Shipboard battles, for instance, are seen but not heard. Even a close-up of Blood clearly speaking has no diegetic sound. Music functions here not unlike its counterpart in the silent film, compensating for and covering this void.

In the same way that music compensates for the absence of diegetic sound in the montage, it also compensates for its spasmodic rhythms. Korngold's musical cue, marked **allegro furioso** (furiously fast), embodies a kind of metronomic function in a quick, continuous pulse which provides a rhythmic framework for a series of edited images lacking temporal and spatial coherence. Finally, music's continuous presence, structurally organized around repetition of the Blood motif, offers its own structural unity as a frame for that of the images. Music thus provides a variety of functions in the montage: it elides the boundary between narrative exposition and virtuosic technical display; it compensates for the absence of diegetic sound; it marks out a regular rhythm often lacking in the complex structure of the montage; and it helps to provide unity through conventions of musical form.

Music and Narrative Action

If formal concerns provided the film composer with a definable set of access points for musical intervention, the starting point for the creation of a musical cue was the image. Its content was gauged in two ways: that which was explicit in the image, such as action, and that which was implicit, such as emotion or mood. What Hollywood film scoring conventionalized was a set of practices for guiding composers in responding to the image musically.

From the nuance of facial expression and bodily gesture to the sweep of movement across the screen, music punctuated narrative. At the heart of this practice was the relationship between music and action. Structural properties of music, such as tempo or rhythm, were harnessed to the visual representation of movement in order to create a particular speed or rhythm. Explains Hugo Friedhofer: "You know the old idea—the horse runs: the music runs."[23] Sequences most likely to be scored in this manner were those which embodied a consistent tempo and/or rhythm which was visually discernable and could easily be matched to a musical accompaniment. In *Captain Blood* there are numerous examples of musical tempo matched, though not necessarily synchronized, to narrative action. Three examples of such cues occur within the first five minutes of the film. The first, a horseback ride at breakneck speed, is accompanied by a passage Korngold marked **ancora piu mosso** (even more agitated), the tempo of the music reproducing and reinforcing the frenzy of the ride. Within a few moments the opposite effect is achieved when Korngold uses the deliberate tempo of the **largo** (slowly) to accompany the lugubrious procession of accused traitors toward prison. Between these two cues is yet a third in which Korngold scores the entrance of loyalist troops with a cue he marked **quasi marcia** (like a march), matching the tempo of the music to the pace of the soldiers' step. Throughout the film similar musical cues contribute to the action, from the extended **allegro** (fast) and **presto** (very fast) in the duel between Blood and his rival Levasseur (Basil Rathbone), to the *sforzando* chord, known as a **stinger**, which marks the sword's fatal thrust. In fact, swashbucklers like *Captain Blood* contained so many action sequences that Korngold initially refused the studio's follow-up, *The Adventures of Robin Hood* (1938), because of its imposing action format and the sheer amount of music he would need to compose. As he wrote Hal B. Wallis, "*Robin Hood* is no picture for me. . . . I am a musician of the heart, of passions and psychology; I am not a musical illustrator for a 90% action picture."[24]

The relationship which existed between music and narrative action did not preclude the possibility of deliberate disjunction for thematic resonance. (There is a striking sequence in *Force of Evil* (1948), for instance, where the protagonist races down a staircase looking for his dead brother to a musical accompaniment of very slow tempo.) But the use of music for this purpose in the classical film score was limited. A more common practice involved using tempi or rhythm in disjunction with narrative action in order to increase a pace perceived lacking in the images. Explains Max Steiner: "There may be a scene that is played a shade too slowly which I might be able to quicken with a little animated music; or, to a scene that is too fast, I may be able to slow it down a little and give it a little more feeling by using slower music." [25] Skiles's text offers this practical advice for those scenes which "played a shade too slowly." "Intelligent chord progressions, changes of color. . . , the use of such melodic percussion instruments . . . can give the feeling of movement an [sic] sustain the audience interest through periods such as these." [26]

In *Captain Blood* Korngold uses the standard musical device of the **ostinato**, a repeated melodic or rhythmic figure, to propel scenes which lack dynamic and compelling visual action. One such sequence involves a clandestine meeting between Blood and his fellow slaves to plan their escape. By necessity dialogue is whispered and character movement is minimal. Korngold begins the musical cue before the cut to the meeting. As guards patrol the grounds, a simple *basso ostinato,* a repeated figure in the bass line, creates a rhythm for the sequence. Following the lap dissolve to the interior of the slaves' quarters, this *ostinato* is joined by two distinctive musical figures, one for cello and tuba, the other for trombones, which add rhythmic intensity to a pan over the motionless men. As the meeting begins, the volume of the music gradually decreases and eventually drops out so that information crucial to the plot—relayed through dialogue—can be heard unobstructed. Music returns during the emotional scene between Blood and a fellow slave and continues to the end of the sequence.

At its extreme the practice of matching music to narrative action resulted in the direct synchronization between visual action and music known as Mickey Mousing. Although it is often associated with silent film accompaniment, Mickey Mousing is a product of sound technology, named for the animated cartoons in which it developed. Mickey Mousing was a well-established practice by the mid-thirties, and it is particularly prominent in the scores of Max Steiner. In *The Informer*, for instance, the protagonist, Gypo Nolan, lumbers down the street in direct synchronization to the leitmotif Steiner wrote for him, every step accompanied by a note of music. To the modern listener, Mickey Mousing may seem excessively obvious and even distracting, but ironically it was a practice founded in the very principle of inaudibility. The vocal track in classical cinema anchors diegetic sound to the image by synchronizing it, masking the actual source of sonic production, the speakers, and fostering the illusion that the diegesis itself produces the sound. Mickey Mousing duplicates these conventions in terms of nondiegetic sound. Precisely synchronizing diegetic action to its musical accompaniment masks the actual source of sonic production, the offscreen orchestra, and renders the emanation of music natural and consequently inaudible. Musical accompaniment was thus positioned to effect perception, especially on the semiconscious level, without disrupting narrative credibility.

Mickey Mousing, like other elements of the classic score, was harnessed to the narrative, catching an action to solidify its importance. Korngold did not depend on Mickey Mousing in his scores (his lengthy cues made its use problematic), but there is a textbook example in *Captain Blood*. As Colonel Bishop is thrown overboard, a rising musical figure imitates each swing of his body as the men prepare to fling him aloft. His entry into the water is caught with a stinger.

Music and Emotion

Music, however, not only responded to explicit content, but fleshed out what was not visually discernible in the image, its implicit content. In this capacity, music was expected to perform a variety of functions: provide characterization, embody abstract ideas, externalize thought, and create mood and emotion. For the fitter of film music in the silent era visual reference was the surest indicator of content. In the sound era the dialogue also helped mark intent. But ultimately the interpretation of implicit content was left to the individual prerogative of the composer. Frank Skinner's admonition to students of Hollywood scoring echoes the familiar advice dispensed to silent film accompanists: "train yourself to grasp situations fast."[27]

Scenes that most typically elicited the accompaniment of music were those that contained emotion. The classical narrative model developed certain conventions to assist expressive acting in portraying the presence of emotion, primarily selective use of the close-up, diffuse lighting and focus, symmetrical mise-en-scène, and heightened vocal intonation. The focal point of this process became the music which externalized these codes through the collective resonance of musical associations. Music is, arguably, the most efficient of these codes, providing an audible definition of the emotion which the visual apparatus offers. Samuel Chell compares the musical score in classical Hollywood narrative film to the laugh track of television situation comedy.[28] Music's dual function as both articulator of screen expression and initiator of spectator response binds the spectator to the screen by resonating affect between them. The lush, stringed passages accompanying a love scene are representations not only of the emotions of the diegetic characters but also of the spectator's own response which music prompts and reflects.

Composers of the Hollywood film score were drawn almost compulsively to moments of heightened emotional expression which afforded them what they perceived to be the most direct access to the spectator. Steiner said of his score for *The Informer*: "I put the music in the harp when McLaglen sold this guy down the river and in the very end, I had him sing when his mother forgave him in church. It brought a few tears."[29] That power of music to elicit emotional response is often ascribed to music's ability to transcend the limitations of the visual image. Elmer Bernstein typifies this position when he argues: "music can tell the story in purely emotional terms and the film by itself cannot." For Bernstein film is "a visual language and basically intellectual. You look at an image and you then have to interpret what it means, whereas if you listen to something or someone and you understand what you hear— that's an emotional process."[30] This position, frequently articulated by film composers, posits music's ability to transcend cognitive mediation as the source of its emotional appeal. But it may be more accurate to attribute music's power not to its presumed innocence but to the fact that its forms of mediation are less immediately discernible.

Korngold's score for *Captain Blood* contains some interesting examples of how music is used in the classical film score to create emotion. Predictably, many of these scenes are related to the romantic plot concerning Blood and the niece of the governor of Jamaica, Arabella Bishop (Olivia de Havilland). At cross-purposes for most of the film, these two lovers acknowledge their feelings for each other only at the last possible moment. Thus Korngold's music responds not to what is explicitly stated in the dialogue (they are either coy or insulting to each other), but to what is implicit in their demeanor and reinforced by conventional expectations of classical narrative (that two attractive stars of the opposite sex belong together). When Blood, for instance, responds to the inquiries of Miss Bishop with a cavalier attitude and high-handed remarks, the music reassures us that he is hardly as indifferent as his demeanor suggests. Similarly, when Arabella Bishop tells Blood that she hates and despises him, the soaring violins of the love theme soften, even negate, her rejection, pointing to her true feelings, thinly disguised beneath the surface. Music draws out the emotional content of the scene, hidden from the characters but not from the spectators.

The leitmotif Korngold used to represent the love between Peter Blood and Arabella Bishop facilitates such a reading. It depends upon several standard devices for emotional expression: dramatic upward leaps in the melodic line; sustained melodic expression in the form of long phrases; lush harmonies; and reliance upon the expressivity of the strings to carry the melody. Because of the nature of the romantic entanglement in this film, Korngold gives the love theme extended expression not when the lovers are together on the screen, but when they are apart, during "private" moments when they are free to rhapsodize about each other. One such example occurs when Blood sends Arabella Bishop ashore moments before the final sea battle. The love theme enters beneath Bishop's dialogue and is turned up to full volume as the dinghy bearing her toward safety moves farther and farther away from the ship. Her gaze, as well as Blood's in the reverse shot, is encoded as melancholic by the extended reprise of the love theme.

From the first violin part for "Love Scene." It accompanies the conversation between Peter Blood and Arabella Bishop on the governor's lawn. This cue embodies many of the techniques Korngold used for heightening emotional expression. Note the musical markings, "*Andante Espressivo*" and "Flowingly"; the soli violins at measure eight; dramatic upward leaps in the musical line; and the use of parallel thirds to fill out the chordal harmony.

Music and Subjectivity

The preceding example is particularly interesting for in it music encodes not only emotion but point of view. The classical narrative model developed a number of conventions for internal thought including voice-over, specific editing patterns (the eyeline match especially combined with the dissolve), and musical accompaniment. Together or separately, these techniques offered an analogue for a character's consciousness. That Bishop is explicitly thinking of Peter Blood, whom she has left behind, is denoted through editing and camera movement. A dolly-out on Blood aboard ship is positioned as the object of her eyeline match. What she is thinking about him, however, is only implicit in the scene, made explicit by a combination of generic expectation (given the conventions of Hollywood romance, what else would she be thinking of?) and the presence of the love theme.

Earlier in the film there is a sequence which this one mirrors. Blood, freed from his imprisonment, is poised on the brink of a pirate career. He stands on the deck of a captured Spanish galleon as his crew prepares to depart, and for a moment he gazes at the faraway shore. A dissolve to a close-up of Bishop at the dock reveals the contents of his mind and reinforces what we have already presumed—that his gaze indicates regret about leaving her. A soaring string melody which modulates into the love theme authorizes this interpretation.

Music and Mood

The creation of mood and atmosphere also relied on the ability of the composer to discern implicit content and respond with appropriate music. "To understand moods in music and to be able to grasp a mood in a pictorial situation,"[31] a skill crucial to the silent film accompaniment, remained central to the sound composer's task. Establishing shots were the most typical point of access for atmospheric music, especially those which made direct reference to geographic location or historical period. Mood music tapped the power of collective associations to create the time and place represented in the image. Korngold had ample

The miniature for the set of Port Royal, Jamaica. Music is instrumental in the creation of time and place; it lends credibility to what might otherwise appear "phony." Korngold's cue for Port Royal is arranged for triangle, celesta, harp, muted trumpets, and percussion, lending an exotic, foreign flavor to the setting.

opportunity for atmospheric music in *Captain Blood*, its Caribbean setting providing exotic locales and its historical context offering a wide spectrum of national types. Korngold's Port Royal cue, for instance, uses unusual instrumentation to define the exotic nature of the port (triangle, celesta, harp, and muted trumpets), and assigns percussive instruments the job of carrying the melody. (A **celesta** is a percussive instrument resembling a small upright piano.) Other examples of music's function in establishing geographic context or national identity include the motif heard during the Spanish pirates' conquest of Port Royal and the motif composed for Tortuga. Both are built upon the pronounced syncopated rhythms associated with Latin cultures. Korngold takes advantage of even the smallest opportunity in *Captain Blood*. A variation on the opening motif of "God Save the Queen," labeled "The Good King William," can be heard when either England or King William is mentioned. The lowering of the French flag is accompanied by a variation on the bugle call from Bizet's *Carmen*.

The classical score, however, relied not so much on actual imitation of music indigenous to other cultures as on a more generic concept of exoticism. Fred Karlin and Rayburn Wright in their 1990 manual for film and television composing, *On the Track: A Guide to Contemporary Film Scoring*, describe it as "quasi authenticity."[32] Instruments not typical of the symphonic complement and rhythmic patterns associated with

Tortuga. The cimbalom, a large dulcimer associated with Hungarian gypsy music, is used here to create an "authentic" sound for Tortuga, a pirate haven in the Caribbean.

foreign cultures represented, often interchangeably, anything from Tortuga, Peter Blood's seventeenth-century pirate haven, to Skull Island, the twentieth-century home of King Kong. A prominent example is the cue Korngold composed for the Spanish "Street Scene." Here Korngold exploits the horns playing in parallel thirds characteristic of the Mexican mariachi bands which developed during the nineteenth century to represent Spanish pirates roaming the Caribbean during the seventeenth century. Similarly, "Tortuga" suggests the exoticism of the pirate haven through an exceptionally unusual complement of instruments. Hand cymbals, tambourines, triangles, harp, celesta, saxophones, vibraphone, and guitar are joined by a **cimbalom**, a Hungarian instrument in the dulcimer family frequently associated with gypsies! (Watch for the cimbalom solo diegetically produced by a musical pirate.)

Atmospheric or mood music was not limited to that generated by the spatial and temporal necessities of the plot. Music was called upon to create a mood sometimes only dimly suggested by the images and thus ready the spectator for a heightened response to narrative development. One of the most important of these moods is suspense, and the Hollywood film score depended upon a core of musical conventions, a shorthand if you will, for encoding tension. A sequence which takes place during Blood's enslavement on the Bishop plantation exemplifies many of these practices. A prisoner who has attempted escape is about to be branded as a fugitive traitor. Korngold's music intensifies the suspenseful potential of the scene through the use of *tremolo* strings, cymbal rolls, horn flutters, an exceptionally high flute part, and *crescendo*. At the moment when the iron sears the man's flesh, the *crescendo* reaches a *fortissimo,* and a *sforzando* attack marks the action transpiring out of the camera's range.

Another technique Korngold uses to create tension is the *ostinato.* Repetition of a specific musical figure can provide a rhythmic intensity to fill an otherwise unremarkable scene. An *ostinato* can also create tension through sheer accumulation, a kind of musical Chinese water torture. Korngold heightens this effect during the men's escape when he introduces a descending *basso ostinato* to infuse their stealthy and circumspect movements with urgency.

Music and Dialogue

An important constraint on the presence of music was dialogue. Privileged above all other elements of the soundtrack, dialogue had priority in the classical system's hierarchy of audibility. Music, even that diegetically produced, must not detract from the power of dialogue in the exposition of narrative. In the crucial early period of sound film, **underscoring**, or musical accompaniment to dialogue, was avoided. The artificiality of nondiegetic music was particularly at odds with the "naturalism" of the spoken word, and the earliest recording techniques prohibited mixing dialogue and music. By the early thirties technology permitted limited underscoring, but the process proved difficult and often produced distortion. Leonid Sabaneev, in his text for film composition translated in 1935, argued that "music should cease or retire into the background when dialogues and noises are taking place. Except in rare instances, it blends but poorly with them." [33] Yet as early as 1931, a film like *Cimarron* used musical accompaniment under dialogue (Sabra Cravat's monologue about her husband, Yancey, is accompanied by music).

Conventions for underscoring developed to bring the expressive possibilities of music to the human voice. These included relying on the strings; avoiding the woodwinds, whose timbre tends to obscure dialogue; avoiding extremes in register; using melody and avoiding counterpoint; and relying on simple rhythms, slow tempi, and low volume. All of these conventions, however, could be violated for a specific thematic purpose. Nonetheless, conventions for underscoring were tacitly assumed throughout the industry. Even contemporary scoring practices reflect these conventions. Karlin and Wright's manual, for instance, advises would-be composers to avoid textures that are "intrusive." Above all, "Don't overwrite." [34]

A recurrent refrain in Wallis' music notes for *Captain Blood* concerns the audibility of dialogue. Wallis indicated where music should be lowered in volume to accommodate the spoken word or eliminated entirely. Typical of his instruction is the following note. "The music when BLOOD's ship sails, we keep all the music in, but every time BLOOD gives a command or there is any dialogue from WOLVERSTONE or PITT, or any of them, drop the music way down and bring the voices up and then raise the music when the dialogue is over." [35] As Wallis puts it: "Under the dialogue, let's hear the dialogue." [36]

Korngold was particularly noted for underscoring, and in *Captain Blood* he experimented with a variety of approaches from the sustained melodic underscoring of the love scenes to the uniquely constructed cues which punctuated key words or phrases in a line of dialogue. One of the longest sustained sequences between Peter Blood and Arabella Bishop, a horseback ride, is entirely underscored. Violins at low volume carry the melody with simple harmonic accompaniment in the strings. There is not even a pause for the dramatic slap which greets Blood's kiss, the modulation to the Blood motif and the change in instrumentation from strings to a horn solo shifting the mood. Similarly, the sequence on Tortuga which results in the partnership between Blood and Levasseur

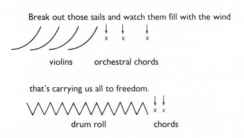

Figure 4.1

is almost continuously underscored. Here the only concession to dialogue is volume. The unusual instrumental texture, however, remains, unmodified to accommodate the spoken word. Not surprisingly, Korngold eliminates music entirely from Blood's final close-up and crucial interior monologue.

Perhaps the most interesting examples of Korngold's underscoring are the unique cues he customized for specific lines of dialogue, punctuating vocal rhythms with musical rhythms to heighten a line's delivery. Blood's final order as the escaped slaves make ready to get under way is an interesting example: "Break out those sails and watch them fill with the wind that's carrying us all to freedom!" The first words are spoken against a rising sequence in the violins, which create a sense of anticipation. At the pause after the phrase "Break out those sails," an orchestral chord punctuates Blood's speech, almost as if it were the musical equivalent of the comma. The next phrase is "punctuated" similarly, with chords after "and" and "watch" speeding up the delivery of the line and lending an urgency to Flynn's intonation. The final two chords punctuate the line after "the wind." A drum roll culminates on the last word in the line, "freedom," obviously drawing attention to its importance. The tension set up by the drum roll is resolved when the fully orchestrated version of the Blood motif returns at the conclusion of Flynn's dialogue. The line of dialogue, with musical "punctuation," is shown in Figure 4.1.

For his next film, *Anthony Adverse* (1936), Korngold would develop this technique, composing music just under the pitch of the voices and "rushing" it into pauses left open in the dialogue.[37] As Korngold explained the process: "I wrote the music in advance, conducted—without orchestra—the actor on the stage in order to make him speak his lines in the required rhythm, and then, sometimes weeks later, guided by earphones, I recorded the orchestral part." [38]

The precision of such underscoring is amazing considering that in recording sessions Korngold shunned the standard devices for synchronization. The common technique for insuring coordination between music and image (and the one favored by Max Steiner) was the **click track**, basically a soundtrack with audible clicks. The precise tempo necessary to fit music to image in a particular sequence was prerecorded on a magnetic track in the form of a series of holes. When run over a playback head these holes produced pops or clicks, creating an audible metronome fed to the conductor and musicians via earphones. Since the click track was variable, any tempo could be produced. Two other devices used to facilitate the synchronization of musical effects were the punch and the streamer. Both were visual cues on the image track itself. A **punch** was a perforation in the film which caused a flash of light during projection. It could be seen without looking up from the score. A **streamer** was a diagonal line scratched into the film's emulsion, creating a vertical line which moved across the screen. Punches and streamers readied the conductor for especially difficult or tricky points of synchronization by signaling their approach. Korngold did not use the click track, relying instead on his eye, an innate sense of timing, and an occasional punch or streamer as "insurance." [39] He avoided even a simple stopwatch and was renowned for his sense of timing. "If a sequence called for forty-two and two-thirds seconds of music, he would write a piece of music and conduct it so that it would fill forty-two and two-thirds seconds." [40]

One final example warrants analysis. In the cue which accompanies King James's speech about the fate of the rebels and which precedes the transition to the colonies, Korngold violates the conventions for unobtrusive underscoring. Here the incongruity of sonorities between the bass voice of actor Vernon Steele and a flute high in its register is heightened by unusual instrumentation such as the celesta and the vibraphone, a nonmelodic and arresting musical line, and dissonant harmonies. Korngold has obviously exploited these devices to provide a distracting and discomforting musical background for the callous cruelty of James and his decree.

Music and Spectacle

Although dialogue received the highest priority on the classical sound-track there were moments when music was privileged in the same way, that is, when dialogue and sound effects were mixed to accede to its priority. The creation of spectacle in the classical narrative model afforded music this position, where virtuosic technical display was heightened by the substitution of music for sound. The closer narrative moved toward pure spectacle and away from the naturalistic reproduction of sound, the more music moved toward the forefront of conscious perception in compensation. Wallis' music notes reflect this relationship: "Lift it way up on that long shot of the boat and right up to where the man says 'Ahoy! Port Royal!' The music should lift up there on those silent shots."[41]

Both the montage and transition analyzed earlier provide examples of music's reciprocity with spectacle, music responding to the presence of spectacle with continuous playing and increased volume. Another example occurs during the sequence in which Blood's ship makes ready to sail from Port Royal. It begins with the narrative justification necessary in the classical model for the eruption of spectacle. In a series of quickly edited shots, Blood barks orders to his crew to ready the ship for departure, and the spectacle of sails unfurling and the ship under way immediately follows. The leap from narrative to spectacle, evidenced in the increased length of shots, the virtuosic camera angles and movements (a stunning vertical pan of the ship under full sail), and close-ups of the film's stars, is marked by the music. Naturalistic sound drops out, and the music, turned up to full volume, provides the only sonority on the soundtrack.

The greatest opportunities for sustained musical expression, however, were extradiegetic, the main title and end title cues. Freed from the restraints of the diegesis, title music was structured more by the conventions of musical form than by the dictates of narrative development. Typically a main title presents the principal leitmotifs later developed in the score. The **end title**, the musical accompaniment to the final credits, was more freely structured and appreciably shorter. It often comprised little more than a memorable restatement of an important leitmotif.

The lengthiest, uninterrupted musical cue in the classical narrative film was typically the main title, which because it preceded the actual diegesis had increased power to set atmosphere and mood for the entire production. The main title for *Captain Blood* was arranged by Ray Heindorf of Warners Brothers' music department. It was quite common within the industry to turn the main title over to an arranger who created an overture from the composer's own material, saving the composer for more important work. Although it is somewhat atypical of Korngold (he did arrange the main titles for most of the other scores he wrote), such was the case with *Captain Blood*. Rhythm, instrumentation, harmony, and melody work together to create a heroic opening which announces as clearly as the pirate ship and crossed swords emblazoned on the title cards that this is a swashbuckler. The main title begins with a musical flourish suggesting the heraldry to come: a drum roll, cymbal crash, and string *glissandi*. Heard immediately after this introduction is the leitmotif associated with Captain Blood, arranged as a horn fanfare. Brass instruments with their connotations of the military are a classic convention for the heroic. Here harmonic structure adds stability and weight (the use of triads, the most fundamental chord in tonal harmony, and strong cadences), as does the use of a major key. Dotted rhythms add vitality to a melodic line which incorporates several dramatic upward leaps. The contrasting B section introduces a second motif quite different in character. The strings carry this new melody which incorporates even rhythms and lyrical phrasings.

Typically, the main title was conceived in terms of the structure of concert music, here a variation of the **sonata-allegro** which encapsulates exposition, development, and recapitulation of one or more themes. Following the exposition is a developmental section in which the musical material is developed through instrumental variation: woodwinds with **pizzicato** (or plucked) string accompaniment and later strings with a horn countermelody. A bridge passage which modulates upward in gradual *crescendo* builds to the climactic moment when the main theme returns for a final reprise in its original instrumentation. A brief musical coda concludes the main title.

By 1935 it had become commonplace to connect the main title to a film's first diegetic cue in order to create a continuous musical background. In *King Kong*, the main title cue extends twenty seconds into the diegesis. *Captain Blood*'s first cue extends from the initial orchestral flourish which opens the main title to the final chord which concludes the first sequence, over a minute into the film. Such continuity covered the entrance of nondiegetic music, naturalizing its presence in the diegesis. End title music functioned in reverse, the last diegetic cue connected to the end title cue. This musical practice helped to negotiate the rift between the hypnotic darkness, which facilitates an absorption into the cinematic image, and the startling bright light of the theater, which disrupts it.

The Placement of Music

As important to the classical film score as conventions for where to place music were conventions for how to place it, that is, techniques for introducing music into the narrative. Steiner admitted that "the toughest thing for a film composer to know is where to start, where to end; that is, how to place your music."[42] By the mid-thirties, conventions for placing nondiegetic music into the diegesis coalesced, guided by the principle of inaudibility and the technological realities of sound editing and mixing. The key was introducing music into the narrative without calling conscious attention to it. As Herbert Stothart, a contemporary of Korngold, put it, "If an audience is conscious of music where it should be conscious only of drama, then the musician has gone wrong."[43] Karlin and Wright advise that "music starts most effectively at a moment of shifting emphasis."[44] Thus music might be introduced at a scene change or a reaction shot or on a movement of the camera. A sound effect could also distract the spectator from the music's entrance. In *Captain Blood*, for instance, the sound of Colonel Bishop whipping Blood's horse or the sound of cannons aboard the captured Spanish galleon masks the entrance of musical cues. Another technique involved **sneaking**, an industry term for beginning a musical cue at low volume usually under dialogue so that the spectator would be unaware of its presence. Many of *Captain Blood*'s musical cues at transitions and montages depend upon this kind of entrance. The accompaniment for the pirate montage in *Captain Blood*, for example, begins not at the montage itself but under the masking effect of the pirates' noisy cheer preceding it. Even a distracting visual action could cover the entrance of music. The dramatic drawing of Blood's sword in the duel or the unexpected arrival of James's troops at the rebels' hiding place allows for music to enter with some volume. Ending a musical cue proved easier. In general, it was timed to conclude with the end of the sequence it accompanied, the shift in time and place covering the sudden absence of music. Cues ending within a sequence were masked by dialogue or sound effects or typically depended on **tailing out**, a term which designates a gradual fade-out of sound.

The Idiom of the Classical Score

The classical Hollywood film score developed an idiom for its expression based on musical practices of the nineteenth century, particularly those of romanticism and late romanticism. The silent film score's reliance upon these practices offered a clear precedent for their use in the sound era, and composers in the crucial decade of the thirties, themselves trained in the late romantic style, reinforced the connection. Max Steiner's grandfather owned the Theater an der Wien, one of Vienna's operatic showplaces, and by the age of sixteen Steiner himself had written an operetta which ran for a year. Korngold was a child prodigy (Mahler pronounced him a genius at age ten) and by the age of seventeen had written two operas widely performed throughout Europe. Dimitri Tiomkin, Franz Waxman, Bronislau Kaper, and Miklós Rózsa were all emigrés who brought with them a musical predilection for the nineteenth century. In fact with the exception of American-born Alfred Newman, the development of the classical Hollywood film score in the crucial decade of the thirties was dominated by a group of composers displaced from the musical idiom in which they had been trained. It was in Hollywood that they were able to reconstitute what John Williams has called "the Vienna Opera House [in] the American West." [45]

Certainly historical factors contributed to Hollywood's adoption of the romantic idiom. It may be more than tradition, however, that coupled them. Film is a discontinuous medium, made up of a veritable kaleidoscope of shots from different angles, distances, and focal depths, and of varying duration. Romanticism, on the other hand, depends upon the subordination of all elements in the musical texture to melody, giving auditors a clear point of focus in the dense sound. Given the high value placed on the spectator's focus on, indeed absorption into, the narrative by the classical Hollywood narrative film, the romantic musical idiom may be its most logical complement. And as Carol Flinn has argued, there may be something particularly seductive about romanticism in a place where individuality was largely suppressed. "The discourse of romanticism offered a means of escaping then-perceived deficiencies—problems such as an increasingly alienating work milieu and industrialized setting, one that would be antagonistic to workers whose backgrounds had led them to believe that 'music was not a business.' "[46]

The musical idiom of the nineteenth century influenced the conventions of orchestration and harmony basic to the classical film score and determined its medium as symphonic. Romanticism and late romanticism relied on lyrical melody as a means of expression. Hollywood's adaptation of this model was characterized by the transcendence of melody, doubling of individual parts, and a reliance on strings to carry melodic material. The romantic attraction to the vast possibilities of orchestral color provided a natural model for film composing which combined orchestral color and the power of collective musical association for thematic resonance. In *Captain Blood*, for instance, Korngold scores the principle leitmotif for Peter Blood as a brass fanfare, relying on the power of the horns to suggest heroism; uses the pathos of two violins for the love theme; and exploits the gypsy associations of the cimbalom to evoke the exoticism of the pirates on Tortuga.

Finally, the nineteenth century bequeathed to the classical film score a symphonic medium. As it had done with other conventions of its nineteenth-century prototype, Hollywood adapted the late-romantic orchestra of ninety-plus players for the recording studio, recreating the deployment of instruments typical of a late-romantic symphony, but reducing the number of players, sometimes by half. The orchestra for *King Kong*, for instance, reported to be as high as eighty musicians, actually numbered about forty-six.[47] In 1933 Warner Brothers had eighteen

Max Steiner at a recording session for *King Kong* in 1933. Compare the size of this orchestra with the one hundred plus players of a late-romantic symphony.

players under contract; by 1938, the year Korngold conducted *The Adventures of Robin Hood*, its orchestra had expanded to only about sixty players.[48] Orchestra size was influenced by genre, from the costume epics which warranted a big sound to the contemporary dramas which evoked a leaner one. A swashbuckler like *Captain Blood*, of course, warranted the former, a full, rich, symphonic sound. In fact, Korngold's neoromantic score for *Captain Blood* so precisely reconstitutes the musical idiom of late romanticism that most listeners cannot distinguish between Korngold's original composition and the two extended selections he borrowed from Franz Liszt.[49] Other musical idioms, such as jazz and pop, found their way into the classical film score during the forties and fifties. Despite the divergence of the musical idioms on which they are based, jazz and pop scores preserved the structure of the classical model. More important, their failure to adopt the pervasive

The duel between Blood and Levasseur. Korngold was running out of time on *Captain Blood* (he scored the film in a little over three weeks) and used selections from Franz Liszt for a few cues. The duel was accompanied by Liszt's symphonic poem *Prometheus*. Because the score was not entirely his own, Korngold insisted on the credit "Musical Arrangement" in the film's titles.

romantic idiom was to some extent narratively justified. Alfred Newman and Alex North both used jazz for films set in contemporary New Orleans, *Panic in the Streets* (1950) and *A Streetcar Named Desire* (1951), respectively. The famous theme song in *High Noon* (1952) is accompanied by a guitar, the quintessential western instrument. Contemporary musical elements eventually took on a life of their own in response to their growing marketability, but at least initially, pop and jazz grew out of the demands of the narrative.

The Leitmotif

A final characteristic of the classical film score is the importance it places on its own structural unity. Marlin Skiles's text on film scoring cautions that "scoring involves more than merely mood-matching, for the music should be capable of standing up alone as an integrated whole." [50] The most typical though not the only method to accomplish an overall unity was the use of the leitmotif. (Chapter 6 is devoted to the analysis of Bernard Herrmann's score for *The Magnificent Ambersons* which offers another possibility.) The precedent of silent film accompaniment with its structural imperative that "every character should have a theme," and the operatic backgrounds of Steiner, Korngold, and others, facilitated a practice that linked musical themes to character, place, object, and abstract idea. To the sound film score, with its piecemeal construction and gaps in musical continuity, the leitmotif offered coherence. According to Karlin and Wright in *On the Track*, "The development of motifs is a powerful compositional device for the film composer, allowing him to bring an overall sense of unity to his score and still leave room for variety." [51] Through repetition and variation, leitmotifs bound a series of temporally disconnected musical cues into an integrated whole. Further, leitmotifs functioned in an interdependence with the visual text. Music responded to the dramatic needs of the narrative and in turn clarified them, sealing music and visual text into mutual dependence. Finally, leitmotifs heightened spectator response through sheer accumulation, each repetition of the leitmotif bringing with it the associations established in earlier occurrences.

The use of the leitmotif in Hollywood touched off a wave of response in the musical community, most of it negative. The first entry on film music to appear in *Grove's Dictionary of Music and Musicians* claims, "The last technique [the leitmotif] is intelligible only in relation to musical structures developed on a very large scale; it is quite inappropriate to the episodic technique of the cinema." [52] Aaron Copland leveled his criticism in print, also citing the leitmotif's inappropriateness for the screen as well as decrying its formulaic predictability. [53] But the most outspoken and virulent critics of the leitmotif are Hanns Eisler and Theodor W. Adorno who launched a pointed attack in *Composing for the Films* on the structural model of the classical film score. Like Wilfrid Mellers in *Grove's*, Eisler and Adorno assert the incompatibility of the leitmotif and film. Because film lacked the "gigantic dimensions" of Wagnerian opera, leitmotifs were destined in film to simple repetition without significant or expressive expansion.[54]

Yet it was around this very issue of scale that Hollywood composers formed their defense.

> A composer in writing his symphonic works, can develop his thematic material to the fullest extent of the message he wishes to express. . . ; his themes can be worked out in their original entirety without being subjected to forced cutting. . . . This limitation forced upon the composer in writing for the screen . . . has, of necessity, compelled me to use the *Leitmotif* technique which Richard Wagner so successfully originated in his *Nibelungen Ring*.[55]

In Gerard Carbonara's apologia, the leitmotif's power to bind is not only unaffected by the strictures of time but in fact generated by them.

One of the primary functions of the leitmotif was its contribution to the explication of the narrative. As Steiner explains: "Music aids audiences in keeping characters straight in their minds."[56] To this end composers created musical identifications for characters, places, and even abstract ideas in a film. In Korngold's score for *Captain Blood* there are leitmotifs for Peter Blood as well as for King James and King William; for all the important locations, Port Royal (also used to accompany the governor of Jamaica), Tortuga, Virgen Magra, England, and France; for the love between Peter Blood and Arabella Bishop; and for the torturous slavery on Colonel Bishop's plantation (which doubles as a motif for Colonel Bishop). An analysis of the leitmotifs associated with Peter Blood demonstrates how the leitmotivic score depended upon the principle of repetition as a means to structure diverse and discontinuous musical cues and the principle of variation as a means to clarify the visual text.

The leitmotif Korngold composed for Peter Blood is presented initially in the main title. It is an extended theme consisting of two shorter motifs: the heroic brass fanfare analyzed earlier and a second, contrasting, lyrical string melody. Throughout the film Korngold separates and recombines these motifs, the A motif underscoring moments of Blood's heroism and the B motif emphasizing his more human and vulnerable

Figure 4.2A.   Copyright 1935 Warner Bros. Music
Captain Blood, A motif, *Captain Blood*

Figure 4.2B.   Copyright 1935 Warner Bros. Music
Captain Blood, B motif, *Captain Blood*

side. The initial appearance of the heroic motif coincides with Blood's first appearance in the film. Summoned at his home in the middle of the night to attend a wounded rebel, Blood agrees to treat a traitor even though he disagrees with his politics. The initial statement of the motif is reminiscent of the martial opening, but it is cast here at low volume in the lower register of the horns and succeeded by reprises first in the woodwinds and then in the strings. Instrumentation here reflects and defines narrative content. The brasses are used under soldier Jeremy Pitt's desperate pleas for aid, but strings underscore Blood's declaration of pacifist principles. These variations set up the groundwork for a climactic return of the original brass orchestration of the motif later in the film. Each repeated variation, and there are several in the first third of the film, accompanies some aspect of Blood's heroic persona. Thus the leitmotif operates on two levels simultaneously: in terms of the narrative it helps to create the heroism of the protagonist; in terms of the music it creates both a thread of repetition and variation which binds the score, and also, through anticipation of a return to the original version, a climactic center for the score's overall design.

Blood's dedication and self-sacrifice are embodied in the contrasting B motif. This initially appears in the sequence where Blood ministers to the wounded rebel. (He will be tried and convicted as a traitor as a consequence.) The volume of the music is low, the tempo is slow, and the instrumentation is primarily string. In fact, much of the pathos of the drama emanates from instrumentation: a solo violin can be heard when Blood refuses to abandon his charge.

For the transition which takes Blood and his fellow convicts from their home in England to their enslavement in Jamaica, Korngold recombines the two motifs. The heroic A motif returns to the score here in an orchestral setting, but significantly it is transposed to the minor and its tempo is slowed. These changes infuse the cue, marked **lento con dolore** (slowly with sadness), with a sense of dislocation contributing to the mood of uneasiness that attends the unfortunate change in Blood's circumstances. The contrasting B motif forms the B section, accompanying Blood's ministrations to his fellow slaves. Like the A motif, it is played in an unfamiliar setting: woodwinds (flutes and clarinets) and strings played in a low register. When the A motif returns it does so with a horn solo. It is then fractured into developmental variations, coalescing into a familiar phrase only as the sequence ends.

During Blood's enslavement on the Bishop plantation short variations of both motifs accompany moments of Blood's daring (outwitting the governor to return to the stockade in time for the escape, for instance) and compassion (attending to his beaten and battered friend, Jeremy Pitt, and risking his life to do so). The climactic musical center of the

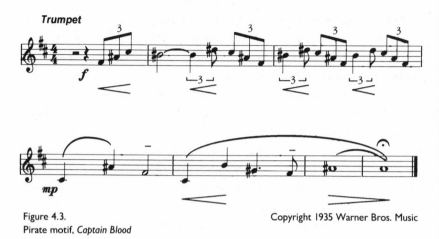

Figure 4.3.   Copyright 1935 Warner Bros. Music
Pirate motif, *Captain Blood*

film occurs when Blood is free at last. As captain of a captured Spanish galleon he becomes what the film's title foretells. Visual and musical text mark the scene as momentous. Inspiring camera work (a series of low-angle close-ups) combines with the dynamic return of the A motif in the original brass fanfare of the main title (here "plumped" by the addition of some strings). It is followed, as it is in the main title, by the contrasting B motif. This aural reminder of Blood's emotional vulnerability is heard during the shot-reverse shot dissolve where he imagines Arabella Bishop's melancholy at his departure.

At this point in the score a new leitmotif is introduced for Blood's career as a pirate. The leitmotivic score achieved an integral structure through repetition and variation. This structure was tightened through relationships constructed among the various motifs. Steven Wescott has called this quality "interconnectedness," achieved through "the common use of prominent melodic contours and intervals" and "shared melodic and rhythmic motives."[57] I would add shared instrumentation and harmonic construction. The relationship between the Captain Blood A motif and the pirate motif provides a case in point. The most apparent connection between them is instrumentation. Both motifs depend on the brasses. (The initial appearance of the pirate motif is played on a French horn with brass accompaniment.) In addition, each motif is built on a melodic contour derived from arpeggiated triadic chords. Finally, each motif incorporates a rising third at the end of the first major phrase.

From the point at which Blood embarks on his pirate career until the end of the film when he accepts a commission in King William's navy, it is this motif which most often accompanies his appearances. Korngold preserves the martial definition of the pirate motif with most of the variations highlighting some type of brass instrument and occurring at moments which define Blood's success as a privateer. Developmental variations of the Captain Blood A motif occur only briefly in the second half of the film and can be heard during the montage of Blood's piracy as well as during Blood's commands to ready the ship for its voyage to Port Royal. Transposed to the minor the Captain Blood motif lends a solemnity to Levasseur's death. But a full reiteration of the Captain Blood motif in its original setting is withheld from the second half of the film and reserved for the climactic naval battle where Blood eschews the life of a pirate for the patriotism of king and country. Significantly, the contrasting B motif appears only minimally in Blood's pirate life, suggesting perhaps that the qualities it represents in Blood have diminished. This motif can be heard in connection with his constant affection for Arabella Bishop, first when Blood unknowingly allows the ship on which she is traveling to pass unmolested, and second during a shipboard meeting between them.

When Blood accepts the pardon and naval commission from King William, the pirate motif relinquishes its place to the Captain Blood motif which dominates the busy musical texture of the ensuing sea battle. With the decisive conclusion of the struggle, the pirate motif disappears from the score entirely and the Blood motif returns to its initial preeminence accompanying the final two sequences in the film. There are two telling variations here: the first in the minor for the pirates' disarmament and the second in a slow, string setting appropriate for the embrace of newly appointed governor Peter Blood and Arabella Bishop. This final variation modulates into the brass fanfare of the opening credits for the end title.

Erich Wolfgang Korngold's score for *Captain Blood* assumed a legendary reputation in Hollywood. Fostered by Korngold's preeminent position as a composer of art music, this legend outlived Korngold himself

Erich Wolfgang Korngold and the Warner Brothers' orchestra at a recording session for what is probably *The Constant Nymph* (1943).

who returned to Vienna after World War II. He died in 1955 without having reestablished his place there. Yet even in 1965, in an era when the neoromantic sound of the classical score was largely abandoned for more contemporary idioms, Gene Roddenberry, creator of *Star Trek*, explained the sound he wanted for this futuristic series by referring to *Captain Blood* as the archetypal example.[58]

Part 2

Textual Analyses

"Every character should have a theme"

The Informer: Max Steiner and the Classical Film Score

Every character should have a theme. In *The Informer* we used a theme
to identify Victor McLaglen. A blind man could have sat in a theater
and known when Gypo was on the screen.

Max Steiner

The development of the classical Hollywood film score parallels the
early career of Max Steiner, one of its most influential practitioners
and clearly its most prolific. Steiner was so productive that legend had
it he composed effortlessly. In fact he spent decades in Hollywood
overworked and exhausted. From 1929 to 1935 Steiner was head of
the music department at RKO and was responsible, at least nominally
and often substantially, for the music in over a hundred RKO films of
that period. In 1934 alone he is credited with thirty-six titles. During
a career that spanned thirty-seven years, his credits include the music
for over three hundred films.[1] Steiner's scores in the formative years of
sound helped to empower the musical conventions his work exemplified. With the scores for *Cimarron* (1931), *The Most Dangerous Game*
(1932), and *King Kong* (1933), he began to establish his reputation. With
The Informer in 1935 he consolidated his position as one of Hollywood's
most important composers and won his first Academy Award for an
originally composed film score.

Regarded in its day as an outstanding example of film music, Steiner's
score for *The Informer* exemplifies the musical conventions of classical
film: selective use of nondiegetic music; correspondence between that
music and the implied content of the narrative; a high degree of direct
synchronization between music and narrative action; and the use of the
leitmotif as a structural framework. The score is also interesting for a
practice Steiner himself came to exemplify: the exploitation of musical
associations to provide the link between narrative content and musical
accompaniment. Steiner's propensity for references both direct and in-

direct to popular music, folk tunes, and the classical repertoire became a personal stamp in a medium often oblivious to his contribution.

The plot of *The Informer* turns on the betrayal of Frankie McPhillip, Irish rebel outlaw, by his friend, Gypo Nolan, for the sum of twenty pounds. John Ford's interest in the story began in 1933 when he acquired the rights to the Liam O'Flaherty novel. The major studios turned down the property as too risky, so in an effort to make the property more marketable, Ford and screenwriter Dudley Nichols agreed to work for a fraction of their usual salaries. Ford claims that it was Joseph P. Kennedy, then owner of a controlling interest at RKO, who gave him the go-ahead for his Irish picture until the studio could find a more appropriate vehicle (i.e., a western). When Kennedy sold his share in the studio halfway through shooting, the new hierarchy, regarding the $200,000 production budget as insignificant, let the filming continue, but moved the company to a backlot soundstage where the city of Dublin "was just painted canvas."[2]

Ford claims to have shot *The Informer* in less than three weeks, and studio records substantiate at least the basis of that claim. It was shot in twenty-seven days from 11 February to 15 March 1935.[3] With similar speed, Ford and Nichols had produced the shooting script from January 1 to January 11 in Mazatlan, Ford's Mexican retreat. Having often been frustrated by composing music for scripts that bore little resemblance to the final film, Steiner preferred to work from a rough cut. "I never write from a script. I run a mile everytime I see one."[4] But for *The Informer* Steiner composed music before and during the shooting schedule. By January 23 Steiner was seeking copyright clearances on the Irish folk tunes he would incorporate into the score including "The Wearing of the Green," "Rose of Tralee," "Would God I Were a Tender Apple Blossom" ("Danny Boy"), and "The Minstrel Boy." He was also at work on six other RKO films, a practice typical in Hollywood.[5] Despite his other obligations, Steiner completed the score quickly, recording most of the music on March 14, about the time Ford was finishing the production. In fact, Steiner completed his job on *The Informer* at the point when he would usually be just beginning.

Steiner's involvement in the film before and as it was being shot provided him the opportunity to reverse the usual practice of postsynchro-

Figure 5.1. Copyright 1935 Bourne Music
"The Informer" (Gypo's theme), *The Informer*

nizing the score to edited footage. Steiner composed music for several scenes before they were filmed, and Ford actually shot them in synchronization to it. This procedure not only facilitated direct synchronization in postproduction but accorded Steiner a determining influence in the development of the film's protagonist, Gypo Nolan. Victor McLaglen, who played Gypo, was rehearsed to walk in the lumbering gait dictated by the accented rhythms Steiner had scored for his leitmotif. Gypo's oafish quality, which is at least partially responsible for the sympathy his character elicits, is demonstrable in the walk Steiner created for him.

The score for *The Informer* begins with a main title that immediately binds music and narrative action. The titles in the film are unusual historically in that they initiate diegetic action behind the credits. The more usual practice involved title cards. The score takes advantage of this opportunity to establish music's presence as a narrative agent through Mickey Mousing, beginning with the shadowy presence of Gypo in direct synchronization to the leitmotif Steiner entitled "The Informer."[6] All of Gypo's brief appearances in the credits are directly synchronized to his leitmotif. An extended example of his connection to this musical theme follows the opening intertitle as Gypo hulks down a Dublin street in synchronization to it.

Mickey Mousing is a structural device which authorizes nondiegetic music. Its perfect synchronicity with narrative action masks its presence so that the music can create certain effects on a semiconscious level without disrupting narrative credibility on a conscious level. Mickey Mousing can also function thematically. In *The Informer*, for instance, the direct synchronization between Gypo's footsteps and the distinctive rhythm in his leitmotif dictates his singular walk. Annotations in Steiner's sketches, such as "heavily," "very heavily," and "**marcato**" (marked), suggest how deliberately Steiner created Gypo's gait.

Finally, Mickey Mousing can indicate extradiegetic meaning. In a film as heavily laden with purpose as *The Informer*, Mickey Mousing is put in service to the symbolic level of the narrative. The score has numerous examples of Mickey Mousing which function on this level. One particularly pointed example occurs in the scene where Gypo tears down Frankie's wanted poster. Its crumpled remains dog him (it stops when he does), finally attaching to his leg before he realizes its presence and discards it. Music's mimetic capacity is here employed to simulate the wind which propels the paper along the street in defiance of the laws of nature. (Steiner uses a harp with a celesta added for the last chord.) The point of this fatalistic gesture seems to be to foreshadow the ineradicable guilt Gypo's betrayal of Frankie will engender, but the improbability of such a natural coincidence, and the music's emphasis of this improbability, seldom fail to raise a guffaw from incredulous contemporary audiences.

But Mickey Mousing can be no more obvious or distracting than the often blatant and sometimes awkward attempts of the camera to prompt a symbolic reading. In *The Informer* the music may be synchronized to the footsteps of various characters, but the camera also makes those feet the focus of the frame. In a later scene, each of the four coins tossed on a table is accompanied by a note of a descending arpeggio, but the camera is there for a close-up. It is interesting that Mickey Mousing has come to represent the worst excesses of the Hollywood film score. Perhaps as contemporary spectators we are no longer used to hearing Mickey Mousing in films (its use radically diminished in the fifties and after). Still the practice of catching every movement with music has a visual equivalent, and Mickey Mousing has been made to bear the brunt of the criticism for an overobviousness that it only partially creates.

The junction of narrative action and music in *The Informer* is largely achieved through a reliance upon Mickey Mousing. The classical Hollywood film score also developed conventions for correspondence between the implied content of the narrative, particularly its emotion, and the music. As discussed in Chapter 4, classical narrative film developed certain conventions to aid expressive acting in the representation of emotion including close-ups, specific patterns of lighting and mise-en-scène, and most critically, music. The power of this process was such that it could create emotion in lieu of performance and frequently did.

In *The Informer* a combination of visual and musical strategies are employed consistently in those sequences which require McLaglen to emote. In the opening, for instance, the upheaval Gypo experiences upon learning of the price on McPhillip's head is created by a combination of editing (specifically the shot-reverse shot) and musical accompaniment. During his nocturnal meanderings, Gypo discovers the wanted poster with a twenty-pound reward offered for information leading to Frankie's capture. As the camera dollies in for a close-up of the poster (an over-the-shoulder medium shot which includes the back of Gypo's head and Frankie's image on the poster), it is accompanied by a musical evocation of tension, a descending bass line in combination with a **pedal point**, a sustained note, usually in the bass, which holds a single pitch while the other parts change. Gypo's anxiety is set up by the dolly-in (a cinematic metaphor for contemplation) and articulated by the music; his face does not appear in the frame.

The poster dissolves into a flashback of Frankie and Gypo at a local pub, the Dunboy House. Steiner's use of the popular Irish ballad "The Wearing of the Green" connects Gypo to Frankie as they sing in unison while the associations of the popular tune evoke Ireland as the cause which binds them. The flashback dissolves back into the wanted poster followed by a straight cut to Gypo's face. In a medium close-up Gypo stares at the poster, rubbing his chin in contemplation. The look on Gypo's face is ambiguous. (It's often hard—with McLaglen's acting—to tell what Gypo is supposed to be experiencing.) The shot-reverse shot construction connects that look to the shot of the poster which precedes it and the close-up of "£20 Reward" that follows it, but what Gypo is feeling is still unclear. He mouths the words "Frankie McPhillip," but is he emoting hatred for the British, thinking about the reward money for himself, or simply staring absentmindedly?

Music here is crucial in delineating Gypo's response. During the close-up of his face, the first five notes of an ascending minor scale introduce a short fragment of the tune "Rule! Britannia" which accompanies the next shot. Steiner has cast the quintessentially British melody into the unfamiliar minor, displacing its associations with British power and supremacy. These musical cues provide the key to McLaglen's cryptic facial expression. I am suggesting here that the music operates in a way similar to and in support of the Kuleshov effect. Gypo's blank face quite literally "usurps" the sinister associations that this variation of "Rule! Britannia" has constructed for it; his reaction becomes anger toward or possibly hatred of the British. A visual confirmation of this reading is offered immediately afterward. Gypo pokes Frankie's image in a gesture of camaraderie.

The next musical cue is diegetic, "Rose of Tralee" sung by a street musician. Because the music is diegetic Steiner could expect his audience to be conscious of it, and he exploits the opportunity by choosing a popular song that tells the story of loss, of a boy far away from home who, cut off from his Irish heritage, comes to cherish its memory. This Irish ballad not only provides an authentic text for the street singer but through its lyrics verbalizes the vague patriotic sentiment and loyalty that Ford has been trying to establish. Other examples of diegetic music include "The Minstrel Boy," sung at Frankie's wake, and "Believe Me If All Those Endearing Young Charms," sung at a brothel. The film depends upon these standard ballads to evoke a mythic representation of Ireland which it has neither the budget nor the time to create visually.

Throughout these first few scenes, Gypo's centrality has been reinforced by his position in the narrative, the mise-en-scène, and the editing, and by the dominance of his leitmotif in the musical score. The classical film score was typically structured by the leitmotif which organized accompaniment around the repetition of recognizable musical themes, developed or varied in response to the image track. The leitmotif could also function as characterization. Gypo's leitmotif, as an example, reproduces his bulky clumsiness in its rhythmic structure. His theme also incorporates a familiar rhythmic trope known as the **Scotch snap**. A distinctive feature of Scottish and Irish folk music ("The Wearing of the Green" is a typical example), the Scotch snap is a dotted

A shot-reverse shot sequence. Gypo's emotional response is not entirely clear visually: is he glaring with hatred at the British; thinking about the reward money; angered at Frankie; or simply absentmindedly staring? The music, a sinister version of "Rule! Britannia," particularizes Gypo's response.

Figure 5.2.
"I Adore Him" (Katie's theme), *The Informer*

note which follows its complement, usually an eighth note, instead of preceding it, the more usual practice. Gypo's theme exploits a version of the Scotch snap, further connecting Gypo to the Irish cause he will die for.

The second major character, Gypo's girlfriend Katie, is introduced by a leitmotif Steiner entitled "I Adore Him." Katie is a prostitute. Because of the strictures of the Production Code, prostitution could not be conveyed directly on the screen, and certain cinematic conventions evolved to convey the necessary information indirectly. The scene in which she first appears presents a clear visual metaphor for her trade. She poses under a streetlight with her head veiled in a shawl. As a well-dressed man passes by and gives her the eye, she dutifully lowers the shawl to expose her shoulders.

Like the Hollywood film itself which created an image of woman as the projection of its own (male) fear and desire, the classical Hollywood film score collaborated in the dominant ideology which punished women for their sexuality. Visual displays of female sexuality were accompanied by a nucleus of musical practices which carried implications of indecency and promiscuity through their association with so-called decadent forms such as jazz, the blues, and ragtime. These included a predilection for woodwind and brass instrumentation, particularly saxophones and muted horns; a dependence upon unusual harmonies, including chromaticism and dissonance; the use of dotted rhythms and

Katie Madden. Publicity still. Note the visual signifiers for "easy" virtue: make-up, costume, lighting, even the cigarette. The music externalizes these codes through "jazzy" instrumentation (like the saxophone), syncopated rhythm, chromaticism, and *portamento*.

syncopation; and the incorporation of **portamento**, a style of playing in which the instrument slides between notes, and **blue notes**, shifting intonation of the lowered third and seventh degrees of the scale.[7] Katie's theme dispels any possible ambiguity about her profession through a combination of these practices: jazzy rhythms, characterized by syncopation; brass instrumentation; chromatic harmonies, blue notes, and *portamento*. Although the narrative clearly posits Katie's prostitution as a direct consequence of economic necessity (she sighs, "I'm hungry and I can't pay my room rent"), Katie retains the taint of promiscuity through a visual representation (unmistakable in its use of lighting, costume, and makeup) and a musical accompaniment which are unforgiving. In an interesting and not unconnected example later in the film, Steiner actually changed the instrumentation of Katie's motif to "make more sense." Gypo passes Katie the money he has earned for informing. Katie's motif had been scored by Steiner for the flute. This manu-

Figure 5.3.
"Mary," *The Informer*

script page, however, was accompanied by a note, presumably from orchestrator Bernard Kaun: "Dear Max: Try it with solo sax. I think it will make more sense."[8] The final version uses the saxophone.

On the other hand, the leitmotif Steiner composed for Mary McPhillip, Frankie's sister and devoted girlfriend of rebel leader Dan Gallagher, embodies none of these pejorative musical conventions. Played initially by violins, and in one memorable reiteration a harp, her leitmotif is accompanied by simple triadic harmonies. Various musical markings used in conjunction with her motif suggest its intent: "**dolcissimo**" (very sweetly); "**poco appassionata**" (a little impassioned); "**legato**" (smoothly); and "Heaven music." Interestingly, this final marking appears in the music which accompanies Katie's confrontation with Mary. Despite the fact that Mary inadvertently prevents her brother's escape from the British death squad and seems to do little else in an emergency than wring her hands, she is ennobled by her leitmotif rather than censured by it.

Up until and including the sequence which introduces Katie the music has been continuous. By 1935 the length of the musical score was expanding significantly. Steiner's score for *Cimarron* included only a few minutes of nondiegetic music. In *The Informer*, by contrast, the first six minutes have an unbroken musical accompaniment, and music is used either diegetically or nondiegetically in almost every scene in the film. (There are only two exceptions: a short scene which transpires on the street and Frankie's visit to his mother's house which culminates in his death.) Steiner's scores exhibit this growing dependence on music.

Gone With the Wind (1939), for instance, begins with nearly twenty-three minutes of continuous music.

Steiner's predilection for a seamless sound is demonstrated in his careful bridging between musical selections. For instance, at the point when "Rose of Tralee" is introduced into the score, any potential disruption is covered by an aural match between the harp, which accompanied the crumpled poster, and a single violin accompanying the singer. The initial low dynamic level of the violin and its similarity in timbre to the harp make its entrance almost imperceptible, and elides the musical cues from one scene to the next.

When Gypo meets Katie (and deals with her potential customer), he walks with her past a shop window with an advertisement for passage to America. The cost is ten pounds. Here the seed is planted in Gypo's mind of the possibility of a fresh start with Katie. The presence of "Yankee Doodle Dandy" on the soundtrack fleshes out the promise of opportunity that America embodies. "Yankee Doodle" is a particularly interesting choice since that particular song is associated with the revolution in which America won its independence from Britain. But the strikingly unfamiliar instrumentation (one variation for celesta and flute, one for bassoon) incorporates Katie's perception of the advertisement: "Look at that thing handing us the ha-ha." A descending chromatic line encodes her despondency.

Internal thought had always posed a problem in Hollywood's narrative model, and a number of conventions developed to convey this process. Voice-over was one solution. Often editing simulated connections made in thought, or dialogue was used to render as naturally as possible the content of a character's mind. Music is another of these conventions. In *The Informer* music functions as part of the cinematic process that offers an analogue for Gypo's consciousness.

An extended example occurs during the sequence where Gypo decides to inform. The sequence begins in the Dunboy House, a local restaurant where Frankie surprises Gypo. The process of thought is encoded in the film through a combination of focal distance (the close-up), facial expression (this generally emerges from McLaglen as a blank stare), and physical gestures appropriate to the act of contemplation (Gypo rubs his chin, wipes his forehead, or scratches his head). When

Frankie appears there is a cut to a medium close-up of Gypo rubbing his forehead and staring at him. What is transpiring in Gypo's mind is suggested visually through a superimposition of the reward money under the reverse shot of Frankie's reaction.

As Frankie leaves, Gypo begins to ponder the opportunities Frankie's appearance has afforded him. Now music becomes a crucial part of the process which simulates thought. Ascending chords accompany the reappearance of the superimposed image of Frankie's face with the twenty pounds reward money emblazoned beneath it. Gypo's ruminations continue after he leaves the restaurant; he pauses outside the shop window which contains the advertisement for passage to America. In a medium close-up, he stares at the poster rubbing his forehead. The reverse shot focuses the content of Gypo's thoughts, but it is the music which provides information to help specify the nature of Gypo's mental process. A quotation from "Yankee Doodle Dandy" played on a muted trumpet represents one factor that figures in Gypo's decision: the promise of opportunity that America offers. The other is his love for Katie, whose leitmotif follows "Yankee Doodle Dandy" on the soundtrack. Her centrality in Gypo's decision to inform is musically encoded in a series of upward modulations of the opening phrase of her leitmotif. The culmination of the final repetition coincides with Gypo's arrival at British headquarters. When the door closes behind Gypo, Katie's motif is repeated yet again. (Is the score suggesting that Gypo's decision to inform is her fault?)

The consequences of Gypo's betrayal are graphically demonstrated in the McPhillips' home. Soon after Frankie arrives, the British, tipped off by Gypo that he has returned, gun him down as he attempts to escape. His death scene is followed by a direct cut to British headquarters where Gypo is paid his twenty pounds. The act of payment disgusts the British officer in charge who lays the money on the table but leaves it to an underling to pass along to Gypo with the tip of a cane. As the officer does so, Steiner introduces the leitmotif entitled "The Money" against a pedal point. This theme, frequently heard on solo instruments in the film, is composed of four notes: a descending tri-tone followed by an augmented triad arpeggiated downward. The **tri-tone**, the interval between a fourth and a fifth on the scale (called a tri-tone because it comprises three whole tones) has powerful musi-

Figure 5.4.
"The Money," *The Informer*

cal connotations. It is the most dissonant interval and historically has been associated with evil (labeled "*diabolus in musica*") and avoided in early music. Steiner set up this association of money and evil earlier, using the tri-tone in the music which accompanies Katie's response to the America poster: "Look at that thing handing us the ha-ha." In the money motif Steiner has found a musical analogue for the gesture of the British officer. The leitmotif symbolically incorporates the taint of evil attached to the money through the tri-tone and creates tension through the unstable tonality of its harmonic base.

Gypo leaves the building by the back door accompanied by a musical passage which juxtaposes a six-four chord (a variation of the tonic chord) and the money motif. In Western harmonic practice this particular juxtaposition craves a strong resolution which a return to the tonic chord would provide. In this case, however, Steiner doesn't resolve the chord, setting up the spectator for the appearance of the blind man who materializes out of the fog. In place of resolution the score offers yet another leitmotif, that of the blind man who follows Gypo from the British headquarters. His musical accompaniment, entitled "The Blind Man," is initially orchestrated for an English horn and woodwinds and repeated by violins. Ford creates a symbol of Gypo's conscience in the blind man who follows Gypo wherever he goes. (The blind man is the only one who can connect Gypo to the British headquarters.) Steiner composes a leitmotif which functions in complicity with Ford's intentions. It represents simultaneously a physical manifestation (the blind man) and a symbolic manifestation (Gypo's guilty conscience).

Figure 5.5.
"The Blind Man," *The Informer*

Gypo will never realize the dream he thinks he buys with twenty pounds, and the remainder of the film chronicles his downfall. The successive stages of his destruction are signaled by a series of horn calls based on the opening motif of his theme. These include the opening five-note phrase of Gypo's leitmotif (what I will call Variation I); a distillation of that phrase into its last two notes, an open fifth (Variation II); and a version which diminishes the last interval of the motif from an open fifth to a tri-tone (Variation III). Instrumentation (horns) and melodic contour (the attention on the intervals of the open fifth and the tri-tone) evoke the hunt, and this musical metaphor marks the trail of evidence Gypo leaves for his pursuers to follow.

The first of these horn calls occurs in the pub where Gypo heads after being paid his twenty pounds. When he enters, Variation I is heard. Gypo orders a whiskey to ease his conscience, but in doing so he only draws suspicion and loses part of the money he needs for passage. When Gypo actually handles the notes themselves, the money motif is heard low in the woodwinds' register against *tremolo* strings. As Gypo drinks his whiskey, Variation III is repeated twice. Its incorporation of the tri-tone is particularly telling, attaching its sinister connotations to Gypo himself while inextricably joining Gypo to the money motif through the shared use of that distinctive interval. Gypo's anxiety in the sequence is musically evoked through the use of several elements: the repetition of the money motif; the continued use of *tremolo* strings; the alternation of tonic and six-four chords; and the repetition of Gypo's theme in the unfamiliar instrumentation of the cello.

When Katie enters the pub her theme returns, reinforcing her connection to Frankie's death. The instrumentation is particularly "bluesy" here: a saxophone, the quintessential blues instrument, plays the melody against an accompaniment of a string and harp pedal point. Steiner marks it "*triste*" and "*doloroso*." Since Katie is now implicated in Gypo's guilt (she provides the motive, however unwittingly, for his crime), the music is harsher toward her, and her theme is played in the classic instrumentation of promiscuity. The implication of this instrumental change becomes explicitly stated a few moments later when Gypo says to her, "I did it for you." This is the first time the dialogue has verbalized the motivation that the music and the visual text have already suggested a number of times.

The horn calls return a few sequences later during Gypo's interrogation by the commandant of the Irish rebel forces, Dan Gallagher, and his captain, Bartley Mulholland. A number of musical practices Steiner used earlier reappear: the use of "The Wearing of the Green" (played "*mysterioso*") to provide a barometer for the magnitude of Gypo's deed against his heritage; the use of the money motif to reinforce Gypo's guilt in a scene in which he denies any responsibility for the crime; and the use of *tremolo* strings, pedal point, and dissonance to create tension. After Gypo is interrogated, Variation III can be heard in the background. When he is dismissed, Bartley shouts, "It's him, Dan." Steiner underscores Dan's response with variations of "The Wearing of the Green" and "Mary's Theme." Bartley will tail Gypo for the remainder of the night. The sequence ends with the repetition of Variation II, the open tonality of the fifths creating anticipation, even anxiety.

Gypo's next stop is a fish-and-chips shop where he spends even more of his money buying food for the assembled crowd. This sequence is one of the most allegorical in the film and, like much of the rest of it, is overladen with a religious symbolism that is not always consistent. An analogy is drawn between Gypo and Christ (suggested by his new title, "King" Gypo, his address as "m'lord," and his act of feeding the multitude with fishes). But he is also connected to Judas, who got thirty pieces of silver, through an attention to the money and to the apostle Peter, who betrayed Christ when the cock crowed three times. (Gypo claims, "I'm going to be the cock of the walk around here.") The melee which attends the serving of the food is intercut with a dolly-in to Bartley at the shop's window, accompanied by a variation of the blind man's leitmotif associated with Gypo's guilty conscience. At the end of the sequence, Variation III returns to mark yet another bit of evidence Gypo leaves behind. This time it is the two pounds he has squandered on fish and chips.

Throughout the film Gypo has been desperately trying to avoid the consequences of his crime. The spectator, however, is frequently reminded of Gypo's guilt, visually through the insistent close-ups on the silver coins, and aurally through repetitions of the leitmotifs associated with the money and the blind man. A crucial sequence follows in which the film attempts to enter Gypo's consciousness. Like other sequences which reveal internal thought, this one relies heavily on music to suggest what is transpiring in Gypo's mind. Gypo passes the shop window again and spies the advertisement which initially inspired him. The sequence begins with Gypo and his drinking companion pausing in front of the window. The shot-reverse shot exchange which structures the sequence consists of a medium two-shot of the back of the two men's heads and the reverse angle which focuses on their faces. This time Gypo scratches his head with the same cryptic look McLaglen has produced before. Katie's theme, scored for solo violin, accompanies the gesture. Moments afterward Gypo verbalizes the thoughts that the music has already suggested: he tells his companion he wants to see Katie.

But before he can find her, Gypo is lured into Aunt Betty's brothel. He will try one last time to ease his guilty conscience through a series of desperate acts: drunkenness; an attempt at social acceptance; an appeal to Irish loyalty; and finally, an effort at retribution. A honky-tonk piano, a musical convention equated with the bordello, establishes the nature of the saloon. Gypo spies a young blonde obviously out of place in her surroundings. That he imagines her to be Katie is prefigured by the music: Katie's theme is heard on the soundtrack before the dissolve which signals the blonde's visual metamorphosis into Katie herself. By this time Bartley has caught up with Gypo and enters Aunt Betty's to retrieve him. As Gypo leaves the brothel, he sees the young blonde once more. The film implies that she is being forced into prostitution. The fact that she cannot pay the rent connects her again to Katie, and Gypo compassionately hands her the money she needs to return to her home. As Bartley surreptitiously tabulates Gypo's bill, the money motif serves as a reminder of Gypo's guilt.

Intercut with this sequence is a reconciliation scene between Dan Gallagher and Mary. Its placement draws a striking contrast between Gypo's retreat to the brothel and the chaste lovers' reunion. Mary's leitmotif underscores the lovers' embrace, but when the discussion turns to politics, specifically to the murder of Frankie, her theme is replaced by other music. Dan questions Mary about her brother's death. As he tells her that he is convinced Frankie's death was the work of an informer, Mary confesses that her brother mentioned seeing Gypo earlier that night. Gypo's theme can be heard in a sinister instrumentation, a musical evocation of the implications of her statement. Gallagher begins to make the connection. The opening phrase of "The Wearing of the Green," in a rising sequence, provides a musical equivalent for the mental process that leads Gallagher to a recognition of Gypo's guilt. Gypo's theme follows, played now by the cello.

Gypo is arrested and brought to the kangaroo court of the Irish rebels. His trial opens with a horn call of an open fifth (Variation II) played on a bugle. Personal testimonies reconstruct the night's events, weaving suspicion more and more tightly around Gypo. As is typical of Steiner's practice, visual references are "caught" with music, the appropriate leitmotif responding to the image track. The blind man's theme is heard when he gives his testimony; the money motif accompanies Bartley's accounting of Gypo's expenses; Gypo's theme, in the horn instrumentation, accompanies his testimony; Mary's theme accompanies a close-up of her; and when Gypo cries out in anguish, "Isn't there a man here who can tell me why I did it?" a variation of Katie's theme is heard in the background as if to answer the question. When deviation occurs in this design, it is especially striking. Gypo's confession, quite unexpectedly, is accompanied by Mary's leitmotif played by violins. This unusual coupling draws attention to the relationship between them, and the lyrical string instrumentation associated with Mary elicits sympathy for Gypo.

Imprisoned, Gypo awaits his execution. A dripping ceiling in Gypo's cell is Mickey Moused to the money motif played on a plucked harp. Steiner himself describes the process.

> There was a sequence toward the end of the picture in which McLaglen is in a cell and water is dripping on him. This is just before he escapes and is killed. I had a certain musical effect I wanted to use for this. I wanted to catch each of these drops musically. The property man and I worked for days trying to regulate the water tank so it dripped in tempo and so I could accompany it. This took a great deal of time and thought because a dripping faucet doesn't always drip in the same rhythm. We finally mastered it, and I believe it was one of the things that won me the [Academy] award. People were fascinated trying to figure out how we managed to catch every drop.[9]

The repetitions of the money motif continue through the cut to the adjoining room where the rebels draw lots to determine Gypo's executioner. In all, the motif is repeated for two minutes and forty seconds.

These repetitions function in several ways: as a chronometer, ticking away the final moments of Gypo's life; as a device to produce tension through the motif's unstable harmonic base; and as a referent to the off-screen drama of a frantic Gypo in the next room. Gypo is able to escape through his own brute strength. When his disappearance is discovered the horn call in Variation II returns.

When Gypo is free, he seeks the shelter and safety of Katie's room. As he confesses his crime, the horn call returns in the tri-tone variation (Variation III). Katie vows to lay down her life for him. The reiteration of her motif, underscoring her dialogue, reflects the sincerity of her motives. String instruments play in a slow tempo with a harp in the background. A note on Steiner's sketch reads: "very light—strings and harp only, maybe Harp and cello in places (no W.W. [woodwinds] ever)." It is interesting to note how the change in instrumentation ennobles Katie and how it does so at a moment in the narrative when Katie proclaims her love for Gypo.

Her devotion is reinforced by similar orchestration in the following scene at the McPhillips' home. As Katie appeals to Dan and Mary to spare Gypo's life, her theme is heard in the string and harp accompaniment usually reserved for Mary. Dan is immovable. But a connection between Mary and Katie, reflected in their shared instrumentation, becomes apparent. Katie reminds her: "I'm not the kind of girl you are. There was a time when I was. And I love Gypo no less for being what I am." A solo violin plays Katie's motif. Moments later, she unwittingly betrays Gypo, telling Dan of his whereabouts in hopes of clemency. The dialogue is underscored by a dissonant passage played by *tremolo* violins marked *"furioso,"* a musical foreshadowing, surely, of impending consequences. An annotation in Steiner's sketch reminds his orchestrator that the dissonance is intentional: "Dissonance on purpose." At this moment, Bartley eavesdrops and takes matters into his own hands.

As Gypo waits for Katie's return, repetitions of the money motif create a palpable musical tension. His strength allows him to escape the ambush at Katie's room only to be gunned down in the street by Bartley. Immediately before he is shot the money motif is heard once more as he walks to the church. Dying, he seeks its refuge. Gypo pauses at the iron gates which mark the church's entrance, and spreads his arms in the crucifixion pose. He enters the church accompanied by a dramatic cymbal crash. Here he meets the mourning Mrs. McPhillip praying for the soul of Frankie. Gypo's motif, played on a solo violin, accompanies his painful walk down the aisle toward her as well as his tortured confession. Steiner's annotations, "pathetic" and "*dolcissimo,*" make explicit his intentions and, in fact, Mrs. McPhillip's forgiveness is foreshadowed by the music. As she repeats the phrase "You didn't know what you were doing," a choir (presumably nondiegetic) sings the "Ave Maria." Gypo calls out to Frankie before he crumples to the ground in death. Rising chords herald his salvation. The choir's "Amen" is accompanied by the church bells.

There is one final characteristic of Steiner's work that is exhibited in this score: his appropriation of the classical repertoire as thematic referents, a practice which allows him to draw extracinematic meaning into the score by incorporating established musical associations. Although the score was described by most critics as uniquely Irish,[10] its true debt lies more with nineteenth-century romantic and late romantic composers than with Irish folk song. Perhaps the most far-reaching example is the motif Steiner composed as the blind man's motif, which draws upon an aria from Giacomo Puccini's opera *La fanciulla del West.* Based on the play *The Girl of the Golden West* by David Belasco, *La fanciulla del West* tells the story of an American frontier saloon keeper, Minnie, and her love for the bandit Ramerrez, alias Dick Johnson. Homesickness, love for one's family, loneliness, the quest for money and its consequences, and the redemptive love of a woman are all important thematic elements in this opera. In fact, the plot of *La fanciulla del West* bears a striking resemblance to that of *The Informer*: a man with a price on his head; a woman pleading for her condemned lover's life; a large sum of gold. Even structural elements are similar: *La fanciulla del West* opens with the camp minstrel singing about homesickness; *The Informer* opens with a street singer intoning "Rose of Tralee" which embodies similar sentiments.

Melodically, "The Blind Man" evokes the aria Puccini composed for his blind man, Jake Wallace: "Che faranno i vecchi miei." Jake's distinguishing characteristic is his blindness. The placement of this aria in the opera (Jack, the camp minstrel, emerges from the chorus in the beginning of the first act) is similar to the placement of the song in *The Informer* (the camera passes a street musician who sings "Rose of Tralee"). Finally, the lyrics of both "Rose of Tralee" and "Che faranno i vecchi miei" detail the loneliness and homesickness of a boy cut off from his loved ones and country.

There is another echo of *La fanciulla del West* later in the film. When Gypo is awaiting his execution, tension is produced both visually and musically by foregrounding dripping water, a chronometer which ticks away the final moments of his life. Steiner matches the drips to the notes of the money motif. A similar scene occurs in *La fanciulla* when Minnie hides her lover Ramerrez in the loft of her cabin. Drops of Ramerrez's blood give him away, however, and, as they drip onto the scene below, Puccini's score catches the drops.[11]

The leitmotif Steiner used as a love theme for Mary and Dan is also strongly indebted to operatic literature. The actual melody, with its highly chromatic line, is reminiscent of one of the most famous love themes in musical literature, the "Liebestod" from Wagner's *Tristan und Isolde*. The reference to these legendary figures, whose passionate love consumed them both, is perhaps stretched in this context (Mary and Dan hardly seem the counterparts of their musical progenitors), but its evocation of passion is unmistakable. And Steiner's "The Money" has a clear antecedent in Giuseppe Verdi's *Requiem Mass*.

When *The Informer* was released it was dubbed "a brilliant work . . . a stirring and profoundly moving tragedy, certain to take its place as a clear-cut model in the future for film artisans who are intent on creating works of art as well as beguiling entertainments."[12] Significantly, Steiner's score drew similar attention and acclaim. *Musical America* reported: "Mr. Steiner in this film has . . . composed remarkably vital music."[13] Richard Watts of the *Los Angeles Herald Tribune* saw the film initially without a score. After a second viewing with the music he wrote: "With a really stirring score . . . the picture is even finer than it seemed to me on first sight."[14] *Hollywood Citizen News* asserted: "Without the masterful musical genius of Max Steiner the picture would not be one-third the picture it now is."[15] What these critics recognized very early in the history of the sound film was the power of the film score to bring a film to fruition. Steiner's scores seem almost operatic

_151_

RKO RADIO PICTURES, INC.

Date: **April 29th, 1935**

JOHN G. PAINE, Agent and Trustee
1501 Broadway
New York City

Production No. **817**

Application is hereby made to use the following musical compositions in connection with

(Title of photoplay) **"THE INFORMER"**

(Studio) **RKO STUDIOS** on or about (date) **3/14/35**

(Location) **Hollywood, California**

*all
Scored music -
4 2 11 ft ·*

Producer: **RKO STUDIOS, INC.**

By: **Max Steiner**
　　　　　Musical Director

		USE Part-Entire
(REEL I)		
1.	Composition: THE INFORMER (BI) (as yet un-published) Composer: Max Steiner Publisher: Irving Berlin, Inc.-RKO Property	Entire
2.	Composition: IRISH SOLDIER SONG (VV) (as yet un-published) Composer: Max Steiner Publisher: Irving Berlin, Inc.-RKO Property	Partial
3.	Composition: BRITISH GRENADIERS (BI) Composer: Unknown Publisher: Irving Berlin, Inc.(Max Steiner arr.) RKO Property	Partial
4.	Composition: ROSE OF TRALEE (VV) Composer: Glover & Spencer Publisher: Movietone Music Corp.	Entire
5.	Composition: I ADORE HIM (BI) (as yet un-published) Composer: Max Steiner Publisher: Irving Berlin, Inc.-RKO Property	Entire
6.	Composition: YANKEE DOODLE (BI) Composer: Unknown Publisher: Irving Berlin, Inc.(Max Steiner arr.) RKO Property	Partial
7.	Composition: I ADORE HIM (BI) (as yet un-published) Composer: Max Steiner Publisher: Irving Berlin, Inc.-RKO Property	Partial
8.	Composition: WEARING OF THE GREEN (BI) Composer: Unknown Publisher: Irving Berlin, Inc.(Max Steiner arr.) RKO Property	Partial
9.	Composition: WEARING OF THE GREEN (BI) Composer: Unknown Publisher: Irving Berlin, Inc.(Max Steiner arr.) RKO Property	Partial

G-1-1

From the cue sheet for _The Informer_. The cue sheet for a sound film enumerates all musical selections heard in the film, whether originally composed or quoted from existent musical literature. As such it is a source for determining musical authorship. Here it can be used to identify the folk songs Steiner employs and to differentiate them from his originally composed material.

in this regard, exploiting each and every opportunity for music, creating a nearly seamless stream of accompaniment. This hyperbolic quality of Steiner scores reaches its apex in *Gone With the Wind* four years later, a film with three hours and twenty minutes of music! The critical success of the score for *The Informer* and the formal recognition it received in the form of an Oscar suggest that Steiner's extravagant, lavish version of the classical score was a viable option for composers working in Hollywood, and many followed his lead in saturating a film with music. One who didn't was Bernard Herrmann, and his score for *The Magnificent Ambersons* constitutes the subject of the following chapter.

CHAPTER 6

The "hysterical cult of the director"

The Magnificent Ambersons:
Music and Theme

Making a film is a cooperative effort of many talents and gifts working together.
But, you see, at the present time there's this hysterical cult of the director.
Bernard Herrmann

The Magnificent Ambersons opens with a characteristically Wellesian touch: a lengthy prologue delays narrative enactment and creates the nostalgic, evocative mood that permeates the film. Critical commentary on Ambersons has been drawn to this cinematic prelude in attempts to define precisely what empowers it and, by extension, the film itself. Ironically, although musical terminology permeates these discussions there is little acknowledgment of the actual contribution of music to the exposition of the film's theme.[1]

Although it would seem to be a truism that filmmaking is a collaborative art, the nature of artistic collaboration in the medium has remained elusive. The developing discipline of film studies initially focused critical attention on film's literary heritage, analyzing the script, the screenwriter, and issues of adaptation. With the advent of auteurism, the "hysterical cult of the director" tended to obscure the nature of individual contribution. Nowhere is this tendency more pronounced than in the lack of attention to a film's score.[2]

In The Magnificent Ambersons this critical reticence obscures a crucial component in the film's signifying system: its music. As the preceding analyses of Captain Blood and The Informer demonstrate, music is an integral part of the process that constructs meaning. In The Magnificent Ambersons the score is an important element in the construction of theme as well, providing a structural and thematic analogue for the film's primary opposition between nineteenth-century aristocratic grace and twentieth-century technological progress. In fact, the score for The Magnificent Ambersons prefigures both the terms of that opposition and its resolution.

Despite its fate at the hands of studio executives and its reputation as a flawed masterpiece, *The Magnificent Ambersons* retains a prominent place in the history of American cinema. Yet the relationship of the score to the film's narrative construction, the nature of the collaboration between its director and its composer, and the fate of the score in the studio's recut version (no composer's name appears on any release print of the film) remain virtually unexplored. It is my intention here to offer a reading of a classical text which takes into account the musical score as part of the process that produces a film's explicit theme.

Bernard Herrmann's score for *The Magnificent Ambersons* was the second filmic collaboration between Herrmann and Orson Welles. Their first was *Citizen Kane* (1941). Welles's precociousness is a matter of record (he was only twenty-five when he made *Kane*), but Herrmann was only twenty-nine when he wrote the score, already a seven-year veteran of composing and conducting. Herrmann seemed more at home in the world of art music than in the frenzied world of film composing. In fact he never considered himself a film composer, but rather a composer who also scored films. Trained at New York University and Juilliard, Herrmann was hired by CBS Radio as a composer and conductor at the age of twenty-two. As musical director of two of the network's musical showcases he promoted the cause of modern music. When the name of Charles Ives was still unknown, CBS listeners heard his music on Herrmann's programs. In 1936 Herrmann's tenure began on the Mercury Theatre of the Air, founded jointly by Welles and John Houseman, where he scored many of the radio dramas done weekly by the company. When Welles came to Hollywood to film *Citizen Kane* he brought the Mercury Theatre company with him, and Bernard Herrmann scored his first film.

Herrmann's score for *Kane* matches the ingenuity of Welles's conception. The instrumentation is striking, avoiding strings and emphasizing brasses, woodwinds, and percussion. The musical forms are equally surprising, particularly dance forms such as the can-can, polka, waltz, hornpipe, and gallop. Herrmann's use of leitmotifs provides a field day for the trained ear. Kane's power theme is a musical permutation of the Rosebud theme. Slowed down in tempo it becomes Kane's campaign song. In fact, if one listens carefully, the identity of Rosebud is revealed first in the music. (It accompanies the medium shot of the sled at the end of the first section of Thatcher's narration.) The score also offers a stunning recreation of nineteenth-century French grand opera in *Salaambo*, complete with the aria "Ah, Cruel" composed by Herrmann. The libretto, based on Racine's *Phèdre*, was contributed by John Houseman.

It was Herrmann's second film however, *All That Money Can Buy* (1941, also known as *The Devil and Daniel Webster*), that brought him commercial success, an Oscar, and the recognition of the Hollywood community. From a point very early in his film career Herrmann had the power to choose his assignments. Because of a demand for his services both as a radio composer and as a conductor in the concert hall, Herrmann never depended upon his film career and worked on carefully selected films. His taste for the bizarre and the fantastic, for instance, led him to such otherwise forgettable films as *White Witch Doctor* (1953); *The Seventh Voyage of Sinbad* (1958); and *Journey to the Center of the Earth* (1959). During his first ten years in Hollywood Herrmann scored only nine films. (Contrast to Max Steiner who in 1933 alone worked on thirty-five.) Herrmann made his home in New York and later London, traveling infrequently to Hollywood.

Late in life Herrmann would contend that his work for Welles was his only opportunity for collaboration during a long and noteworthy career in Hollywood. As Herrmann has said, "Orson is the only one with any musical, cultural background. All the other directors I worked with haven't had the temerity to tell me anything about music."[3] At least part of the cement that joined them was Welles's musicality. Raised by a mother with a prodigious musical talent (at one point there was talk of a concert career for her), Welles was encouraged in his inclination toward music at an early age. At five he appeared in the walk-on role of Trouble in the Chicago Lyric Opera's production of *Madama Butterfly*. He also demonstrated, not surprisingly, a precociousness at his mother's piano. The theater ultimately seduced Welles, but music left its mark in the form of a solid if informal musical education upon which he drew in many phases of his career. (As a young director, for instance, Welles staged a notorious production of Marc Blitzstein's opera *The Cradle Will Rock*.) Welles's musical acumen and Herrmann's respect for it allowed

Orson Welles and Bernard Herrmann at a recording session for *Citizen Kane*. Herrmann and Welles enjoyed a unique relationship in Hollywood for a composer and a director: Herrmann contended that in his long career in Hollywood, Welles was the only director with whom he discussed the score for a film.

Welles to make musical suggestions and work them out with Herrmann (the idea of writing an original aria in *Kane* for Susan's operatic debut, for instance, was thrashed out between them). In return Herrmann got Welles's unfailing support in studio disputes over his musical decisions.

The Mercury Theatre company in Hollywood was noted for its encouragement of experimentation and innovation and its antagonism toward any studio interference. As a member of Mercury, Herrmann exemplified its character. His own philosophy of composition avoided many of the conventions developed in Hollywood for film scoring. The working conditions under which he expected to carry out his duties were unconventional to say the least. And his adamant stance on the integrity of the composer's musical material often thrust him into bureaucratic power struggles within the studio.

The conventions that constitute the classical film score were firmly established during the decade of the thirties, and composers who came to Hollywood in the forties encountered a powerful, institutionalized model for setting image to music. As discussed in Chapter 3, however, the classical model was not so monolithic and rigid that divergence was impossible, and composers began to test its limits. One such composer was Bernard Herrmann. Unlike Max Steiner who loaded a film with music, Herrmann scored a film sparingly. Further, Herrmann avoided a direct correlation between music and screen action, often leaving the most climactic narrative scenes unscored. Instead of privileging melody, Herrmann composed extremely short and frequently nonmelodic musical cues, as he had done in radio, some lasting only a few seconds. He also avoided emotional underscoring. Harmonically, Herrmann was daring, moving away from a dependence on late romanticism, using dissonance, unresolved chordal structures, and **polytonality**, the use of two or more different keys simultaneously.

Herrmann also avoided the standard symphonic orchestra. Instead, he used smaller ensembles, employing unorthodox combinations of instruments to create unusual textures. The instrumental colors he employed and the unique textures he scored for them are a trademark of his film scores. (In *Psycho*, for instance, Herrmann used an ensemble made up entirely of strings, for the discarded *Torn Curtain* [1965] score, an ensemble entirely of brass.) Herrmann was also one of the rare composers to orchestrate his own film scores, a touchy point among those Hollywood composers such as Steiner, Korngold, and Newman who were capable of orchestrating their own material, but who were prevented from doing so by a studio system which utilized them exclusively for their compositional talents. Herrmann's strident insistence that orchestration was a necessary part of composition was not calculated to endear him either to his colleagues or to the Hollywood establishment.

Because of a relationship between Herrmann and Welles and their base at Mercury which developed over the course of several years and dozens of productions, as well as the unique set of circumstances which brought Welles to Hollywood (as reigning wunderkind he was accorded relative autonomy at RKO), Herrmann and Welles were able to sustain a collaboration within the Hollywood system. During *The*

Magnificent Ambersons this translated into Herrmann's inclusion in the planning stages of the film, his ability to come and go on the set as he pleased, and his immediate access to as well as unwavering support of producer/director Welles.

For Herrmann time was a crucial element. A Hollywood composer typically was given about four to six weeks to complete a score. Since Herrmann was part of the *Ambersons* production team from the beginning, he had the entire length of the shooting schedule as well as the pre- and postproduction stages to complete his work, from its initial planning stages in August through the final recording session in February. The one creative prerogative Herrmann lacked was final approval of the musical portion of the soundtrack. After the painful lesson of *Ambersons*, he would be uncompromising in protecting his music.

Preproduction on *The Magnificent Ambersons* began in the summer of 1941. Booth Tarkington's novel had long held a fascination for Welles. In 1939 he wrote, directed, and produced a radio drama based on the novel for the Mercury Theatre of the Air.[4] Floundering for a vehicle in the wake of *Kane*, Welles returned to it, utilizing again the prodigious talents of the Mercury Theatre: Joseph Cotten, Agnes Moorehead, Erskine Sanford, William Alland, Everett Sloane, Paul Stewart, and of course Bernard Herrmann.

RKO, however, was growing ever more wary of Mercury's autonomy, and contract negotiations with Mercury personnel demonstrated their deep reservations. Herrmann's initial contract agreement was with Mercury Theatre, which frequently made its own deals and turned them over to the studio which was expected to honor them. Mercury hired Herrmann to compose, score, orchestrate, and conduct the score. The fee was to be divided into six equal payments. Herrmann would also receive sole musical credit on a separate title card.[5] A six-month battle of wills was fought between the RKO hierarchy, who insisted that Herrmann ultimately be responsible to them, and Herrmann, who insisted that his responsibility was to the Mercury Theatre, which meant, in essence, to Welles himself. RKO balked and negotiated for delayed payment, withholding a portion of Herrmann's salary against completion of the score, giving them control over a portion of Herrmann's salary and, according to their logic, assuring his compliance. Herrmann resisted and won—six equal payments. As it turned out, he had good reason to insist on the original agreement. The studio assigned another composer, Roy Webb, to complete a score for the final release version.

Herrmann's participation in the production of The Magnificent Ambersons can be dated almost from the film's inception. In August, when Welles was still at work on the screenplay, Mercury Productions was seeking copyright clearance under Herrmann's directive for period pieces to be used as part of the turn-of-the-century musical background. Shooting began in October with a production schedule that was to extend through February of the following year. Early in the schedule were the ballroom scenes. By November 19 Herrmann was conducting a recording session for music to accompany them.[6] This pattern of composing and/or selecting and arranging music as the footage was being shot, and recording it almost immediately after it was in rough cut (and before the entire film was completed), was continued throughout the production schedule so that by January 29, only nine days after principal shooting was completed, almost all of Herrmann's score had been composed and recorded. (A typical Hollywood composer would not have seen any footage by this stage.) In fact, by the time Herrmann's contract negotiations were concluded on February 27, he had completed virtually all of his work on the film.

The Magnificent Ambersons is a film steeped in lost innocence, a nostalgic reverie for America's collective mythical past, distilled into the history of one family. When Welles introduced the radio version of The Magnificent Ambersons, he described the novel as "the truest, cruellest picture of the growth of the Middle West."[7] The film's sympathy for the values of the nineteenth century amid the inevitability of the "progress" technology offers, embodied in Welles's narration and Cortez's cinematography, is exemplified in Herrmann's score. Music inspired by and in one case borrowed from the nineteenth-century repertoire is set in opposition to the nonmelodic and strikingly dissonant music associated with the twentieth century. Orchestration, harmony, rhythm, tempo, and dynamics delineate the binary opposition between pastoral grace and industrialization that the film explores.

Ambersons opens with a long expository sequence, with Welles in voice-over, introducing an idyllic picture of the nineteenth-century Midwest of small towns and leisured life-styles. Music accompanies this voice-over which actually precedes the visual image. *Ambersons* opens without the fanfare of typical Hollywood credits—two title cards are followed by a dissolve to a blackened frame, establishing the soundtrack as the initial system of address between the spectator and the screen. Welles's voice and Herrmann's music "speak" directly to the spectator, preempting the power of the visual image. This privileged introduction defines the vanishing world of the Ambersons, and when the visual image does appear, it does so as heir to the representation the music and voice-over have constructed.

Welles's voice-over evokes the transience of this world: "The magnificence of the Ambersons began in 1873. Their splendor lasted throughout all the years that saw their midland town spread and darken into a city." Herrmann cast the vulnerability of the Ambersons into a single, muted violin playing a period waltz, "Toujours ou jamais," in a languorous tempo (Herrmann marked it simply "*valse tempo*").[8] The violin, one of the most plaintive instruments, is joined by the celestial background texture of arpeggiated harps. The melody itself incorporates a hesitating, arresting quality emanating from the suspension of forward motion on irregular or unexpected tones of the scale, dramatic upward leaps in the melodic line, and deceptive cadences.

Herrmann's use of the waltz and the instrumentation he employs for it define the sympathies of the film as allied with the nineteenth century. Immediately following is the music representing progress. Thus the score introduces the film's structuring dichotomy, the conflict between the nineteenth century and the twentieth, before the image track does through the juxtaposition in the prologue of a waltz and a gallop. While the voice-over, narrative construction, and elements of mise-en-scène continue to delineate a mythic past (a way of life in which Eugene Morgan has time to keep up with fashion and men still gather for an evening in the local tavern), the score introduces opposition through contrasting musical selections.

The most noticeable change is that of tempo from the slow $\frac{3}{4}$ meter of the waltz to the gallop's alternation of $\frac{2}{4}$ and $\frac{6}{8}$ meters marked variously from *moderato* to **allegretto vivace** (quite fast). The violin and harps of the waltz have been replaced by the woodwinds and muted

Figure 6.1.
"Toujours ou jamais," *The Magnificent Ambersons*

Copyright 1942 Bourne Music

brasses. Rather than playing high in the register, as the earlier violin had done, the woodwinds and brasses play low in their register. A flute line in an arresting pattern of alternating sixteenth and eighth notes appears, its rhythmic intensity accentuated by the strings. Much of the music is written in dotted rhythms, in direct contrast to the even rhythms of the waltz. The opening with its fluid rhythms and dependence on strings is juxtaposed with this section of rhythmic intensity orchestrated for brass and woodwinds. The prologue does not merely evoke a bygone way of life, it foreshadows musically the seeds of the conflict the film develops between men and women, romanticism and technology, idealism and progress.

Both musical themes which structure the prologue come from a piece by Emile Waldteufel. A contemporary of Johann Strauss, Jr., Waldteufel is generally considered the lesser of the two composers.[9] Of his several hundred waltzes only a handful are remembered, "The Skater's Waltz" being his most famous composition. Herrmann nevertheless rejected the more obvious choice, Strauss, and settled on a Waldteufel waltz, having used his music in the *Ambersons* radio score. The head of RKO's music department, Constantin Bakaleinikoff, however, objected to its use. The nature of the Welles-Herrmann collaboration (and Welles's power on the RKO lot) is reflected in the chain of command settling the matter. In December Herrmann wired New York for the Waldteufel waltz. It was in the public domain in the United States, but controlled abroad, necessitating extra cost to secure foreign copyright clearance. Strauss, on the other hand, had no such financial impediments. Bakaleinikoff approached Herrmann initially with his suggestion for changing to Strauss, but by January he was appealing to Welles directly, emphasizing the cost of Waldteufel and the relative economy of Strauss and suggesting that "the entire cost could be eliminated if an original theme were to be used." [10] The intention is clear: use Strauss or make Herrmann compose an original theme. Welles's directive, "Use 'Toujours ou Jamais' as decided by Herrmann," [11] reveals the extent to which Welles deemed Herrmann and not the studio responsible for decisions about the musical score and the lengths to which he would go to insure that prerogative.

After establishing "Toujours" as the Ambersons' musical identification, Herrmann develops its motifs as the barometer of their fortunes. In the Christmas ball sequence, at the height of the Ambersons' wealth and power, "Toujours" permeates the score. The sequence begins with a musical prelude, a brief statement of the "Snow Ride" theme (discussed below) played on a solo celesta (marked "*Lento*"). A series of typical waltzes and dance tunes of the era comprise the musical accompaniment, the centerpiece being a lushly orchestrated version of "Toujours." The sequence ends with a final reiteration in the instrumentation of the opening. "Toujours" enjoys a privileged place in the score here, transplanting the other dance tunes preceding it and providing the musical accompaniment for the courtship ritual of the film's central couple. It is the last time Herrmann intended it to be played in its entirety and in a clearly perceptible major key.

"Toujours ou jamais" relinquishes its position at this point and will gradually disappear from the score. It returns only in fragments, arranged for unfamiliar combinations of instruments and in increasingly dissonant harmonies. Three scenes in particular return to its original in-strumentation: Fanny's hysterical outbreak on the stairs, Isabel's reading of Eugene's letter, and Isabel's death. In each case familiar instrumen-tation is used as a reminder of the past and serves to underscore the present's incongruity. A stronger reminder is heard in the cue Herrmann entitled "Garden Music" played during Eugene and Lucy's metaphoric conversation about Indian legends. The first three notes of "Toujours," cast in the minor, form the opening, and brief variations of "Toujours" are woven into the musical texture. When Jack visits Eugene and Lucy to report Isabel's ill health, the opening phrase of "Toujours" returns in a lugubriously slow tempo in a predominantly minor key. A sense of dislocation is heightened by reiteration of the familiar tune deprived of its identifying instrumentation, tonality, and tempo. And in Herrmann's original ending for the film the opening phrase from "Toujours" was to have been heard as the final six notes of the score.

In place of "Toujours ou jamais" are musical cues for the Amber-sons motivically instead of melodically oriented, employing low strings, brasses and muted brasses, and woodwinds, slow tempi, and chordal progression. A cue which exemplifies this practice can be heard as a pre-lude to Wilbur Minafer's funeral. It begins with a repeated note played in the dark instrumentation of muted horns and basses, each repetition progressively louder. A three-note phrase marked "**subito**" (suddenly) and "ppp" is played against it. Although the cue is only four measures long, it lasts a full twenty-two seconds. Dark instrumentation as well as slowly moving chords are also heard after Eugene is refused permission to see Isabel on her deathbed, and similar instrumentation is heard in the scene in which Major Amberson has lost his mind. Herrmann scores this passage for trombones, a timpani, bass drum, cello, and basses, and emphasizes this dark instrumentation with mutes and slow tempi.

What must surely be the most celebrated of all the sequences in *Ambersons* is the sleigh ride and car excursion scene. The film posits a juxtaposition between the Ambersons' pastoral world and the world of technology represented by the automobile. A key characteristic of Herrmann's score is its embodiment in musical microcosm of this nar-rative conflict. The score in the snow ride sequence recapitulates the narrative opposition of gentility and progress through the juxtaposition of two very different musical pieces. The first is "Snow Ride." It appears initially in a brief quotation during the prologue, is recapitulated as a fragment during the prelude to the Ambersons' Christmas Ball, and is given full expression here. "Snow Ride" is scored almost exclusively for percussion—celestas, piano, small and large triangle, jingle bells, and harps (the one exception)—instruments which cannot sustain sound as long as brass or string instruments can. The ephemeral quality produced by the instrumentation is reinforced by its structure. The subtitle of "Snow Ride," "Perpetual Motion," is a phenomenon demonstrated by the repeated four-note motif. Although the music moves at a quick tempo, it does not move in any discernible direction. The harmony is vague; it is so highly chromatic that it borders on atonality. This short piece is typical of Herrmann with its absence of melody, gravitation toward atonality, repetition of key motifs, and unusual instrumental color. As such it embodies the evanescence of the Ambersons' way of life.[12]

The second "piece" is the sound of the automobile itself, established initially as an unpleasant, squeaking monotone (the sound of its engine being primed) and becoming an annoying roar when its engine catches. As in the prologue and the Christmas ball sequence, the score encapsulates the film's dual concerns with leisure and speed in this case by associating them with music and noise respectively. The sleigh, in rounding a corner too fast, topples over, and its occupants, George and Lucy, must be rescued by Eugene and his automobile. When the expanded touring party crowds into Eugene's car, "Snow Ride" is replaced by a vocal rendition of "The Man Who Broke the Bank at Monte Carlo." At the end of the sequence, the car moves confidently into the distance as the camera irises out on a bygone way of life. Music capitulates to noise. The song drops out and the automobile provides the music of the future.

Music which represents the new technology dominates the remainder of the film. Short, nonmelodic phrases, often highly chromatic and devoid of harmonic support with increasingly percussive instrumentation, represent industrial progress. A dramatic example of music in the machine age is heard during the montage in which George walks home through the progressively industrialized city of his youth. As he passes

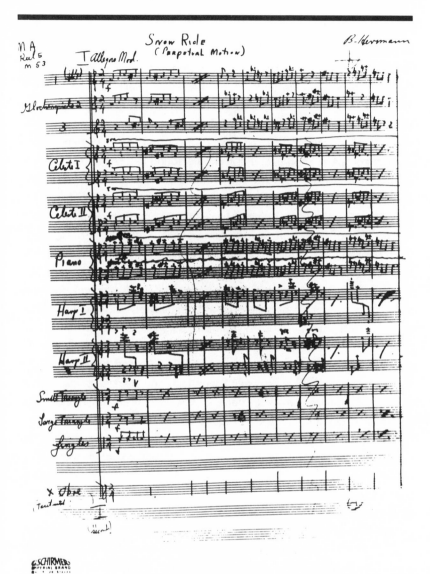

From Bernard Herrmann's autograph score for *The Magnificent Ambersons*. Note the last-minute cross-outs in the eighth, and across the third and fourth measures (where they are barely visible). Herrmann eliminated these measures at the recording session, trimming to fit the final edited sequence.

telephone posts, rooming houses, and billboards, Welles's voice-over outlines the unwelcome changes. Low chords played by muted trumpets and trombones rumble beneath the narration. Herrmann then introduces three vibraphones playing short, nonmelodic phrases in a highly chromatic progression. Herrmann's intention to make the music sound mechanical is reflected in the directive on muting: "cup mute more nasal; mechanical; reed like; music should sound like character." Unfortunately eliminated from the final release print, the music Herrmann composed for the tour of Eugene's automobile factory made the point even more emphatically. Using unconventional orchestration, Herrmann scored "noise" to accompany the birth of the assembly line.

Herrmann's use of music as thematic analogue structures the score in a direct relationship to the film's narrative organization. There is a further sort of complicity between Herrmann and Welles: scenes involving climactic action or emotional force are deliberately left unscored. (The typical scene that a more conventional Hollywood composer would sink his teeth into Herrmann avoids.) There is no music at all, for instance, during the fight between young George and his taunter, the postparty gossip session between Fanny, Jack, and George, or the dinner party when George attacks Eugene. Fanny's first breakdown under the taunting of Jack and George as George wolfs down strawberry shortcake, her final hysteria in the decaying mansion, George's proposal to Lucy and their farewell scene are similarly unaccompanied by music. Yet, these scenes are not silent. Vocal intonation generates its own aural texture: Agnes Moorehead's high-pitched hysteria; Joseph Cotten's flat monotone; Tim Holt's whining tenor; Ray Collins' resonant baritone. In order to emphasize the power of speech and to give the actors a chance to shine, Welles keeps expressionistic camera techniques to a minimum. In those scenes in which Welles moves toward a less visible style, Herrmann does too, dropping musical accompaniment altogether.

Like Welles, Herrmann gravitated toward moments of transition in films (influenced, no doubt, by techniques of radio scoring at Mercury Theatre of the Air), concentrating many of his musical resources on those moments which serve as temporal or spatial mediation. These are the same moments to which Welles is drawn over and over again, from the lightning mixes of *Citizen Kane* to the languid iris-out of *Ambersons*.

In fact, in moments of transition there is what might be termed a symbiotic relationship between Welles's omniscient narrator and Herrmann's musical score.

Both the omniscient voice-over and the musical score are mediatory. In *Ambersons*, they are also interactive. A case in point is the transition between the scene in which the town gossips prophesy the future of Isabel Amberson's children and the scene in which Georgie fulfills that prophecy. The music which precedes Welles's narrative bridge incorporates lively rhythms but, when Welles's voice-over comments that the gosspis were wrong, Isabel "didn't have children, she only had one," the music sustains a long-held note in the oboe. This musical pause, coming unexpectedly in the quick tempo, draws the attention of the listener, and the impact of the spoken line recited against it is heightened. Complicity between Welles's voice-over narration and the music thus functions to privilege a key passage.

The relationship between narration and musical text is even more pronounced in an earlier scene. Welles as narrator suggests that the magnificence of the Ambersons is out of place in rural Indiana: "against so homespun a background, the magnificence of the Ambersons was as conspicuous as a brass band at a funeral." He is interrupted by a clarinet after pronouncing the word "Ambersons." The clarinet plays a descending ninth suggesting the cadence of a laugh, imitating Welles's intonation and encouraging a conspiratorial response between narrator and spectator. Indeed, the musical cue encapsulates the interactive relationship between music and text, composer and narrator, which mediates between the spectator and the screen.

The contribution that Herrmann made to *The Magnificent Ambersons* was not destined for posterity. In spite of or perhaps because of his relationship to Welles, Herrmann was disenfranchised at RKO, and his score was altered and appended during the final weeks of postproduction when the studio seized control of the film and both recut and reshot portions of it. Reports of what happened to the original version of *The Magnificent Ambersons* depict a nightmare of chaos, mismanagement, and studio shortsightedness.[13] World War II was declared in December 1941 about halfway through the shooting schedule. Welles had a number of uncompleted projects on his hands when the United

States government extended him an invitation to make a documentary in Brazil. (The project, *It's All True*, was never completed.) *Ambersons* had not yet finished shooting; another film due RKO, *Journey into Fear* (1943), was also before the cameras, with Welles playing the role of Major Haki and directing (Norman Foster was eventually called in and retains screen credit); and Mercury Theatre of the Air was still claiming his time. Welles left for Brazil on 3 February 1942 barely two weeks after principal shooting on *Ambersons* was completed.

A rough cut was complete by mid-March when it was shown in Pomona and then in Pasadena. Viewing conditions for the previews were hardly ideal. *Ambersons* followed either *The Fleet's In* (in Pomona), a Dorothy Lamour musical comedy, or *Captains of the Clouds* (in Pasadena), an action-packed World War II film about the heroics of the Royal Canadian Air Force. Editor Robert Wise claims that sneak previews were "a disaster. . . . Audiences were in a completely different frame of mind now that the war was on, everybody was keyed up and they just didn't have the patience for this artistic piece of work." [14] A government restriction on civilian flying prevented Wise from joining Welles in Brazil so a copy of the film was sent to Welles in his place. Wise then began the process of reediting the film according to long and often confusing instructions cabled back by Welles. Wise recalled the confusion:

> He [Welles] ran the film and called us by long distance with dozens of suggestions and things he wanted improved and changed. At one time I had a 35 page cable of instructions from him. I've lost it over the years moving—I should have had sense enough to have kept it. Anyway, we did everything that we could that Orson wanted done.[15]

RKO wavered and eventually lost patience with the whole project. Welles's original contract with RKO, under which he made *Citizen Kane*, would have protected him; the contract he negotiated in order to insure the possibility of making *Ambersons* did not.[16] It came back to haunt him. Drastic recutting was ordered (supervised by Wise), and retakes began May 19. The question of textual authorship in the recut version is muddied by sketchy production records and conflicting and sometimes unreliable personal testimony. To wit: Wise claims to have directed a few scenes himself and contends that Freddie Fleck, production manager, directed the final hospital scene. Stanley Cortez recalls that both Russell Metty and Harry Wild photographed re-takes; he also claims that Wise shot the final hospital scene. Welles himself insisted that Norman Foster be brought in. Production records indicate that some footage, including the final hospital scene, was not shot by Welles and Cortez, and that almost a full hour of their original work is missing from the extant print.[17]

Stanley Cortez blames Charles Koerner, the new RKO West Coast production chief (he replaced Charles Schaeffer, a Welles ally in the RKO hierarchy), for the massive cuts. According to Cortez, Koerner "was obsessed with the idea of the double feature. He came out with the arbitrary edict that no film left the studio longer than 7,500 feet, no matter what the picture was."[18] But the deathblow for Welles's and the Mercury Theatre's further involvement with *Ambersons* was delivered by Ross Hastings of RKO Legal on 1 June 1942. Based on Welles's renegotiated contract, Hastings claimed that RKO had the legal right to edit the picture as it liked and did not need the approval of Welles or the Mercury Theatre. Although Welles was reportedly returning to the United States to do battle with RKO executives, the lot was legally closed to him and he never got his opportunity.[19]

The massive recutting of the film was accompanied by an equally massive recutting of the music. When Welles left for Brazil, Herrmann completed postproduction work and left shortly afterward for New York. Herrmann had no power of his own with RKO as the episode with Bakaleinikoff demonstrated. His position was dependent upon Welles's, and it was in the nature of their collaboration for Welles to back Herrmann unhesitatingly. Unfortunately when Welles lost power, so did Herrmann. As early as April, the studio was making changes in Herrmann's score. But because Welles was out of the country (and Mercury was losing control of the production), Herrmann was never consulted or even informed about any of them. Unknown to Herrmann, RKO assigned another RKO composer, Roy Webb, to do the work.

By 22 June 1942, thirty minutes and forty-three seconds of Bernard Herrmann's music had been deleted from the film. To make matters worse, six minutes and fifty-four seconds of music (or almost one-fifth of the score heard in the release print) was not composed by Herrmann. As early as April musical sequences composed by Roy Webb were being recorded. "End Title" and "Eugene and Lucy at Desk" recorded on April 28 were used in the film. The cue sheet of 21 June 1942 shows that two dance pieces selected by Webb were eventually added to the ball sequence, and his incidental music for Isabel's bedroom scene was used.[20] Webb scored the trailer for *Ambersons* using his own music almost exclusively with the exception of brief quotations from "Toujours ou jamais" and a Herrmann cue, "Chorale," deleted from the final release print. In all, less than half of the music Herrmann had composed or arranged for *Ambersons* was used, and one-fifth of the revised version was written by Webb.

Bernard Herrmann's autograph full score includes eleven selections not heard in the final release version: "Fantasia," "*Tocatta* [sic]," "Chorale," "Second Reverie" (the first was used in the film), two nocturnes, and cues Herrmann entitled "Major and Jack," "First Letter Scene," "Second Letter Scene," "Where Now?" "Back to the Sun," and "Uncle Jack Tells Isabel." Most of these cues disappeared from the final release print when the film was recut by the studio and the companion scenes were reedited or eliminated. One of the most interesting of the missing cues may have been cut even earlier. "*Tocatta*" is a piece Herrmann composed for the factory scene where Eugene gives Fanny, Isabel, and Jack a tour of his automobile plant. It is a stunning musical recreation of "noise," scored for xylophone, steel plate, two anvils (high and low), bass drum, and four timpani. Presumably the sounds of the factory itself made Herrmann's cue superfluous.[21]

Changes to the ending of the film are the most disruptive. Herrmann intended that the end title be a somber, dirgelike culmination to the fall of the Ambersons with a coda restating "Toujours ou jamais" in a minor key. The end title opens with cellos and basses playing low in their registers, the melodic material played by the ubiquitous instrumentation of the new technology: woodwinds. Herrmann avoids the Hollywood convention of privileging music during a film's final moments by deliberately obscuring it, marking the entire passage "pp." Instead of offering a solid harmonic resolution, the music flirts with chromatic

The tour of the Morgan automobile factory. Publicity still. This was the sequence that was to have been accompanied by "*Tocatta* [*sic*]."

harmony and only at the last chord is resolved. A solo vibraphone ends the score, playing the opening motif from "Toujours ou jamais" against the film's last chord, an evocative musical commentary on the demise of the Ambersons.

But Herrmann's "End Title" was never used, and new pieces by Roy Webb accompany the last scenes of the film. Webb's musical cues are more clearly in keeping with conventional Hollywood scoring practice and provide a stark contrast to Herrmann's idiom. In the scene in Eugene's library, Lucy has just learned that George has been seriously injured in an automobile accident and tells her father that she is going to the hospital for a reconciliation. Webb's accompaniment rests squarely within the classical tradition: a full chordal harmony is employed with a transcendent melody played by violins. (Webb uses eight; Herrmann never used more than four at any given moment in the score.) Melody underscores the entire conversation, a practice Herrmann scrupulously

From Bernard Herrmann's autograph score for *The Magnificent Ambersons*. Although "*Tocatta*" was recorded, it does not appear in the final release print. Herrmann intended it for the sequence in which Eugene Morgan gives a tour of the Morgan automobile plant. Note the unusual instrumentation such as the steel plate and the anvils.

avoided. In fact, Webb's accompaniment to this scene, culminating in the performance directions for the last two measures "almost triumphantly,"[22] contradicts the entire thematic concept of Herrmann's approach.

On the musical cue sheet, the name of the composer for music accompanying the hospital scene is absent. But it is consistent with the musical style of the preceding scene and in all likelihood was also composed by Webb. Eugene forgives George and (is it possible?) suggests a renewed romantic interest in Fanny. Violins play "Toujours ou jamais," providing an emotional catharsis for the happy ending. Musically there is little justification for an eleventh-hour return to the orchestral sound and melodic tag of the Ambersons' earlier days. It not only violates the structural unity of the score but seems incongruent with the blank faces of Eugene and Fanny.

Webb's end title is a restatement of "Toujours ou jamais" in the orchestration of the opening, contradicting the thematic progression that Herrmann had created in the music. Herrmann intended that the music which closed the film be somber and elegiac, a funereal dirge for a bygone era. Webb's return to the music of the opening matches the ending put on the film by the studio, but works against the thematic integrity of Herrmann's score and bears little if any resemblance to what Herrmann intended.

Although changes in Herrmann's score had clearly been made, RKO Studio Publicity released the following information about the music:

> Behind the film is heard a nostalgic score by Herrmann, who scored "Kane," and who is the youngest American composer to have had a work performed by the New York Philharmonic orchestra. Long the musical director for all the Welles radio productions, Herrmann chose a Waldteufel waltz for the thematic approach to scoring the "The Magnificent Ambersons," and his original music built around this is heard through the entire film.[23]

But after attending a New York preview, Herrmann claimed that only one-third of his music had been used. (In fact, the film uses about one-half of his music.) Herrmann demanded that the studio remove his

From Bernard Herrmann's autograph score for *The Magnificent Ambersons*. Note the restatement of "Toujours ou jamais" in the last line, the vibraphone part.

name as musical director.[24] On 22 June 1942 RKO East Coast executive Gordon E. Youngman wired West Coast legal chief Ross Hastings that Herrmann

> demands that we refrain from giving him any screen credit for score. Perfectly willing to have us use his music but wants all mention of him elminated [sic]. Mention is made in Welles reference to him as composer of score. Please discuss [with] Koerner and Depinet and advise because Hermann [sic] insists cut be made before trade showing.[25]

The following day Youngman sent a more desperate wire:

> Had lengthy discussion [with] Weissberger [about] Bernard Hermann matter and am convinced in view of man's temperament he will bring injunction proceeding and cause all other trouble he can. His theory is that statement is made score is by Bernard Herrmann while it is not entirely so and that this is deception to public and injurious to his reputation. Doubt he would ultimately recover on this theory but there is some chance and urge re-consideration by studio of desirability of making cut. Please wire.[26]

Herrmann's contract contains the standard Hollywood compliance clause stating that the musical director will "change and revise any music . . . as often and to such extent as the corporation may require in order that the same shall be satisfactory to the corporation."[27] The contract itself makes no mention of exclusivity in terms of Herrmann's score for *Ambersons*, but Herrmann had returned to New York to continue his radio work, and much the same argument that the studio leveled at Welles (if he isn't here to recut the picture, we'll do it ourselves) was leveled at Herrmann.

It does seem doubtful that Herrmann's contract would have given him the legal right to have his name removed from the credits.[28] But he was known to be outspoken, aggressive, and temperamental. As long as he was willing to relinquish control of his music, RKO was willing to avoid a lengthy, and assuredly vituperative, legal battle at all costs. It remains one of the greatest ironies of film history that, despite the fact that Herrmann composed a score for *The Magnificent Ambersons* which became an integral part of the film's complex and deeply moving interpretation of America's idyllic past, and that his work with Welles represented a unique instance of musical collaboration in Hollywood, his participation was never to be acknowledged; his name does not appear on any release print of the film.

The Magnificent Ambersons was the last film collaboration between Welles and Herrmann. Although Herrmann was originally hired to compose Welles's *Macbeth* (1948), his tenure on that production was short; the score was eventually composed by Jacques Ibert. According to Richard Wilson, intermediary between the production company and Herrmann, Herrmann quit in a rage and left for New York. "Benny had said from the very moment we had originally discussed the film that he wanted to be in on it as it went along, that it would take him a long time to write, and he wanted to see a rough print." Herrmann's major complaint was that "he wasn't let in on things"; he insisted that "Orson must be here for scoring and dubbing."[29] Without a position of relative independence backed by Welles and an acknowledged part in the production as it was being filmed, Herrmann would no longer be involved. Almost thirty-five years after his collaboration with Welles, Herrmann still spoke of it with admiration: "I have the final say about my music; otherwise I refuse to do the music for the film. The reason for insisting upon this is that all directors—other than Orson Welles, a man of great musical culture—are just babes in the woods."[30]

CHAPTER 7

"Not exactly classical, but sweet"

Laura: New Directions

Waldo: "Would you mind turning that off?"
Mark: "Why? Don't you like it?"
Shelby: "It was one of Laura's favorites. Not exactly
classical, but sweet."
Mark: "You know a lot about music?"

The classical film score was dominated in the thirties by a triumvirate of composers, Max Steiner, Erich Wolfgang Korngold, and Alfred Newman, who set the prevailing idiom for musical accompaniment to narrative film as neoromantic and established its medium as symphonic. As the chapter on *The Magnificent Ambersons* demonstrates, however, the conventions which constituted this model were not so stringent and unilateral that variation and innovation were impossible. In fact, during the forties both the idiom and the medium of the classical film score began to diversify due to the influx of new composers to Hollywood who brought with them the musical language and styles of the twentieth century. The most consistent and distinctive feature of the classical score, however, a structural foundation which bound music and image in service to the narrative, remained constant. A score such as David Raksin's for *Laura* reveals the force of that structural foundation and the flexibility of its idiom.

David Raksin's experience as a film composer differs markedly from that of Steiner and Korngold, who were trained in Europe in the style of late romanticism and turned to film composing after some success in art music. Raksin was an American-trained musician whose background included a father who was a conductor at Philadelphia's grandest movie palace, the Metropolitan. Raksin started in Hollywood as a staff musician. After arranging Chaplin's *Modern Times* (1936) he found work at Universal where, as part of a team of musicians who scored "B" films, he specialized in main titles, montages, and battle sequences. Raksin eventually moved to Twentieth Century-Fox where he graduated to scoring

159

entire films. His speciality was horror; screen credits from this period include *The Man Who Wouldn't Die* (1942), *Dr. Renault's Secret* (1942), and *The Undying Monster* (1942). His assignment to *Laura* in 1944 gave Raksin the opportunity to work on an "A" picture, and it substantially changed the conditions under which he worked.

> The first picture at Fox where I ever talked to anybody other than one of the music department people was *Laura*. It was the first time I went to a meeting with producers and directors, and also the first picture that got me out of the rut of doing only grue & horror movies or battle movies or westerns.[1]

Raksin's initial typecasting as a composer of horror films was due, in large part, to a musical style that incorporated such unfamiliar elements as complex counterpoint, jazzy instrumentation, and what he called "freaky" harmonies.[2] Like Herrmann, Raksin departed from the nineteenth-century idiom that dominated scoring practices in the thirties. The harmonic structures of his scores are more impressionistic and postimpressionistic than romantic or late romantic; their texture tends toward the contrapuntal or fugal rather than chordal. Raksin seldom adopted the symphonic medium of the thirties score, using instead the pared down and smaller ensembles more characteristic of twentieth-century music. The dominance of strings, and indeed the very concept of melody, is not characteristic of Raksin's music. If anything, the instruments of jazz—brass, woodwinds, percussion—dominate his work. In fact, Raksin's score for *Laura* introduced elements of popular music into the vocabulary of the Hollywood score, creating what *The New Grove Dictionary of American Music* calls "a remarkable synthesis of the serious and popular aspects of film music."[3] Raksin's most experimental scores, for *Force of Evil* (1948) and *Too Late Blues* (1962), rely solely on the contemporary idioms of jazz and blues. Such progressive musical practices, like those of Bernard Herrmann, Aaron Copland, and others, did not displace the neoromantic language of the preceding decade. Rather the practices embodied in a score such as *Laura* were gradually absorbed into the classical model, enlarging and diversifying its possibilities.

Laura is the kind of film Hollywood pointed to as the epitome of its craft. It was directed and produced by Otto Preminger, a man who would become a Hollywood legend for efficient and distinctive film-making; it had a clever plot with a unique twist; and it enjoyed immediate and resounding success with both the critics and, more important, the moviegoing public. The plot turns on the trick of mistaken identity: Laura Hunt (Gene Tierney), an attractive, highly successful advertising executive, is found murdered in her apartment, her face rendered unrecognizable by a shotgun blast. Lieutenant Mark McPherson (Dana Andrews), in an attempt to solve the crime, delves into Laura's life and falls in love with her. Halfway through the film Laura reappears, very much alive. McPherson's task, more and more clouded by his love for her, is to find the murderer of Diane Redfern, a Laura look-alike mistakenly killed in her place. The suspects include Laura and the two men closest to her: Waldo Lydecker (Clifton Webb), her mentor, and Shelby Carpenter (Vincent Price), her fiancé. McPherson solves the crime just as the murderer returns to finish the job. Waldo Lydecker is gunned down as he is about to murder Laura. He dies with her name on his lips.

The final release version of *Laura* is a film in which structural ambiguity and ideological confusion impede a consistent reading. Criticism, most notably by feminist film critics, has exposed this structural ambiguity and posited its ideological consequences. *Laura* has become an archetypal example of the ways in which female sexuality threatens classical narrative and of the processes by which classical stratagems both contain and fail to contain that threat.[4] *Laura* provides a particularly interesting case study because of a thorny production history in which these concerns were made explicit. The role of the score has not been explored in this connection despite the fact that music has a crucial function in the film's textual system and represents a major component in the film's ambiguous ideology and structure.

The sources of this structural and ideological tension in *Laura* are evident in the production history which brought Vera Caspary's novel to the screen. Caspary contended that the studios were indifferent to the synopsis that made the rounds in 1942; she considered adapting the property for the stage at this point with collaborator George Sklar. (The play was eventually produced on Broadway in 1947.) When Twentieth Century-Fox showed interest in 1943, she sold it. Caspary initially relinquished any claim to writing the screenplay, but her interest in the project was renewed when she read a first draft.[5] Angered over a change in the plot that she felt weakened the film, she confronted Preminger. In the novel Waldo Lydecker conceals the murder weapon, a custom-built shotgun, in his cane. Preminger felt the gimmick was unbelievable, and in the screenplay Lydecker uses an actual shotgun which he hides in an ornate clock in Laura's apartment. Caspary responded: "Would a man as elegant and self-conscious as Waldo Lydecker, an authority on murder and a potential killer, be so dumb as to carry a shotgun through the streets of New York on his way to a murder?"[6]

Although Caspary's point now seems minor (the screenwriters adopted Preminger's version), her story conference with Preminger reveals another, more crucial tension between the source novel and the film and one that was not resolved: the characterization of Laura. How she would be represented on the screen hinged on the attitudes of the film's producer and director toward her sexuality. Preminger disapproved of Laura because of what he perceived as her promiscuity, claiming that she had "no character" and pointing out that she had "to pay a gigolo" to get a lover.[7] Caspary, on the other hand, admired Laura's sexual freedom—the novel terms her a "modern woman"—and suggested that it was an important part of her attraction for the reader.[8] Her Laura was "wonderful, warm, sexy," a woman who "enjoyed her lovers."[9] Preminger would later call Laura "a whore."[10] Darryl F. Zanuck, production chief at Twentieth, shared Preminger's reservations, objecting to any references in the screenplay which alluded to Laura's attraction to the male physique.[11] Such vastly disparate attitudes toward Laura's sexuality as Caspary's, Preminger's, and Zanuck's resulted in a confusing characterization for her on the screen.

The film's narrative structure compounds problems in Laura's representation. In the novel, Laura is one of three narrators from whose point of view the story unfolds. (Lydecker and McPherson are the other two.) To Laura, however, falls the prerogative of narrative resolution: she narrates the final third including the denouement. (A coda is supplied by McPherson's commentary on the police report.) The original draft of the screenplay by Jay Dratler (30 October 1943) reproduces the novel's narrative construction through voice-over for Lydecker,

McPherson, and Laura. A later draft (25 January 1944) reduces Laura's voice-over narration to one scene, the party where she is arrested by McPherson. In later revisions it was dropped entirely. While McPherson's voice-over was eventually eliminated also, much later versions of the script (the shooting final of 18 April 1944 and revisions of 24 April 1944) still contain his narration. In fact, Dana Andrews actually recorded a voice-over for the film.[12] Some of the material originally narrated in the novel by Laura was eventually transferred to McPherson through the device of Laura's diary which he discovers and reads. The elimination of Laura's point of view leaves certain aspects of her character, in particular the nature of her relationships with Lydecker and Shelby Carpenter, ambiguous.

Lydecker's narration was the only one of the three to survive into the release print. Another tension in the film emanates from the ambiguity surrounding his character, the result of an equivocal attitude toward his sexuality. The film ostensibly posits Waldo as Laura's lover; yet filmic conventions encode him as homosexual. At least part of this ambiguity can be traced to the source novel. Despite Caspary's disclaimers to the contrary, the novel includes several references to Waldo's sexuality that are ambiguous at best, including a scene in which Waldo enacts a completely convincing imitation of Laura.[13]

Negotiations over the casting of the part suggest that Waldo's sexuality was very much an issue in the film version. Laird Cregar was originally considered for the role but eliminated because as an established heavy he would tip the plot. Preminger wanted a Hollywood unknown, Clifton Webb, then a Broadway actor. But Zanuck objected on the grounds that Webb was too effeminate.[14] Preminger made a screen test and Zanuck acquiesced. Whether or not Preminger was conscious of the ambiguity surrounding Waldo's sexuality in the novel, his casting of Webb highlights the very aspects of Waldo's character that Caspary's novel had least under control.

All of the novel's references to Waldo's homosexuality were removed in the process of adaptation. But in their place the screenwriters adopted filmic conventions for transmitting Waldo's sexuality to the screen. Ironically, the film's allusions are even more pointed than the novel's. The opening sequence, for instance, begins with a lengthy track-

The set of Waldo's apartment. Note the "fussiness" of the decor, its visual excess encoding Waldo's sexuality.

ing shot of Lydecker's apartment. Its ornate decor, baroque furnishings, and art objects displayed prominently in the design scheme establish a type of cinematic excess ("It's lavish, but I call it home"), a frequent signifier of homosexuality. The shooting script describes it as "too exquisite for a man." [15] This excess, further exemplified in Waldo's fastidiousness and preoccupation with taste and breeding, sets him apart from the spartan "masculinity" of McPherson. As Richard Dyer points out, even Waldo's opening lines emphasize his difference: " 'I should be sincerely sorry to see my neighbor's children devoured by wolves' calls attention to his childlessness and hence sexual unnaturalness." [16] We first glimpse Waldo seated in a bathtub with a typewriter over his lap. The entrance of McPherson prompts Waldo to get out of the tub, exposing himself. McPherson's response (he does take a good look before he turns his back) is a smirk. The entire bathroom sequence is a creation of the screenwriters. In the novel Waldo is seated in his study when McPherson arrives.

McPherson asleep in the chair beneath Laura's portrait. Originally Darryl F. Zanuck wanted Laura's reappearance to be part of McPherson's dream. The score, which is artificially manipulated at this point, helps to set up Laura's reappearance as an apparition. Notice the portrait of Laura which dominates the mise-en-scène.

Ambiguity created through adaptation and casting was further compounded by structural problems which threaten the coherence of the narrative itself. Zanuck envisioned the entire second half of the film, from that point where Laura herself reappears, as a figment of McPherson's imagination. Laura's reappearance was thus filmed using a standard convention for the dream: the camera dollies in on McPherson as he falls asleep in Laura's apartment, then immediately dollies out when he loses consciousness. An ending was shot in which McPherson awakens from the very armchair in which he fell asleep.

According to Zanuck "everything was a dream and now we're going to tell the truth." Walter Winchell reportedly talked him out of this ending after a preview, and a new version was shot.[17] But the structural device for the dream version remained. This results in narrative confusion—is Laura's appearance real or imagined—which the film fails to resolve. Kristin Thompson argues that *Laura*'s structure is "duplicitous," one of a group of rare classical films which consciously or unconsciously expose the apparatus of classical narrative construction.[18] Although this will be discussed in greater detail later in the chapter, I would here note that the musical score is a part of the textual operation that creates this duplicity. Another source of ambiguity is Lydecker's structuring voice-over which opens the film, but fails to close it. Indeed since Lydecker dies at the film's climax, closure is impossible, except perhaps as an otherworldly afterthought in the manner of *Sunset Boulevard* (1950).

The production was plagued by yet another problem—its director. Preminger wanted to direct the film himself, but it was Rouben Mamoulian who was hired. After eighteen days Mamoulian was replaced, and Preminger finished the film. There are varying accounts of the circumstances under which this transferral took place.[19] At least one sequence of Mamoulian's, the opening in Waldo's apartment and the ensuing dialogue with McPherson, remains in the final release print.

A final source of textual ambiguity is generated by the music, or more specifically by the composer, David Raksin. Like Caspary, Raksin saw Laura as a sensitive romantic and not as the fallen woman envisioned by Preminger and Zanuck; he wanted to compose a score reflecting this conception of her. In attempting to do so he challenged prevailing musical conventions for representing female sexuality. Certain stereotypes evolved as a type of shorthand for sexual experience, subconsciously affecting spectator response through a kind of musical censorship. As *The Informer* demonstrates, these conventions included brass and woodwind instrumentation, unusual harmonies, and bluesy rhythms. As Raksin himself explained to me:

> You see, in the old days, there would've been a muted trumpet, the prostitute's music and all the rest of that. . . . It's principally the nature of the tune and the harmonization that does it. And then it's the kind of colors you use for it and the manner of playing. . . . It was, in a small way, let's say, a plague.[20]

Like Katie Madden in *The Informer*, Laura, a woman of sexual experience, would typically be characterized by elements of this same stereotype.

It was clear that Preminger was thinking along these lines when Raksin was assigned to the film. Preminger's original choice of a theme song for Laura was "Summertime" by George and Ira Gershwin. When Ira Gershwin refused permission, Preminger turned to the music of Duke Ellington, specifically "Sophisticated Lady." The choice of these pieces, both of which rely on jazz conventions, demonstrates the force of musical stereotypes in the representation of female sexuality and reveals the connection between gender and race that underlies it.

The classical score frequently encoded otherness through the common denominator of jazz. For white audiences of the era, jazz represented the urban, the sexual, and the decadent in a musical idiom perceived in the culture at large as an indigenous black form. Playing upon these culturally empowered stereotypes, the classical score used jazz as a musical trope for otherness, whether sexual or racial. Difference could thus be encoded into a text not only by visual representation but by music as well.

Raksin objected to "Sophisticated Lady," precisely because it embodied what he has called "the usual Hollywood approach to a woman of relatively easy virtue."[21] Raksin's recollection of his story conference with Preminger merits quoting at length.

> At our first conference Preminger announced that he was going to use "Sophisticated Lady." I suggested right away that it was wrong for the picture, whereupon Preminger said, "What do you mean, dear boy, the wrong piece? Don't you like it?" I assured him that I liked the piece and its composer, but that did not make it the right theme for his film. He wanted to know why not, so I said, "Because it already has so many associations in the minds of people that it will arouse feelings that are outside the frame of this picture. I also think that you have made some connection between the title, 'Sophisticated Lady,' and your conception of this girl." At this, he blew a fuse and almost shouted, "The girl is a whore—she's a whore." I said, innocently like a child tormenting a parent, "By whose standards, Mr. Preminger?"[22]

Because Laura had had lovers in the past, she was a woman of sexual experience which required a certain type of music to characterize her. Raksin argued for an original theme and Preminger gave him the chance to compose one. What Raksin produced became the melody immortal-ized as "Laura," a theme which represents a direct reaction against the classical score's formulaic conventions for the representation of female sexuality. The film offers textual evidence that at least three differing conceptions of Laura survived into the final release version: Caspary's, Preminger's (and Zanuck's), and Raksin's. At least part of the film's ambivalence toward Laura's sexuality can be attributed to the tension between the image track and the music track.

The tension between Raksin's Laura and Preminger's is most appar-ent in the initial shot of the film, a freeze-frame of Laura's portrait over which the credits appear. Her portrait reflects the double-bind of female sexuality in film noir: it attracts and threatens; allures and repels. Both the contents of the portrait (the way Laura is posed as well as her attire) and the camera angle (a slightly low angle) are constructed to project her sexuality. Laura is dressed in a black evening gown with a black shawl draped off her shoulders. (An earlier prototype of her portrait had her draped in leopard fur!) Her body is turned sideways to emphasize her bustline, and one of her hands is placed strategically over her bosom. But because this display of female sexuality is also threatening, it is constrained by conventions which defuse its threat. Laura is simultaneously cast as sexual temptress and passive object of male desire. She is caught in the portrait in the position of being be-held; her gaze is not directed outward, meeting the eyes of the implied spectator, but rather remains focused indiscriminately, at an oblique angle. The very picture frame around her serves to contain the power of her threatening sexuality. Frozen into a moment of time, immobile, she is literally on display, forever to be beheld in the moment of sexual anticipation.

Raksin's main title is at odds with this representation. The score opens with a typical technique for attracting the spectator's attention and signaling the nature of the images which follow: string *glissandi* and a cymbal crash. (This is similar to the musical gesture that opens *Captain Blood*.) This musical flourish activates certain expectations about the narrative content—that it is heroic, romantic, epic—which rest uneasily with the ideological message of the portrait. The melody of Laura's theme and the style in which it is performed further widen the

Figure 7.1.   Copyright 1944 Twentieth Century-Fox
Laura's theme, *Laura*

gap between music and image track. Although Laura's theme incorporates chromaticism in its melodic contour, and the brass accompaniment to the string theme is marked **rubato** (a tempo which allows for
flexibility in playing), it is also very lyrical and rooted in performance
techniques of Hollywood's neoromantic tradition. Raksin here uses a
standard symphony orchestra, one of the few times in his career that
he would turn to this medium.[23]

Later in the film there is another example of the tension between
the image and music tracks, compounded by the addition of dialogue.
McPherson arrives at Laura's apartment with Lydecker and Carpenter
to search for clues in the investigation of her murder. Laura's portrait
dominates the mise-en-scène, at the top center of the frame, a con-
tinual reminder of the conceptualization of her as a sexual object. In
fact, it is clear at this point that McPherson has adopted an attitude
toward her that is consonant with the message contained in the portrait. Laura is a "dame" to McPherson, one of two possible categories
of femaleness, the other being the type that walks him "past furniture
windows to look at the parlor suites." Interestingly, it is Lydecker who
defends Laura's character, attacking the estimation of her implied in
McPherson's label. ("Will you stop calling her a dame. Look around. Is
this the home of a dame?") In fact, Lydecker actually calls into question
the reliability of the portrait itself, attacking the ability of the painter,
Jacoby, to capture "her vibrance, her warmth."

The filmic text encompasses two divergent characterizations of Laura
at this point. The music adds another. McPherson puts on a recording of

(coincidentally?) Laura's theme, in a symphonic arrangement with strings (including sixteen violins) carrying the melody. Carpenter says that it was Laura's favorite, facilitating a reading of the sequence in which the music becomes a signifier of Laura herself. In describing the music, Carpenter terms it "not exactly classical, but sweet," an evaluation which authorizes a depiction of Laura in the same terms.

With such pervasive use of a single melody, it's little wonder that the audience noticed the tune. The popularity of the theme from *Laura* surprised both the studio (who listens to the music anyway?) and Raksin himself. Its immediate and overwhelming success gave rise to a phenomenon known as the theme score, a stylistic approach to film scoring which privileged a single musical theme. The studio had a marketable commodity that could be lifted from the score and function as an integral piece of music. The classical score did occasionally produce a memorable melody which caught the audience's ear and was quickly reproduced in sheet music or on record. Tara's theme from *Gone With the Wind* is a good example. Steiner's melody with added lyrics was released in sheet music as "My Own True Love." But a hit tune was the by-product rather than the intended result in such cases, and the success attendant upon such songs did not precipitate a change in classical scoring practices.

The most prominent characteristic of the theme score is its persistent use of a single musical theme, and for this reason it has been discussed frequently in terms of opposition to classical scoring. An analysis of a prototypical theme score such as *Laura*, however, reveals that rather than departing from the classical model, the theme score can be seen more accurately as a variation of it. While it does privilege a single theme over the classical score's multiplicity of leitmotifs, the theme score uses that theme in exactly the same way that the classical score used leitmotifs: to provide coherence for a string of discontinuous musical cues. And, like the classical score, the theme score employed variation to clarify and comment on the image track.

In fact, the theme Raksin composed for Laura functions not unlike a typical leitmotif in a classical score. Its presence on the soundtrack is frequently motivated by either Laura's literal appearance, her figurative appearance through the agency of the portrait, or specific allusions to her in the dialogue. Using rhythm, instrumentation, tempo, dynamics, and harmony Raksin develops the theme to clarify visual content (as in the apartment sequence analyzed earlier in which the arrangement of Laura's theme validates Lydecker's opinion over McPherson's) and to comment upon or in certain cases even to undercut the image track (the neoromantic version which is heard under the opening freeze-frame of the portrait).

Although Raksin limits himself in *Laura* more or less to a single theme, he employs the same means to create nuance in its expression that composers such as Steiner and Korngold relied upon. Through instrumentation Raksin can use Laura's theme to characterize McPherson as a tough guy (using French horns in the opening sequence); Lydecker as odd (using distinctive instruments such as the piccolo and the bassoon and unusual combinations of instruments); and Laura as a romantic protagonist (relying on the strings). Through rhythm and tempo, Raksin can use Laura's theme to suggest both Laura's spirit (a rhythmically arresting variation that accompanies her first meeting with Lydecker) and her naiveté (a waltz variation entitled the "Tierney Waltz," which accompanies her ill-fated attempt to secure Lydecker's endorsement for a pen). Later, Raksin arranges a variation with a beguine rhythm to set the mood for a sophisticated cocktail party.

The first sequence of the film, which transpires in Lydecker's apartment, provides a more extended example of how variation functions within a single theme. Here changes in instrumentation, a pedal point, and *tremolo* strings dramatize the difference between Laura and Lydecker. Laura's theme, heard in the main title in a neoromantic arrangement, is now heard in a predominantly woodwind ensemble of alto flute, alto clarinet, contrabass clarinet, and flute. The use of a pedal point and *tremolo* strings further dramatizes the difference between these two arrangements of Laura's theme. Additionally, this variation of Laura's theme is built on a development of its opening phrase. Instead of providing the melody in its entirety, Raksin here thwarts expectation, creating tension by preventing the melody from coming to its natural resting place. As accompaniment to the lavish excess of Lydecker's

Figure 7.2.   Copyright 1944 Twentieth Century-Fox
"Waldo," *Laura*

art-filled apartment and the purple prose of his voice-over narration, the music both projects and reflects the dis-ease attached to these surroundings.

Laura's theme dominates the musical texture of *Laura*, but it is not the only musical material Raksin composed for the film. A second theme can be identified, although its use is more limited. Raksin introduces this theme immediately after the variation of Laura's theme described above. While this theme is clearly related to Laura's theme (it both borrows and extends its chromaticism), its harmonic construction, melodic contour, and instrumentation differentiate it. This theme is so highly chromatic that it borders on the nonmelodic; it consists of one distinctive and extremely short phrase; and it is introduced in the opening sequence by the unusual choice of a solo piccolo. Because this passage is associated with Lydecker—indeed is labelled "Waldo" in both the cue sheet and the score—it is more accurate to refer to this music as a leitmotif for Lydecker. It is tempting to hypothesize that Raksin used chromaticism and unusual instrumentation to draw attention to Lydecker's eccentric personality and perhaps even his sexuality.

As with Laura's theme, Lydecker's motif functions as a typical leitmotif might, accompanying his presence on the image track and varying in response to narrative developments. Lydecker's leitmotif even functions to foreshadow the revelation that Lydecker is the murderer. A reiteration of his leitmotif, for instance, can be heard at the first mention of the word "murder." Later, the theme reinforces the connection between Lydecker and the murder weapon, underscoring key scenes that involve McPherson's discovery of its hiding place. These musical fore-shadowings are confirmed when McPherson reconstructs the crime and Lydecker's theme can be heard under Laura's acknowledgment of his guilt. Finally, Lydecker's motif foreshadows his villainous reappearance at the film's denouement.

Raksin's score for *Laura* did produce a hit song in a nonmusical con-text, and its success precipitated an extension of the classical score's boundaries. But the position that *Laura* represents an alternative model for film scoring is overstated. Raksin has frequently defended his scores, and especially *Laura*, against claims that they represent a departure from classical practices. The term he has used to describe his work is the "dramatic film score."[24] Clearly he saw himself working within clas-sical traditions. In fact, in describing his score for *Carrie* he posits a direct relationship between his music and the conventions of silent film accompaniment:

> It was my hope that the music of *Carrie* would bear the same relationship to the story that existed between the story and music of some of the wonderful silent movies for which my father conducted the orchestra. . . . What a warmth there was between the screen and score in those days, when "heart-songs," *Kinothek* music, and sometimes excerpts of master-pieces followed hard upon one another! The Saturday matinees when I sat in the orchestra pit and responded like a seismograph to the heavings of the Gish sisters had made a deep impression on my young mind.[25]

The classical Hollywood film score was grounded in a structural model for the placement of music in narrative film. Although the theme score challenged its stylistic conventions, principally the number and variety of leitmotifs, it did not undermine this structural basis. Like the scores of Steiner and Korngold, theme scores respond to the needs of the story and remain intricately bound to the narrative. Rather than standing in direct contrast to the principles which defined the classi-cal score, the theme score exemplified them, its music existing in the same interdependent relationship with the narrative embodied in the classical score. Thus the concept of a hit song did not directly challenge the classical model. Even the development of the pop score in the sixties and seventies and marketing strategies, which promoted a policy of inserting pretested music into a film, did not subvert it.

Although Raksin depended upon a single theme and, as argued earlier, employed a musical language which differed from the one developed by film composers in the thirties, his structural approach to film scoring relied upon the same set of conventions. Like Korngold, Steiner, and other composers of the classical score, Raksin used music to sustain structural unity, accompanying those moments in which spatiotemporal continuity is the most tenuous. Raksin tends to avoid simple scene changes. More often than not, diegetic sound (crowd noises, traffic) covers these transitions. But during the film's most complicated structural device, an extended flashback of Lydecker and Laura's relationship, Raksin intervenes musically. The disruption of strictly chronological time and coherent geographic space that the flashback precipitates is elided by the presence of music.

The flashback begins in a restaurant where McPherson and Lydecker are dining. The opening shot is a medium close-up of a trio—an accordionist, a pianist, and a violinist—playing (what else?) Laura's theme. A slow tracking shot moves above and past the musicians; a matched cut to Lydecker and McPherson in a medium two-shot makes the track seem continuous. Gradually the shot is reframed to exclude McPherson. The flashback itself is signaled by a number of conventional devices for the temporal shift: a gradual lap dissolve, voice-over narration, and the absence of ambient sound.

One way that music is able to elide such spatiotemporal gaps is through its continuous presence on the soundtrack. The arrangement of Laura's theme that the trio plays at the beginning of the sequence continues uninterrupted until well into the flashback itself. In addition, Raksin initially casts this accompaniment as diegetic; the trio in the restaurant supposedly produces the version of Laura's theme that plays in the background. Using diegetic music naturalizes its presence—there is no question as to where the music is coming from—and thus masks the entrance of nondiegetic music with its attendant increase in volume and number of instruments. The final chord played by the trio covers the first chord of the orchestra's entrance. It is interesting here to note the sentimental arrangement of Laura's theme with the violinist playing the melody in a tempo marked "*rubato*."

This extended flashback structure in *Laura* is anchored by periodic reestablishing shots of Lydecker and McPherson in the restaurant, facilitated by voice-over narration, and supported by the presence of music at key spatiotemporal transitions. Not surprisingly, the montage of Laura's rise to success and growing intimacy with Lydecker is scored with continuous music, often achieved by chords which are sustained from one cue to the next. The end of the flashback and the resumption of the cinematic present tense are effected without music, the trio presumably having finished their performance. A dissolve to the restaurant is followed by Lydecker and McPherson's exit.

In the same way that the musical score for *Laura* depends on many of the structural conventions of the classical score, it exhibits the same relationship to the narrative that the classical score does. Music does not compete with dialogue. As in a classical score, the spoken word is privileged over musical accompaniment. Although Raksin tends to avoid the dialogue in *Laura*, he does underscore several scenes incorporating pauses and stingers much as Steiner or Korngold would. In the film's denouement stingers played by muted trombones draw attention to the lurid details of McPherson's reconstruction of the murder: "So he let her have it . . . with both barrels right in the face."

Although Raksin tends not to score action to the same degree as composers such as Korngold and Steiner or, for that matter, fill a film with the same amount of music, Raksin does reinforce important narrative action. A good example occurs during Carpenter's search for a shotgun in Laura's country house. An *accelerando* and *crescendo* accompanies his movements, creating a sense of expectation. Stingers punctuate key actions: Carpenter's suspicious entrance to the house and his attempt to remove the shotgun from its place over the fireplace.

More characteristic of Raksin's work is the tendency to score implicit rather than explicit action, what one critic has described as charting "an emotional graph . . . with music." [26] Thus for Raksin the most important sequence in the film becomes, not the narrative denouement or other sequences crucial to the murder-detection plot, but the sequence in which McPherson falls in love with Laura, a woman who he thinks is dead.

Late one night McPherson returns to Laura's apartment and wanders from room to room carrying a packet of her letters. He goes through her lingerie drawer, smells her perfume, opens her closet. He returns to the living room to pour himself a drink and is drawn to the portrait. After a call to a colleague and a brief interruption from Lydecker, he sits down with his drink in an armchair beneath the portrait, and closes his eyes. A slow dolly-in and dolly-out follows. In the next shot, Laura walks in the front door.

Zanuck was dissatisfied with the sequence, feeling that McPherson's wanderings were aimless and that the audience would be confused. He ordered massive cuts, including almost all of the material that precedes Lydecker's entrance. Raksin objected. "But if you cut that scene, nobody will understand that the detective is in love with Laura. . . . This is one of those scenes . . . in which music could tip the balance—tell the audience how the man feels." [27]

Raksin's response echoes a familiar refrain in the literature of film music: that the image is ultimately limited in its ability to convey emotion. Zanuck gave Raksin permission to "save" the sequence and handed him an opportunity to demonstrate music's power to define and refine its implicit content. Raksin took the opportunity to explicate McPherson's emotional response and articulate his thought processes.

The sequence is almost continuously scored. Musical accompaniment begins even before McPherson enters Laura's apartment. To create tension and infuse McPherson's movements with import, Raksin uses a pedal point and avoids melody, using a basically ascending passage played on muted horns. McPherson first enters the apartment to *tremolo* strings against a basically descending woodwind passage. But when McPherson sees the portrait, Laura's theme emerges from this musical background in an arresting arrangement for alto flutes and bassoons. As McPherson leaves the living room and the spell of the portrait, Laura's theme is replaced by the ascending passage played earlier by the horns. Here it is heard in the woodwinds; the *tremolo* strings also return.

McPherson ransacks Laura's desk drawers, finding some letters and a diary. Although his behavior appears innocuous enough (if anything he looks bored to me), the tension created by the music belies his casual demeanor and outward calm. Raksin's use of a contrapuntal variation of Laura's theme, as well as the increased volume, infuses McPherson's listless movements with tension, an example of how music contributes to perception of his actions. Another example is demonstrated moments later when McPherson extinguishes his cigarette. A *crescendo* and *accelerando* mark the action as significant, and McPherson's seemingly casual movement is redefined by the musical accompaniment as a dramatic gesture. An annotation in the score marks this moment as "*dramatico*."

The texture of the music changes at this point. All the instruments drop out under McPherson's gesture except for a double bass and the alto flutes. Raksin now begins to build to another climax. Techniques similar to those in the preceding sequence construct an anxious musical context for McPherson's voyeuristic activities in Laura's bedroom: a pedal point; a stinger; *tremolo* strings; juxtaposition of extremely high and low musical registers; *crescendo;* and chromaticism.

McPherson wanders to the living room and pours himself a drink. A series of three tri-tones, played initially by woodwinds, then by muted horns, and then by woodwinds again, accompanies this action and signals the narrative revelation in the following shot: McPherson is unable to resist the attraction of Laura's portrait. In fact, he is in love with her.

McPherson gazes at the portrait. Lighting and mise-en-scène, in combination with Dana Andrews' acting (downcast eyes, nervous hand gestures, a toss of the head as if to clear it) work to define McPherson's glance as meaningful. Zanuck, however, didn't understand what was happening in the scene and assumed that the audience wouldn't either. The musical accompaniment dispels any ambiguity in the image track. Laura's theme is heard here in a variation for piano solo and string accompaniment, encoding McPherson's romantic longing through classical conventions of instrumentation and harmony. Even Laura's actual reappearance, a few moments later, lacks the potency of this moment. After a brief phone call and an untimely interruption from Lydecker, McPherson slumps into an armchair with his drink. Moments later Laura reappears.

The sequence which follows problematizes the film's narrative through the activation of a dream structure which the film ultimately fails to resolve. This sequence depends upon a well-established convention for the dream: a dolly-in and dolly-out. The narrative is constructed to reinforce the power of this convention. The fact of McPherson's drinking heightens the unreliability of his perception, as does a line of dialogue delivered by Lydecker: "You better watch out McPherson or you'll end up in a psychiatric ward." Earlier McPherson himself accused a colleague of being asleep on the job. When Laura does appear, McPherson's first impulse is to rub the sleep from his eyes.

The musical score is a crucial part of this process, one of the most potent of the textual operators for conveying altered states of consciousness. As McPherson lands in the armchair, an arresting variation of Laura's theme can be heard. Raksin has commented that he wanted to create a particularly unusual effect for the sequence, something "really magical."[28] What he devised was a track with an artificially produced permutation of piano chords. By turning on the recording microphone only after a chord has been played on the piano and at extremely high volume, it is possible to record not the chord itself but the resonance left after the chord has been played. Raksin further manipulated this chord through the "Len-a-tone" process which produced a slight waver or "wow." This unusual sound was prolonged through a loop. Raksin then used it as a kind of pedal point under Laura's theme. In fact, the cue was so arresting that at the time of the film's release *Film Music Notes* was unable to identify its instrumentation, suggesting "the vibraphone or possibly some electrical instrument contributing a weirdly human and menacing quality."[29] This artificially produced sound creates an otherworldliness, offering an analogue for McPherson's altered state of consciousness. The score is here complicit with narrative and cinematic cues for the dream and facilitates a reading of the scene as McPherson's hallucination.

Raksin seems drawn to scenes with highly charged emotion as well as to those which treat states of consciousness. Other types of implicit content, such as atmosphere and mood, however, are also rendered musically. An extended example of classical techniques for the creation of suspense occurs near the film's denouement. Lydecker warns Laura against McPherson, but instead she breaks with Lydecker who leaves in a huff. His exit is rendered sinister by the expressionistic lighting, low camera angle, and the contrapuntal variation of his leitmotif played by the bassoons and a bass clarinet. A conventional technique for creating suspense, an ascending passage, accompanies McPherson's search for the murder weapon with stingers as punctuation to its subsequent discovery.

Laura is struck by remorse, confessing to McPherson, "I'm as guilty as he is. Not for anything I did, but for what I didn't do." Underscoring her dialogue is a poignant string version of her theme (with violin and viola solos) contradicting her. Music instead posits Lydecker's guilt: his leitmotif is heard immediately after McPherson tells Laura he is about to arrest him. When McPherson and Laura kiss, it is against an orchestral version of Laura's theme.

The ending of this variation of Laura's theme shifts the mood of the sequence from romance to suspense. Laura's theme does not come to rest at the end of the familiar melody; it is suspended uncomfortably on the opening phrase which repeats. Lydecker's leitmotif returns at this point, the unusual instrumentation (alto flute, bassoon, and bass clarinet) reinforcing the shift in mood. *Tremolo* strings help to sustain tension. Music drops out entirely for Lydecker's unsuspected reentrance; he retrieves and loads the shotgun to the unnaturally loud ticking of the clock.

The denouement of the film plays out in the succeeding moments as a policeman guns down Lydecker and McPherson protects Laura from imminent death. Frenzied strings (marked "*Mosso Agitato*") accompany Laura's last-minute rescue. The film, interestingly, ends on the connection between Lydecker and Laura: Laura running to his side and Lydecker dying with her name on his lips. A brief restatement of Laura's theme concludes the film.

Laura became one of a rare group of nonmusical films in which the audience paid attention to the music. After its release Twentieth Century-Fox was deluged with requests for copies of its musical theme, and the studio commissioned lyricist Johnny Mercer to collaborate with Raksin on a version of the melody that could be released as a song. "Laura" was the result. It was recorded by the major singers of the

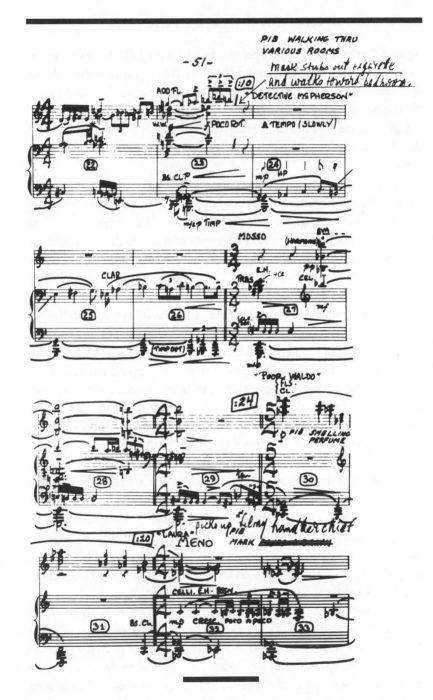

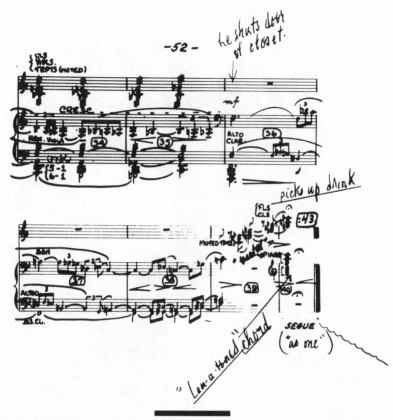

The "Len-a-toned" chord from the piano conductor part for *Laura*. This chord can be heard as McPherson falls asleep in Laura's apartment moments before her reappearance. It was produced by a complicated process that involved recording the resonance of the chord, rather than the chord itself, and "Len-a-toning" it, or passing it through a playback machine to produce a waver. This chord proved so unusual that reviewers at the time of the film's release could not identify the instrumentation used to produce it.

One version of the sheet music for the song "Laura." With the success of the film's music, the studio commissioned Johnny Mercer to write lyrics to Raksin's melody. (Raksin also composed music for the verse.) Robbins Music marketed the song not only through its singer but through its connection to the film.

forties, reaching the top of the hit parade in 1944. Such success pointed to music's commercial potential outside the life of a film, but during the forties and fifties this potential was exploited to generate added revenue for a hit film through marketing its theme song. Using music to actually sell a film was a development of the sixties when the massive demographic shift toward a younger audience precipitated a change in marketing techniques.[30] Music was promoted not only as added revenue but as audience incentive, and songs were premarketed and inserted into a film to insure its success. *Laura*, however unwittingly a progenitor of such practices, remains firmly rooted in an earlier tradition.

CHAPTER 8

John Williams and "The Empire" Strike Back

The Eighties and Beyond:
Classical Meets Contemporary

One would think that faced with the limitlessness of space and the multiplicity
of life forms Williams would explode with ideas. But in composing the sound to
go with the future, Williams doesn't look to any of the "avant-garde" composers
like Varese or Cage. . . . Instead Williams looks to the major-key flourishes
of Wagner . . . and Tchaikovsky . . . and the swashbuckling *Captain Blood* and
Adventures of Robin Hood soundtracks of Erich Wolfgang Korngold.
Greg Oatis in *Cinemafantastique*

The breakup of the studio system, which triggered changes in the creation, distribution, and exhibition of feature films in Hollywood, affected
every aspect of a film's production. The successful attack by the United
States government on the movie industry for monopolistic practices
in distribution and exhibition forced a change in the operation of the
major Hollywood studios. With their theater chains gone, studios lost a
guaranteed market for their films. Television began to siphon off movie
audiences. Production declined. Financial backing went to projects with
proven marketability, and successful formulas produced scores of imita-
tors.

To look at the careers of Max Steiner, Bernard Herrmann, and David
Raksin after about 1960 (Erich Wolfgang Korngold died in 1957), one
might be tempted to think that the classical score virtually disappeared
along with the studio system that engendered it. Steiner composed
only nine film scores after 1959 in a career that encompassed over 360
films; after parting ways with Hitchcock in 1966, Herrmann found little
work until the very end of his life; after a decade in demand, Raksin was
relatively idle. It became commonplace among established composers
to decry the demise of the film score. Complained Elmer Bernstein,
"What ever happened to great movie music?"[1] A central premise of
this book has been that the classical score, as a historical practice, is a
flexible model which embraced numerous innovations as part of a con-

184

tinual process of renewal that insured its vitality. But in the late fifties and especially the sixties the classical score underwent a period of experimentation so intense that it often looked at the time as if it had simply vanished.

The first of many changes to the classical score was precipitated by jazz which, during the fifties, began to dominate the industry. As early as 1937 George Antheil included elements of jazz in his score for *The Plainsman* as did David Raksin in his 1948 score for *Force of Evil*. But it was the early fifties that saw the institutionalization of jazz through the success of such films as *Panic in the Streets* (1950), *A Streetcar Named Desire* (1951), and *Touch of Evil* (1958). One particularly influential score of the period was Elmer Bernstein's *Man with the Golden Arm* (1955) whose hit song, distilled from the main title, enjoyed widespread popularity.

As a proven commodity, the jazz-oriented score became highly marketable in the aftermath of the industry shake-up and was imposed upon many a film with which it had little connection. Yet in the best of these scores (and interestingly enough the most influential of them), jazz is narratively motivated and is exploited in much the same way that the classical score used atmospheric or mood music: to establish the authenticity of geographical and historical context. (Both *Panic in the Streets* and *A Streetcar Named Desire*, for instance, take place in New Orleans.) A comment by Elmer Bernstein is particularly telling in this regard: "my score [for *Man with the Golden Arm*] was not a jazz score, but a score in which jazz elements were incorporated toward the end of creating specific atmosphere for that particular film." [2]

Concurrent with the development of the jazz-oriented score was the proliferation of the monothematic or theme score. Engendered by the success of Raksin's *Laura*, the theme score gained momentum in the fifties, challenging (and sometimes combining with) the jazz score. Dimitri Tiomkin's score for *High Noon* proved pivotal in this regard. No longer was the hit song culled from thematic material; Tiomkin composed a country-western song (with lyricist Ned Washington) specifically for the film: "Do Not Forsake Me Oh My Darlin'," sung by Tex Ritter on the soundtrack. Films such as *Three Coins in the Fountain* (1954), *Love Is a Many-Splendored Thing* (1955), and *Around the World in Eighty Days* (1956) accrued additional revenue from record sales of songs composed specifically for them. Like jazz-oriented scores, theme scores became so institutionalized that composing a hit song as part of a film score became virtually compulsory, a phenomenon composer Irwin Bazelon described as "title-song mania" and Jerry Goldsmith as "a real pain."[3] Yet Bazelon's description draws attention to an important link between the theme score and its classical progenitor. The theme score operates on the principle of the leitmotif and, like the classical score, presents the musical ideas which unify the score in the main title. In the theme score, of course, the "leitmotif" is arranged as an integral piece of music that is extractable from the score. But in the context of the film the theme is treated as a leitmotif: varied and repeated in response to the dramatic and emotional needs of the film.

With the advent of the sixties, the most serious challenge to the classical film score emerged: the "guitar-washed"[4] youth-oriented version based in various kinds of rock and roll. These pop scores, as they came to be known in the industry, represented a loose adaption of the theme scores of the fifties, substituting a succession of self-contained musical numbers, usually nondiegetic songs, for the repeated occurrences of a score's theme. Pop scores were particularly attractive to the industry in an era when changing demographics revealed an increasingly younger audience. Since many composers of pop scores were already established in the record industry, scores such as those for *The Graduate* (1967), *Butch Cassidy and the Sundance Kid* (1969), and *Good-bye Columbus* (1969) were also easily marketed as records, and frequently outgrossed the films they were composed for. In the seventies producers capitalized on the pop score's ability to create an audience for a film and began the practice of premarketing a film's songs. The pop score has, not unexpectedly, produced heated response from established composers who pronounced it the death of the film score. David Raksin, for instance, claims that "this business of having rock and pop in everything is just absolutely absurd,"[5] and it is hard to disagree with Elmer Bernstein's observation that the music in some films "seems to drone on quite unrelated to the events in the picture."[6]

In fact, the pop score represents the most serious challenge to the classical score among the various attempts to update it in the fifties and sixties. Specifically, the pop score's insistence on the integrity and marketability of the nondiegetic song frequently brought it into conflict with some of the basic principles of the classical model. Unlike earlier innovations which added new idiomatic possibilities, like jazz, or demonstrated the adaptability of the leitmotif, like the theme score, the pop score often ignored structural principles at the center of the classical score: musical illustration of narrative content, especially the direct synchronization between music and narrative action; music as a form of structural unity; and music as an inaudible component of the drama. Yet for all that, few would claim that the pop score fulfilled the dire prophecy initially attached to it. Like the jazz-oriented score and the theme score before it, the pop score initially challenged the classical model as a radical alternative, only to find its most iconoclastic characteristics excised in the process of fitting itself into Hollywood. The pop score that emerged from the seventies was much closer to the classical paradigm than the one that was born in the sixties. Nondiegetic songs, which had previously filled the soundtrack, were now reduced to one or two distinctive numbers, or relegated to the main and end titles.

A film such as *Flashdance* (1983) exemplifies the direction the pop score took in the seventies. Though its musical idiom is contemporary, Giorgio Moroder's score for *Flashdance* continues to function structurally within the classical framework. The industry, in fact, has begun to use the label contemporary to differentiate these scores from the earlier pop variety. Music, for instance, sustains structural unity at those moments when narrative continuity is most tenuous. Another important change from the pop score is the return to music's narrative functions: to underscore action (watch for the Mickey Mousing in the opening factory montage); to resonate emotion between the spectator and the screen; and to represent a character's subjectivity. Though the score for *Flashdance* features nondiegetic songs, it embeds them in spectacle, relying on conventions of the classical score to authorize their audibility. Both the nondiegetic "Lady, Lady, Lady" and the diegetic "Flashdance: What a Feeling" work in this way.

The major change to confront the classical score in the seventies and eighties has been the development of synthesized sound as an alternative to, or sometimes replacement for, acoustic instruments. As part of the process to keep on the contemporary edge, Hollywood has begun to turn to synthesized or **synth** scores as a way to update its product. "The synthesizer is an extension in musical history the way automobiles were an extension in transportation history," claims Giorgio Morodor, whose synth score for *Midnight Express* (1978) was the first electronic score to win an Academy Award.[7] Dubbed "the mockingbird of instruments," the synthesizer has an almost limitless ability to create sound, unique and otherwise, including the ability to duplicate acoustic instruments.[8] In this capacity synthesizers can be used to fill out an orchestral texture by doubling traditional orchestral instruments, expanding a string section, for instance, or adding a complement of horns. In some cases, synthesizers have been used to substitute for live musicians in order to reduce expenses. Synthesizers are most commonly used, however, for the unique sounds they can produce. Thus, they are often exploited in sci-fi and futuristic genres to create an otherworldly effect. Giorgio Moroder's reconstruction and rescoring of the 1927 *Metropolis* is such an example, as is Vangelis' score for *Bladerunner* (1982). In more conventional genres, synthesizers can give a film that much-sought-after contemporary edge. Maurice Jarre's score for *Witness* (1985) is a striking example of the influence and prevalence of synthesized sound in Hollywood. Its main title and several opening cues are obviously synthesized, but even the barn-building sequence, which sounds so quintessentially American (it's based on the modal harmonies of American folk song), is scored exclusively for synthesizer. To many listeners, its sound is indistinguishable from that of an orchestra.

Contemporary literature on film music has credited John Williams, virtually single-handedly, with returning the classical film score to its position of preeminence. As the preceding discussion reveals, however, the classical score is hardly in need of resuscitation. It continues to function in Hollywood as a primary determinant on the construction of the film score. Williams was, however, the major force in returning the classical score to its late-romantic roots and adapting the symphony orchestra of Steiner and Korngold for the modern recording studio. Through Williams' example, the epic sound established in the thirties once again became a viable choice for composers in contemporary Hollywood. In fact, the score for *The Empire Strikes Back* is a master example of the continued strength of the structural model which underlies the classical score and the force of the late-romantic idiom which drives it.

Like so many other film composers in both the classical and the contemporary eras, John Williams "stumbled into films" from a career or anticipated career in art music.[9] Trained as a pianist and composer, primarily at UCLA and Juilliard, Williams found his way in the fifties to Columbia and later Twentieth Century-Fox where he played in their orchestras. Unlike Steiner or Korngold who entered the studio ranks with a fair amount of prestige and its attendant power, Williams entered as a contract musician working with "the then giants of the film industry": Alfred Newman, Franz Waxman, and Dimitri Tiomkin.[10] Eventually Williams began to orchestrate, a process he describes as "a natural progression," including work for Adolph Deutsch on *The Apartment* (1960)," and Tiomkin on *The Guns of Navarone* (1961).[11]

Concurrent with the work in films, however, was another apprenticeship—in television. The film industry had begun to consider television a proving ground, as Williams' straddling of the division between the large screen and the small screen at an early stage in his career demonstrates. The growing ease with which composers could move not only from television to film but from film to television blurred distinctions between the two mediums, at least in terms of dramatic scoring, and not surprisingly Williams' television work, such as *Wagon Train* (1957–65), *M Squad* (1957–59), *Kraft Suspense Theatre* (1963–65), and *Lost in Space* (1965–67), reflects many of the principles that underlie the classical model.

Television scoring resembles film scoring in more ways than one. Like the scores for "B" movies churned out by studios, television scores were often the product of more than one creative agent, and all of Williams' credits cited in the previous paragraph are collaborative in this sense. Williams may have composed an opening theme or more likely a few internal cues, "real factory-line work," as he calls it.[12] In fact, his experience rather closely resembles the apprenticeship of David Raksin at Twentieth Century-Fox, where a composer specialized in scoring particular types of generic situations but was expected to fill in if the occasion warranted as orchestrator, arranger, or composer. Such musical typecasting characterized Williams' transition to the big screen where he became known for his work in hip sixties comedies such as *John Goldfarb, Please Come Home* (1964), *How to Steal a Million* (1966), *Not with My Wife, You Don't!* (1966), and *A Guide for the Married Man* (1967).

It wasn't until the seventies that Williams turned to the action-adventure projects with which he has become indelibly associated. A series of disaster films, among them *The Poseidon Adventure* (1972), *The Towering Inferno* (1974), and *Earthquake* (1974), led him to Steven Spielberg and *Jaws* (1975). During this period Williams retooled his style from the sixties-inflected musical idiom which fills his comedies to the late-romantic idiom which has come to characterize his work. Williams' exploitation of the resources of the symphony orchestra is aptly demonstrated in *Jaws*, nowhere more tellingly than in the leitmotif Williams composed for the shark itself, a deceptively simple yet unnerving alternation of two notes, scored for eight basses and five trombones. The phenomenal success of *Jaws*, as both a film and a score, led to the establishment of Williams as the premiere composer of Hollywood big-budget films, action and otherwise, where, as he says himself, he likes to paint "with a big brush."[13]

As an established film composer Williams epitomizes a practice which closely resembles that of Steiner and Korngold in the heyday of the studio system. Like most of the major film composers of that era, Williams works in an extremely constricted time frame (for *The Empire Strikes Back*, Williams had less than eight weeks, from the initial spotting session in early November to the recording sessions in late December and early January); he depends upon an orchestrator or, more likely, orchestrators to produce a finished version; his major musical resource is the symphony orchestra (on the *Star Wars* trilogy, none other than the London Symphony); and he conducts his scores himself.

There are also important structural characteristics which bind Williams to the classical model: the use of music to sustain unity; a high degree of correspondence between narrative content and musical accompaniment; the use of music in the creation of mood, emotion, and character; the privileging of music in moments of spectacle; a dependence on expressive melody and the use of leitmotifs; and the careful placement of music in relation to the dialogue. There are even striking similarities between Williams and Hollywood's classical composers on a personal level. Like Steiner who never reads scripts ("I run a mile every-time I see one"), Williams avoids them also, preferring to "react to the people and places and events . . . of the film itself." [14] And like Korngold, Williams has tried to sustain a career in art music while working in Hollywood.

The practice of orchestration in Williams' work provides insight into the ways in which the contemporary film score has both adopted and adapted the classical model. Like his predecessors, Williams depends on others to orchestrate his material. Given his background as a pianist, it is not surprising that Williams often composes at the piano, but before he gives these sketches to the orchestrator, he transfers them from the two staves of a piano sketch to eight to ten staves: "I try to be *very* careful about my sketches so that I get just what I want." [15] Like Korngold who developed a long-term relationship with his orchestrator, Hugo Friedhofer, Williams has developed an association with Herbert Spencer who is credited with the orchestration of most of Williams' scores. Such detailed sketches and long-term collaboration leave little room for deviation and insure a consistency in terms of the Williams sound.

As Williams' approach to orchestration demonstrates, the classical model's division of labor which separates composition from orchestration continues to influence contemporary scoring practices. If anything, such parceling out of activity has proliferated. On *Star Wars* (1977), for instance, though Herbert Spencer retains screen credit for orchestration (by Williams' own tally, Spencer orchestrated about five hundred of the score's eight hundred pages), four other orchestrators, including Williams, contributed to the final version. [16] Williams still prides himself on his orchestration, and on occasion, for a "small" film, he orchestrates the entire score. But more typical is the situation of *The Empire Strikes Back* in which a veritable army of orchestrators worked on the ice battle alone.

At least one characteristic of the contemporary scoring scene, how-ever, does not have its roots in its classical progenitor, that is, **temp tracking**. This is the practice of accompanying the film during the early stages of editing (before the score is composed) with recorded music of various kinds (pop, classical, or even other movie music) to substitute for a score that has yet to be composed. Temp tracks are used for a variety of purposes, from simply giving a film the effect of music before the score is ready, to providing a specific sound for composers to imitate. While the temp track can be useful as a point of communication between a composer and the production team, it can also function as a straitjacket, locking the composer into certain musical ideas, gestures, styles, and even melodies. The most infamous example of the tyranny of the temp track concerns Alex North's original score for *2001: A Space Odyssey* (1968) which was dumped in favor of the temp track chosen by director Stanley Kubrick: Richard Strauss's *Also sprach Zarathustra*, Johann Strauss waltzes, and works by Khachaturian and Ligeti.

Even a composer with John Williams' stature must deal with the temp track. On *The Empire Strikes Back*, director Irvin Kershner rummaged through the classical record collection of producer Gary Kurtz to create a temp track before Williams spotted the film. Asked whether this would in any way tie Williams' hands or influence him in a certain direction, Kershner answered, "No, it won't make the slightest difference. John has a strong feel for what he wants." [17]

The score for *The Empire Strikes Back* is by anyone's reckoning a massive piece of music. While it was common in the classical era for roughly three-quarters of a film to contain music, changes in the fifties and sixties gradually altered this proportion, and by the seventies it was more likely that one-quarter of a film was scored. *Empire* runs 127 minutes, and Williams initially marked 117 minutes of it for musical accompaniment. He was able to recycle three of the important leitmotifs from the original *Star Wars*: the Star Wars theme, which functions as a sort of all-purpose leitmotif for the Rebel Alliance and especially Luke Skywalker; the Force theme which doubles as a leitmotif for Ben (Obi-Wan) Kenobi; and the opening phrase of Princess Leia's leitmotif, which serves as a love theme for Leia and Han. Williams also reprised the main title from *Star Wars*, but the vast majority of music in *The Empire Strikes Back* was scored specifically for the film. I have chosen three musical cues to analyze in detail here, the main title, Darth Vader's leitmotif, and the ice battle on the planet Hoth, each of which exemplifies Williams' use and adaptation of the classical model. Together they represent a cross-section of the way music functions in the film.

Figure 8.1.   Copyright 1977 Warner Tamerlane Corp. and Bantha Music
"Star Wars," *Star Wars*

The Empire Strikes Back begins with a reprise of the main title of *Star Wars*, a martial overture which contains many familiar classical conventions: the opening gesture for epic genres, a cymbal crash and brass fanfare; a modified *sonata allegro* form; and continuous scoring through to the first cue of the film. The opening chord is particularly effective here following a sustained pause after the Twentieth Century-Fox musical logo and synchronized to the appearance of the title *Star Wars*. (The actual appearance of the title *The Empire Strikes Back* is a bit of an understatement after this. It's buried on the screen after "Episode V" and is part of a lengthy printed text.) Like the titles, the familiar Star Wars theme, with its dramatic upward fifths, tonal harmony, brass instrumentation, and rhythmic underpinning, connects this film to its successful predecessor. The distinctive martial and heroic sound is achieved through an exploitation of brass and percussion (trumpets for the melody, joined later by woodwinds, tubas, trombones, horns, snare drums, and timpani in accompaniment), a driving counterrhythm (on the off-beat) in the accompaniment, and a heroic form—a march marked "**Maestoso**" (majestically).

One motif that is not reprised from *Star Wars* is the musical tag for Darth Vader, the rebels' archenemy. In his flowing black robes and Nazi stormtrooper headgear, Vader is the embodiment of evil. With his amplified heavy breathing and distorted speech, Vader unsettles aurally as well as visually. Not surprisingly, his motif in *Star Wars* plays off musical conventions for suspense: it's a short passage in chordal harmony accompanied by various combinations of timpani, celli, trombones, bassoons, and basses playing low in their register. There is a hint of dissonance in the accompaniment which is a kind of *ostinato,* a single repeated note in a rhythmic pattern driven by triplets with a distinctive descending major third at the end of some phrases.

In *The Empire Strikes Back* Vader has a much larger role, and Williams composed a new theme for him, an extended and richly orchestrated march which activates not only musical conventions for suspense but those for evil as well. The basis of the melodic line is deceptively simple—an inverted spelling of a major triad. But the accompaniment, especially the strings, is predominantly minor, which confuses perception of the tonality. Even the way Williams chooses to spell out the triad confounds a clear major or minor tonality. Instead of spelling, or breaking down the triad into the conventional and familiar pattern of bottom note, middle note, and top note in the chord, Williams shuffles the pattern to middle note, bottom note, top note, with a return to the middle note once again. Thus instead of the expected intervals of an ascending major third, an ascending minor third (and an ascending fifth between the first and last notes of the chord), we hear a descending major third, an ascending fifth, and a descending minor third. The important part to remember here is that this arrangement works to make the melody sound minor even though it is actually major. (The interval of descending major third is the conventional way to begin the spelling of a descending minor chord.) Thus we're set up, in a sense, to expect minor, which colors our perception of the rest of the melody. It is interesting to speculate that Williams capitalized on that crucial descending major third from the original Vader motif in *Star Wars*, developing the new theme around it. (Descending major thirds also turn up in the woodwind and timpani parts in the new theme.) At any rate, it is surely a great irony that one of the most sinister and "minor"-sounding melodies in classical scoring is actually based on a major triad.

Vader's leitmotif in *The Empire Strikes Back*, like the Star Wars theme, has an ABA structure: the main melodic motif, followed by a contrasting section, and a return to the original. This contrasting B section is even murkier in its definition of major/minor tonality than the preceding A section. It is basically a descending chromatic line which develops out of the notes of the triad and flirts with both major and minor before

Figure 8.2.   Copyright 1980 Fox Fanfare Music, Inc., and Bantha Music (BMI).
"The Imperial March" (Darth Vader's theme), *The Empire Strikes Back*.
The G naturals in measures 2 and 5 are from the original score. Technically, they are not necessary. Because of the nature of score recording, however, in which there is little or even no rehearsal time, copyists frequently add such markings as "insurance" to stave off possible mistakes on the part of musicians performing unfamiliar music.

coming to rest in the major for the reprise to section A. In fact, one might even describe Vader's leitmotif as bitonal, playing a predominantly major melodic line against predominantly minor accompanying parts.

The major/minor tonality is only one of the ways in which Williams taps cultural associations to create Darth Vader's evil persona. To return to the A section for a moment, after the motif based on the triad is completed, the melody leaps to the seventh tone of the scale, privileging one of the most potentially disturbing intervals in the pitch system. This is followed by a tri-tone, associated with evil since medieval times, which introduces the return to the triad, momentarily in the minor before resolving back into the major. The instrumentation also carries connotations of darkness as well as militarism, especially in the choice of trumpets, horns, trombones, and basses for the melody and low percussion instruments such as a bass drum and timpani in the accompaniment (denoted "*marcato*"). A marking in the score also indicates a "deep military drum." Finally, Williams has retained the triplet figure from the original Vader theme to drive the rhythm in the new version's accompaniment and recast its *ostinato*-like repeated notes, which build suspense, as a prelude to the new one.

That prelude is first heard in the film as the imperial spaceship bearing Darth Vader enters the frame. Several elements, both visual and aural, build suspense even before Vader appears. Though the screen is filled with various craft careening through space, Vader's command

Darth Vader's leitmotif looms over the film as his literal presence does in this art work for an advertising poster.

ship enters from the offscreen space behind the camera, startling us and creating tension by drawing our attention to a portion of offscreen space we are often unaware of when watching a film. The prelude to Vader's theme is heard here: a series of ascending intervals consisting of two minor sixths and two major sevenths. Each of these intervals creates tension through its instability in the tonal system, especially the seventh which beckons the tonic note which begins Vader's leitmotif. Even Vader's appearance is unnerving. Our first glimpse of him is a tight close-up with his back to the camera, any clues to his feelings or personality hidden under the black helmet that obscures his head.

The placement of Vader's leitmotif and its relation to narrative content both explicit and implicit reveal the power of the classical model in Williams' work. In this scene, as in a typical classical score, music begins before the actual sequence does, covering over the rather arty wipe which ends the preceding scene with a musical cue that continues uninterrupted until the end of Vader's sequence (and beyond). Such continuousness on the part of the music necessitates certain adjustments so as not to challenge the primacy of narrative exposition. Volume, for instance, is controlled by narrative priority: dialogue which requires the subjugation of the music, and spectacle which allows the privileging of it. (Listen, for example, to the marked increase in volume which accompanies the wipe to the vast expanses of space.) Similarly the texture of the music is dependent on narrative exposition: during dialogue the musical texture is sparse so as not to compete with or distract from the spoken word; such constraints are not necessary, however, during the spectacle which precedes Vader's appearance where Williams is freer to exploit intricate rhythmic patterns and unusual combinations of instruments. Even instrumentation itself is tied to the recording of the human voice. Vader's deep bass voice (dubbed by an uncredited James Earl Jones), in conversation with his staff, is accompanied in this sequence not by the distinctive trumpets, horns, and trombones, but by the woodwinds, which provide more of a contrast and allow Jones's voice to be heard more easily.

Vader's leitmotif appears throughout *The Empire Strikes Back* as one might expect when his presence literally or figuratively looms over the narrative. Williams uses the leitmotif again in *Return of the Jedi* (1983) where it is heard so often that it actually competes with the Star Wars leitmotif for dominance of the soundtrack. One of the most evocative occurrences of the leitmotif, in fact, is heard in *Return of the Jedi*, at Vader's death, when his helmet is removed and he is revealed as Anakin Skywalker, Luke's father. Instrumentation here activates celestial associations which encourage the audience to forgive Vader, as Luke does. This quasi-religious mood is set up in the preceding duel between Vader and Luke which is accompanied by hymnlike chanting. Three particularly arresting repetitions of the Vader motif reinforce these associations: one for extremely high violins accompanied by harps; one for a flute solo again accompanied by harps; and finally, one for a solo harp. This monumental change in instrumentation from the brasses which have performed Vader's theme throughout two films to a solo harp extremely high in its register makes this one of the most powerful moments in the trilogy.

As the preceding analysis of the Star Wars and Vader leitmotifs suggests, Williams' score for *The Empire Strikes Back* is steeped in late romanticism: in its expressive use of melody; its exploitation of the effects of instrumentation; its dependence on tonal harmony and especially triadic harmony; and its use of the large-scale resources of the symphony orchestra. George Lucas had originally wanted to use classical music as accompaniment for the first *Star Wars* film, but Williams convinced him to try original music which can be used "in a major key, minor key, fast, slow, up, down, inverted, attenuated and crushed, and all the permutations that you can put a scene and a musical conception through, that you wouldn't be able to tastefully do if you had taken a Beethoven symphony and scored . . . with that."[18] For Williams using a late-romantic sound was "a conscious decision. . . . music should have a familiar emotional ring so that as you looked at these strange robots and other unearthly creatures, at sights hitherto unseen, the music would be rooted in familiar traditions."[19] Williams' apologia hardly seems necessary given the tremendous success of the score, but not all critics were equally enthusiastic about Williams' "return" to the nineteenth-century sound. The *Village Voice* labeled his music "corny Romanticism," and Greg Oatis, in the epigraph to this chapter, bemoans Williams' role models (Tchaikovsky, Wagner, and Korngold),

Luke battles Vader. This climactic duel is given added poignancy when it is revealed that Vader is Luke's father. The music prepares us for this moment through Vader's leitmotif which plays off both major and minor tonalities.

wishing instead for " 'avant-garde' composers like Varese or Cage." [20] Oatis' comment is odd but revealing: why not ask George Lucas for a less classical filmmaking style, or Lucas, Leigh Brackett, and Lawrence Kasdan for a less conventional story, or John Mollo for a more futuristic couture?

Williams' dependence on a late-romantic idiom and medium is no-where more apparent than in the extraordinary battle on the ice planet Hoth. Although the sequence is filled with the synthesized sounds of an ion cannon, blasters, speeders, imperial walkers, and other assorted space hardware, its music is recorded in its entirety by the London Symphony augmented with an additional five piccolos and oboes, a battery of extra percussion, and two pianos and harps. (In fact, the only *musical* cue I could detect in the entire score that employs a synthesizer is entitled "The Magic Tree"; it can be heard during Luke's confrontation with the apparition of Darth Vader on Dagobah.)

The ice battle cue depends upon a number of familiar classical conventions which both lend to the tension of the sequence and help to clarify its key narrative moments. The sequence opens with a familiar musical gesture for the creation of tension—*tremolo* strings and pedal point—here accompanying a vaguely pentatonic xylophone part. It accompanies a shot of the rebels on the frozen landscape of Hoth preparing for an attack from the Empire. Reverse shots reveal an empty snowscape. Although nothing appears on the horizon, suspense about the impending invaders is sustained through a combination of narrative expectation ("General, there's a fleet of star destroyers coming out of hyperspace in sector four"), narrative construction (parallel editing between the ice plain, rebel headquarters, and Vader's spaceship), and the music.

Continuous scoring accompanies the cutaway from the ice plain to the rebel headquarters, helping to facilitate the spatial and temporal transition. Discovered now by the Empire, the rebels must evacuate immediately and run the Empire's blockade to do so. The diegetic sound is quite dense here with numerous distracting sound effects; the quick tempo of the music contributes to the overall sense of chaos and tension. Two important leitmotifs, however, can be clearly differentiated: Vader's, played at an increased tempo, and the rebels', the Star Wars theme itself. The way in which these two musical identifications interact complements the image track: first, the distinctive opening phrase from Vader's leitmotif as the Empire somewhat overconfidently readies to destroy the first rebel transport, then a motif from the Star Wars theme (though not the identifying opening phrase) as the outcome of the confrontation is in doubt, and finally the recognizable opening phrase as the rebels foil the Empire and the transport escapes unharmed. Thus a dense and busy musical score performs a dual function here: it contributes to the creation of confusion crucial to sustaining the tension of the sequence, and it draws attention through the use of leitmotifs to key narrative developments to guide the spectator through it.

This same strategy of simultaneously creating mood and anchoring narrative development can be heard throughout the ice battle. Williams employs a number of tactics here to produce effects of tension: competing musical lines, unusual and intricate rhythmic patterns, and odd instrumentation. Xylophones, for instance, are featured prominently, contributing to a sense of foreboding at the beginning of the sequence

Original art work for the imperial walkers. Music brings to life the technological hardware of the Empire during the ice battle on the planet Hoth.

and coming to be associated with the imperial walkers by the end of it. Simultaneous with these techniques are strategies for drawing attention to key moments in the dense narrative texture. These can be as straightforward as attaching dissonance to the approach of imperial forces and marking the demise of an imperial walker with a descending octave or as complicated as casting the opening motif from the Star Wars theme into the minor when Luke's ship crashes. In fact, a number of leitmotifs are used here: Vader's theme as imperial forces close in on the power generator and later when Vader makes an imposing entrance in rebel headquarters; the Force theme, when the rebel retreat is called; the Star Wars theme during the collapse of the rebels' command center; and the opening fanfare to the Star Wars theme as Luke destroys an imperial walker. Leitmotifs here even foreshadow later narrative developments: the sequence ends with a short quotation from what will become Leia and Han's love theme as the Millennium Falcon, bearing both of them, narrowly escapes capture.

Williams' score for *The Empire Strikes Back* represents one version of the classical film score, a contemporary adaptation of the original model which adopts its idiom and medium as well as its structural imperatives. Due to the phenomenal success of the music from the *Star Wars* trilogy and other Williams work of the era such as *Jaws* and *E.T.* (1982), scores which depended on a late-romantic style and utilized the resources of a symphony orchestra became reestablished as a viable option. The romantic film score took its place once again among the various stylistic practices available to Hollywood composers. This is not to say that the romantic film score replaced other options. There continue to exist other possibilities. Pop music, synthesized sound, and the use of non-diegetic songs all have left their mark on the classical model. Yet, like *The Empire Strikes Back*, all of these practices share a commitment to narrative exposition and to the classical techniques which insure it.

CONCLUSION

This book has been devoted to settling the classical Hollywood film score from its institutionalization in the thirties to its continued presence in the eighties. Its central argument has been that the classical score is defined ultimately by its structural conventions, a set of practices that evolved for the use and placement of music in Hollywood films. The force of these conventions transcended idiom (late romantic or pop, for example), medium (symphony orchestras or jazz combos), and even personal style (the characteristic sound of a Herrmann cue versus the sound of a Korngold fanfare) to exert a controlling influence on what audiences heard when they went to the movies.

The power of the classical paradigm transcends even the historical era which saw its development and proliferation. Given the current state of the art in Hollywood it would be naive to deny the existence of significant changes in the practice of film scoring. But it would be equally hasty to conclude that the classical score no longer wields considerable power over the way contemporary film composers go about their work. In fact, an examination of any number of eighties films (and beyond) reveals that although its idiom has changed, or more specifically has widened to include a variety of new musical styles, the classical score retains a structural basis which is very much in evidence in contemporary Hollywood films. In fact, a comparison between a classical and contemporary film score yields some surprising results.

Upon first hearing, Basil Poledouris' score for *RoboCop* (1987) might seem to bear little resemblance to a classical score such as Korngold's *Captain Blood*. Certainly the musical medium has been altered (synthesized versus orchestral sound). But in other ways the score for *RoboCop* bears a striking similarity to the classical model. *RoboCop* depends upon music to sustain structural unity at those moments when narrative continuity is the most tenuous. Notice the way in which the music extends continuously from the single title "*RoboCop*" into the diegesis, for instance. Like Korngold, Poledouris also employs music to illustrate

203

narrative content, depending upon such conventional devices as *tremolo* and *ostinato* to create suspense, and stingers and Mickey Mousing to delineate individual actions within a scene. Listen to the *tremolo* strings, for instance, when Murphy and his partner, Lewis, enter the building where Murphy is shot down, and to the machine-like *ostinato* that accompanies the appearance of the ED 209. Notice also the stingers as Clarence, the archvillain, attacks the robocop with a spear, and the Mickey Mousing as Lewis is thrown over a balcony. Like the classical score, *RoboCop* exploits cultural associations in a variety of ways. Listen for the use of fourths and fifths in the harmonic texture during the film's two climactic battles, lending a gladiatorial feel to the confrontation between the high-tech warriors. In *Captain Blood* music resonates emotion between the spectator and the screen. In *RoboCop* emotional response is created in the same way, particularly through the emotionally loaded effects of instrumentation. Listen for the strings in scenes of intense emotion such as Murphy's return to the empty suburban house where he once lived, and the martial horn orchestration of the robocop theme during action sequences such as the robocop's heroic first night on the job. As this last example would make obvious, *RoboCop* also shares with *Captain Blood* its penchant for leitmotivic construction, creating identifiable themes for Murphy and his cybernetic manifestation, the robocop, in much the same way as Korngold constructed musical identifications for Peter Blood and other important characters. And, as in *Captain Blood*, dialogue in *RoboCop* is privileged over other elements of the soundtrack, with musical cues placed to encourage its audibility.

The most striking difference between *Captain Blood* and *RoboCop*, however, is the medium of performance: the orchestra versus the synthesizer. But a closer analysis reveals that *RoboCop*'s score depends heavily on the orchestral medium (it was recorded by, among others, the Sinfonia of London); most of *RoboCop*'s synthesizers are reserved to create unusual sounds for the film's various robots and electronic gadgets (the ED 209, for instance). Deploying a strategy not unlike that of *King Kong*, *RoboCop* uses such sound to create an otherworldly dimension and to legitimate the "futurity" of the images, using synthesized music in connection with the robocop itself, sometimes mixed with orchestral sound, sometimes as prelude to orchestral sound. Like jazz in the classical score, synthesized music in *RoboCop* is used for narrative effect, exploiting a contemporary sound to lend authenticity to the visual track. John Williams has frequently been depicted as the virtual holdout against the onslaught of contemporary musical forces. Considering a typical eighties score for an action-adventure film such as *RoboCop*, it would seem fair to say that Williams is not alone.

In closing, let me reveal another purpose I have had in mind throughout this book, one that is both reflected in and masked by my title. *Settling the Score* may at first appear to be a bit of a throwaway, the kind of catchy opening that always seems to be followed by a colon. But I have meant that title very literally, and it has been the unspoken aim of this text to redress the balance between visual and aural contributions to a film. Miklós Rózsa said, "Music is still considered as the salt that makes cinema meat taste better, but not as an equal ingredient which could be used with maximum efficiency in the kitchens of cinema cooks." [1] It is my hope that I have presented music as an "equal ingredient," and that in doing so I have come a little way toward settling that score.

Notes
Illustration Credits
Bibliography
Index

Introduction

1. David Raksin, participant, "Composers and the Creative Process," symposium presented at the Virginia Festival of American Film, Charlottesville, Virginia, 25 October 1990.

2. For a detailed analysis of this period of film history, see David Bordwell, Kristin Thompson, and Janet Staiger, *The Classical Hollywood Cinema: Film Style and Mode of Production to 1960* (New York: Columbia, 1985).

3. David Raksin, quoted in Irwin Bazelon, *Knowing the Score: Notes on Film Music* (New York: Van Nostrand and Reinhold, 1975), 246.

Chapter 1: The Language of Music

1. The methodology I've constructed in this chapter for listening to film music is strongly indebted to the work of Ray Jackendoff and Fred Lerdahl. For a fuller explication of a cognitivist approach to music, see Ray Jackendoff, *Consciousness and the Computational Mind* (Cambridge: MIT Press, 1987), 213–45; Fred Lerdahl and Ray Jackendoff, *A Generative Theory of Tonal Music* (Cambridge: MIT Press, 1983), and "A Grammatical Parallel between Music and Language," in *Music, Mind, and Brain: The Neuropsychology of Music,* ed. Manfred Clynes (New York: Plenum Press, 1982), 83–117; John A. Sloboda, *The Musical Mind: The Cognitive Psychology of Music* (Oxford: Clarendon Press, 1985), especially 1–66 and 239–68; Diana Deutsch, ed., *The Psychology of Music* (New York: Academic Press, 1982); Mary Louise Serafine, *Music as Cognition* (New York: Columbia University Press, 1988); and recent issues of the journal *Psychomusicology.* For a comparison to the cognitive approach, consider the following quotation from a recent text: "It is for these reasons that it is fruitless to attempt to produce a sense of the value of a musical work in anyone who is unmusical. The significance of any musical work can be revealed only to initiates." Malcolm Budd, *Music and the Emotions* (London: Routledge and Kegan Paul, 1985), x.

2. Jackendoff, *Consciousness and the Computational Mind* 216.

3. Lerdahl and Jackendoff, *Generative Theory of Tonal Music* 295.

4. Strictly speaking a pitch refers to any one of the sounds existing within a given musical system while a note refers to the visual sign for a pitch. In practice, however, such a distinction is rarely maintained, and the term "note," especially in English, is used to designate both the sound and its sign. It is this practice that I follow when I use "note" throughout the text.

5. All of the musical examples in this chapter originated as my own transcriptions. I was able to compare these against the autograph copy of the full score in the Bernard Herrmann Archive of the University of California at Santa Barbara. All future references to this score will be quoted from this copy.

6. For an insightful reading of the score for *Vivre sa vie* see Royal S. Brown, "Music and *Vivre sa vie*," *Quarterly Review of Film Studies* 5, 3 (Summer 1980): 319–33.

7. Royal S. Brown, "Herrmann, Hitchcock, and the Music of the Irrational," *Cinema Journal* 21, 2 (Spring 1982): 17.

8. Leonard B. Meyer, *Emotion and Meaning in Music* (Chicago: University of Chicago Press, 1956), vii.

9. Deryck Cooke, *The Language of Music* (Oxford: Oxford University Press, 1959), 90. For a cognitivist response to Cooke's position, see Sloboda, *Musical Mind* 60–65.

10. Jackendoff, *Consciousness and the Computational Mind* 244. See also Leonard B. Meyer, *Music, the Arts, and Ideas* (Chicago: University of Chicago Press, 1969), 9–15.

11. Jackendoff, *Consciousness and the Computational Mind* 245.

12. Franz Waxman, "Franz Waxman," in *Film Score: The View from the Podium*, ed. Tony Thomas (South Brunswick and New York: A. S. Barnes, 1979), 55.

13. Henry Mancini, *Sounds and Scores: A Practical Guide to Professional Orchestration* (Northridge Music, 1967), 131.

14. Craig Safan, quoted in Fred Karlin and Rayburn Wright, *On the Track: A Guide to Contemporary Film Scoring* (New York: Schirmer Books, 1990), 127.

15. H. Stephen Wright, "The Materials of Film Music: Their Nature and Accessibility," in *Film Music I*, ed. Clifford McCarty (New York: Garland, 1989), 4. Other essays on the problems involved in film music scholarship include Robert Fiedel, "Saving the Score," *American Film* 3, 1 (1977): 32, 71; and Martin Marks, "Film Music: The Material, Literature, and Present State of Research," *Journal of the University Film and Video Association* 34, 1 (Winter 1982): 3–40.

16. Wright, in fact, argues that the variability of musical transcription and the general unavailability of scores to check a transcription against "may well be the largest obstacle to the widespread advancement of film music scholarship."

As evidence of the problem, Wright points to the use of the disclaimer by film music scholars who have not been able to locate or acquire access to a score. See Wright, "Materials of Film Music" 4–5.

17. Linda Harris Mehr's *Motion Pictures, Television, and Radio: A Union Catalogue of Manuscript and Special Collections in the Western United States* (Boston: G. K. Hall, 1977), for instance, has obvious geographic limitations. Gillian Anderson's monograph *Silent Film Music 1894–1929: A Guide* (Washington, DC: Library of Congress, 1988) is scrupulously researched but limited to silent film scores in the Library of Congress and MOMA collections. Appendices catalogue the silent film music collections of Arthur Kleiner at the University of Minnesota; George Eastman House in Rochester; the Music Division of the New York Public Library; and Fédération Internationale des Archives du Film in Brussels. D. W. Krummel et al., eds., *Resources of American Music History: A Directory of Source Materials from Colonial Times to the Present* (Urbana: University of Illinois Press, 1981), lists some film composers among its entries.

18. For a reconstruction of its rediscovery see my "Impetuous Rhythm: Edmund Meisel's Score for Eisenstein's *Battleship Potemkin*," *Purdue Film Studies Annual* 7 (1983): 33–43.

Chapter 2: A Theory of Film Music

1. Plato, *Timaeus*, in *Dialogues of Plato*, trans. B. Jowett, 3d ed., Vol. 3 (New York: Oxford University Press, 1892), 488. Similar descriptions can be found in Alcmaeon, Democritus, Anaxagoras, Diogenes, and Aristotle. To the Greeks, an empty space referred not to a vacuum as we know it but to a space with no contents except air.

2. Alcmaeon, quoted in Theophrastus, *On the Senses*, trans. and comp. George Malcolm Stratton, in *Theophrastus and the Greek Physiological Psychology before Aristotle* (New York: Macmillan, 1917), 89; Democritus, quoted in *Theophrastus* 115; Aristotle, *On the Soul*, trans. R. D. Hicks, in *A Source Book in Greek Science*, ed. Morris Cohen and I. E. Drabkin (Cambridge: Harvard University Press, 1958), 289.

3. Empedocles, quoted in *Theophrastus* 73.

4. Heraclitus, *Fragments*, trans. T. M. Robinson (Toronto: University of Toronto Press, 1987), 61.

5. Aristotle (attributed), quoted in John Beare, *Greek Theories of Elementary Cognition* (Oxford: Clarendon Press, 1906), 124.

6. *Theophrastus* 35.

7. Duncan B. MacDonald, "Emotional Religion in Islam as Affected by Music and Singing. Being a Translation of a Book of the *Ihya 'Ulum ad-Din* of al-Ghazzali with Analysis, Annotation, and Appendices," *Journal of the Royal Asiatic Society* (1901): 199. Quoted in Frederick Vinton Hunt, *Origins in Acoustics: The Science of Sound from Antiquity to the Age of Newton* (New Haven: Yale University Press, 1978), 54.

8. Peter Pollack, *The Picture History of Photography* (New York: Abrams, 1969), 19.

9. Hermann Helmholtz, *On the Sensations of Tone*, trans. Alexander J. Ellis, 2d ed. (1877; repr. New York: Dover, 1954), 2, 3.

There is a striking similarity here to what film composers would say about their craft. See, for instance, Elmer Bernstein's comments on the "intellectual" perception of the visual image, versus the "purely emotional terms" of the music and Aaron Copland's claim that "the screen is a pretty cold proposition." Bernstein, quoted in Tony Thomas, *The View from the Podium* (South Brunswick and New York: A. S. Barnes, 1973), 193; Copland in *Our New Music: Leading Composers in Europe and America* (New York: McGraw-Hill, 1941), 261.

10. Edmund Gurney, *The Power of Sound* (1880; repr. New York: Basic Books, 1966), 15, 14.

11. Ibid. 13.

12. Richard Wagner, *The Music of the Future*, trans. Edward Dannreuther (London: Schott, 1873), 29.

13. Sergei Eisenstein, Vsevolod Pudovkin, and Gregori Alexandrov, "A Statement on Sound Film," in Eisenstein, *Film Form*, ed. and trans. Jay Leyda (New York: Harcourt, Brace, and World, 1949), 258.

14. Rudolf Arnheim, *Film as Art* (Berkeley: University of California Press, 1957), 209.

15. Ibid. 216.

16. Béla Balázs, *Theory of the Film: Character and Growth of a New Art*, trans. Edith Bone (London: Dennis Dobson, 1952; repr. New York: Dover, 1970), 236.

17. Siegfried Kracauer, *Theory of Film: The Redemption of Physical Reality* (New York: Oxford University Press, 1965), 139, 142.

18. Ibid. 142.

19. See for instance Mark Evans, *Soundtrack: The Music of the Movies* (New York: Hopkinson and Blake, 1975; repr. Da Capo, 1979); Tony Thomas, *Music for the Movies* (South Brunswick and New York: A. S. Barnes, 1973); and Roy Prendergast *Film Music: A Neglected Art* (New York: Norton, 1977).

20. Tom Levin, "The Acoustic Dimension: Notes on Cinema Sound," *Screen*

25, 3 (1984): 56. Even the term "spectator" reveals the visual bias that continues in film theory today.

21. See also Max Horkheimer and Theodor W. Adorno, "The Culture Industry: Enlightenment as Mass Deception," *Dialectic of Enlightenment*, trans. John Cumming (New York: Seabury Press, 1972), 120–67; and Adorno, "On the Fetish-Character in Music and the Regression of Listening," and "The Sociology of Knowledge and Its Consciousness," in *The Essential Frankfurt Reader*, ed. and trans. Andrew Arato and Eike Gebhardt (New York: Continuum, 1982), 270–99 and 452–65.

22. Hanns Eisler and Theodor W. Adorno (uncredited), *Composing for the Films* (New York: Oxford University Press, 1947), 20. Adorno's co-authorship is unacknowledged in the original English edition. For an analysis of Adorno's contribution see Philip Rosen, "Adorno and Film Music: Theoretical Notes on *Composing for the Films*," *Yale French Studies* no. 60 (1980): 157–82, and Claudia Gorbman, *Unheard Melodies: Narrative Film Music* (Bloomington: Indiana University Press, 1987), 172–73, note 3.

23. Theodor W. Adorno, *Introduction to the Sociology of Music*, trans. E. B. Ashton (New York: Seabury Press, 1976), 51.

24. Ibid. 51.

25. Kristin Thompson, "Early Sound Counterpoint," *Yale French Studies* no. 60 (1980): 118.

26. Sergei Eisenstein, "The Future of Film," interview with Mark Segal, *Close Up* 7, 2 (August 1930): 143.

27. Eisler and Adorno, *Composing for the Films* 8; Irwin Bazelon, *Knowing the Score: Notes on Film Music* (New York: Van Nostrand Reinhold, 1975), 127. The reader is here warned about Bazelon's frustrating lack of documentation. Claudia Gorbman in an important review of Bazelon's book found numerous examples of uncited "borrowings" from both Eisler and Adorno (*Composing for the Films*) and William Johnson (a 1969 article entitled "Face the Music" in *Film Quarterly*). The evidence Gorbman offers is overwhelming. See her "Film Music," *Quarterly Review of Film Studies* 3, 1 (Winter 1978): 105–13.

28. Bazelon, *Knowing the Score* 127.

29. Claudia Gorbman, "Narrative Film Music," *Yale French Studies* no. 60 (1980): 189. A revised version of this article appears as chapter 1 of *Unheard Melodies*.

30. Gorbman, "Narrative Film Music" 190.

31. Adorno, *Introduction to the Sociology of Music* 42.

32. Jacques Attali, *Noise: The Political Economy of Music*, trans. Brian Massumi (Minneapolis: University of Minnesota Press, 1985), 6.

33. Richard Leppert and Susan McClary, eds., *Music and Society: The Politics of Composition, Performance and Reception* (Cambridge: Cambridge University Press, 1989), xii.

34. See Christopher Ballantine, *Music and Its Social Meanings* (New York: Gordon and Breach Science Publishers, 1984); John Shepherd, Phil Virden, Graham Vulliamy and Trevor Wishart, *Whose Music? A Sociology of Musical Languages* (London: Latimer, 1977; repr. Transaction, 1980); Simon Frith, *Sound Effects: Youth, Leisure and the Politics of Rock 'n' Roll* (New York: Pantheon, 1981) and *Music for Pleasure* (New York: Routledge, 1988). See also the work of Lawrence Grossberg, an American, especially "The Politics of Youth Culture: Some Observations on Rock and Roll in American Culture," in *Social Text* no. 8 (Winter 1983): 104–26 and "I'd Rather Feel Bad Than Not Feel Anything at All: Rock and Roll, Pleasure, and Power," in *Enclitic* 8, 1–2 (Spring-Fall 1984): 94–110.

35. Eisler and Adorno, *Composing for the Films* 59.

36. Ibid. 54.

37. See Martin Marks, "Film Music of the Silent Period, 1895–1924" (Ph.D. diss., Harvard University, 1989).

38. Gorbman, *Unheard Melodies* 109. For an excellent summary and critique of Eisler and Adorno's analysis, see Gorbman, *Unheard Melodies* 99–109, and "Hanns Eisler in Hollywood," *Screen* 32, 3 (Autumn 1991): 272–85.

39. Attali, *Noise* 8.

40. Gorbman, *Unheard Melodies* 57.

41. Ibid. 58.

42. Flinn, "Film Music and Hollywood's Promise of Utopia in Film Noir and the Woman's Film" (Ph.D. diss., University of Iowa, 1988), 175.

43. Ibid. 284.

44. See in particular Didier Anzieu, "L'enveloppe sonore du soi," *Nouvelle revue de psychanalyse* 13 (Spring 1976): 161–79; Dominique Avron, "Notes pour introduire une métapsychologie de la musique," *Musique en jeu* 9 (November 1972): 102–10; Guy Rosolato, "La voix: entre corps et langage," *Revue française de psychanalyse* 38, 1 (January 1974): 75–94; Francis Hofstein, "Drogue et musique," *Musique en jeu* 9 (November 1972): 111–15; and Gérard Blanchard, *Images de la musique de cinéma* (Paris: Edilig, 1984). All translations from the French are my own.

45. Anzieu, "L'enveloppe sonore du soi" 161; Rosolato, "La voix" 81; Blanchard, *Images de la musique de cinéma* 95. Kaja Silverman argues that this image is hardly innocent. In *The Acoustic Mirror* she points out that it can also be "sinister," as in Michel Chion's "umbilical net" and "cobweb." For Silver-

man, the alternately positive or negative charge attached to this image points to "an ambivalence which attests to the divided nature of subjectivity." See Silverman, *The Acoustic Mirror* (Bloomington: Indiana University Press, 1988), 72–73; and Michel Chion, *Le son au cinéma* (Paris: Cahiers du cinéma/Editions de l'Etoile, 1985).

46. Chora is a term Kristeva uses in a number of texts. See particularly *Revolution in Poetic Language* (New York: Columbia University Press, 1984).

47. Hofstein, "Drogue et musique" 111.

48. Rosolato, "La voix" 81.

49. Ibid. 82.

50. Another line of inquiry generated by psychoanalytic theory is the concept of suture and its relation to the musical score. For a working out of this perspective, see Samuel Chell, "Music and Emotion in the Classic Hollywood Film: The Case of *The Best Years of Our Lives, Film Criticism* 8, 2 (Winter 1984): 27–38; and Anahid Kassabian, "Unconscious Workings, Emotional Appeals: Gender, Film Music, and Theory," paper presented at the annual meeting of the Society for Cinema Studies, Iowa City, 1989.

51. See Carol Flinn, "The 'Problem' of Femininity in Theories of Film Music," *Screen* 27, 6 (November–December 1986): 56–72.

52. Gorbman, *Unheard Melodies* 64.

53. Ibid. 64.

54. See, for instance, Silverman, *Acoustic Mirror*, and Mary Ann Doane, "The Voice in the Cinema: The Articulation of Body and Space," *Yale French Studies* no. 60 (1980): 33–50.

Chapter 3: The Silent Film Score

1. Thomas Edison, Forward, in W. K. L. Dickson and Antonia Dickson, *History of the Kinetoscope and Kineto-Phonograph* (New York: Albert Bunn, 1895), unpaginated.

2. Hanns Eisler and Theodor W. Adorno (uncredited), *Composing for the Films* (New York: Oxford University Press, 1947), 75.

3. Kurt London, *Film Music: A Summary of the Characteristic Features of Its History, Aesthetics, Technique, and Possible Developments*, trans. Eric S. Bensinger (London: Faber and Faber, 1936; repr. Arno Press, 1970), 60.

4. Siegfried Kracauer, *Theory of Film: The Redemption of Physical Reality* (New York: Oxford University Press, 1965), especially 136.

5. Frederick W. Sternfeld, "Music and the Cinema," in *Twentieth Century Music*, ed. Rollo H. Myers (New York: Orion Press, 1968), 123.

6. See, for instance, Aaron Copland, *Our New Music: Leading Composers in Europe and America* (New York: McGraw-Hill, 1941), 264; Roy Prendergast, *Film Music: A Neglected Art* (New York: Norton, 1977), 213; Sergei Eisenstein, *Film Sense*, ed. and trans. Jay Leyda (New York: Harcourt Brace Jovanovich, 1947), 164; and Rudolf Arnheim, *Film as Art* (Berkeley: University of California Press, 1957), 230.

7. Noël Burch, *Theory of Film Practice* (New York: Praeger, 1973), 100; Jean Mitry, "Music and Cinema," trans. William Frawley, *Film Reader* no. 4 (1979): 142.

8. London, *Film Music* 35.

9. See Martin Marks, "Film Music of the Silent Period, 1895–1924" (Ph.D. diss., Harvard University, 1989).

10. Ernst Luz, cue sheet, *The Sin That Was His*, Cue Sheet Collection, Theatre Arts Library, UCLA (hereafter referred to as Theatre Arts, UCLA); *Moving Picture World* (hereafter referred to as *MPW*) 13, 4 (27 July 1912): 321. See also George W. Beynon, *Musical Presentation of Motion Pictures* (New York: Schirmer, 1921), 139–40; M. M. Hansford, "Preparing Programs for Photoplay Accompaniments," *Dramatic Mirror* (hereafter referred to as *DM*), 4 August 1917, 10; and 11 August 1917, 10; Clarence E. Sinn, "Music for the Picture," *MPW* 8, 1 (7 January 1911): 27, and 8, 8 (25 February 1911): 409; and George Tootell, *How to Play the Cinema Organ* (London: Paxton, n.d.), 82. For a sharp attack on the practices of silent film accompaniment from a musicological point of view, see Harry Potamkin, "Music and the Movies," *Musical Quarterly* 15, 2 (April 1929): 281–96.

11. Gillian Anderson cites four theater organ schools: one in Chicago, one in Boston, and two in New York. I came across schools in Detroit and Rochester, New York. For further background on the practices of silent film accompaniment, see her informative essay "The Presentation of Silent Films, or, Music as Anaesthesia," *Journal of Musicology* 5, 2 (Spring 1987), 257–95. An expanded version of this essay, "A Warming Flame: The Musical Presentation of Silent Films," appears in Gillian Anderson, *Music for Silent Films, 1894–1929: A Guide* (Washington, DC: Library of Congress, 1988), xiii–xliv.

12. Beynon, *Musical Presentation of Motion Pictures* 76.

13. David Mendoza and William Axt, musical adaptation and arrangement, *Ben-Hur*, piano conductor part, Margaret Herrick Library of the Academy of Motion Picture Arts and Sciences (hereafter referred to as Academy). Gaylord Carter, a theatrical organist, remembers accompanying the film at the Million Dollar Theatre in Los Angeles where he was instructed: "Now, Gaylord, while the people are coming in, we want you to keep some music going."

Rudy Behlmer, " 'Tumult, Battle and Blaze': Looking Back on the 1920s—and Since—with Gaylord Carter, the Dean of Theater Organists," in *Film Music I,* ed. Clifford McCarty (New York: Garland, 1989), 25.

14. *DM,* 28 July 1917, 10. Sinn writes similarly: "Sometimes a pause is effective, but, as a general rule I think we should try to preserve the continuity in the music." *MPW* 8, 1 (7 January 1911): 27. See also Edith Lang and George West, *Musical Accompaniment of Moving Pictures* (Boston: Boston Music, 1920), 58, 61; Erno Rapee, *Encyclopedia of Music for Pictures* (New York: Belwin, 1925; repr. Arno Press, 1970), 14; Eugene Ahern, *What and How to Play for Pictures* (Twin Falls, Idaho: News Print, 1913), 44–45; Beynon, *Musical Presentation of Motion Pictures* 137; Tootell, *How to Play the Cinema Organ* 82; and Bert Vipond, "The Art of Playing to Pictures," *Moving Picture News* (hereafter referred to as *MPN*) 3, 18 (30 April 1910): 13.

15. *MPW* 14, 3 (19 October 1912): 235. See also *DM,* 21 July 1917, 11.

16. See Ernst Luz, "The Musician and the Picture," *MPN* 6, 23 (7 December 1912): 20; Sinn, *MPW* 13, 13 (28 September 1912): 1271; *DM,* 28 July 1917, 10; 1 September 1917, 12; and 6 October 1917, 11; Beynon, *Musical Presentation of Motion Pictures* 139; Tootell, *How to Play the Cinema Organ* 82; and Rapee, *Encyclopedia of Music for Pictures* 14–15.

17. *DM,* 11 August 1917, 10.

18. Lang and West, *Musical Accompaniment of Moving Pictures* 35. See also Ahern, *What and How to Play for Pictures* 12, 14; Rapee, *Encyclopedia of Music for Pictures* 14; Tootell, *How to Play the Cinema Organ* 83; Beynon, *Musical Presentation of Motion Pictures* 85–86, 139.

19. Rapee, *Encyclopedia of Music for Pictures* 14; Tootell, *How to Play the Cinema Organ* 83.

20. *That's My Daddy,* Universal Thematic Cue Sheets, Theatre Arts, UCLA.

21. Roy L. Medcalfe, "Hollywood Theater," *American Organist* 7, 11 (November 1924): 643, quoted in Anderson, "Presentation of Silent Films" 288–89.

22. Mortimer Wilson, pencil sketches, *Don Q, Son of Zorro,* Collection of Silent Film Compositions and Arrangements, Music Library, UCLA.

23. Victor Schertzinger, piano conductor part *Robin Hood,* Academy.

24. Lang and West, *Musical Accompaniment of Moving Pictures* 1–2; Beynon, *Musical Presentation of Motion Pictures* 2.

25. Max Winkler, *A Penny from Heaven* (New York: Appleton-Century-Crofts, 1951), 168–69. See also Sinn, *MPW* 13, 11 (14 September 1912): 1082; Kenneth Aiken, "Thoughts for the Pianist," *MPW* 15, 5 (1 February 1913): 470; Vipond, *MPN* 13, 11 (12 March 1910): 6; Luz *MPN* 6, 22 (30 November 1912): 20; and May Meskimen Mills, *The Pipe Organist's Complete Instruction and Ref-*

erence Work on the Art of Photo-playing (May Meskimen Mills, 1922), 7, quoted in Anderson, "Presentation of Silent Films" 279.

26. The very term diegetic is problematic in this context and demonstrates a certain murkiness in current sound theory. As Carol Hamand argues, diegetic and nondiegetic "cannot describe a sound represented in the visuals but left unrendered in the auditorium, a characteristic sound-image relationship found in virtually every silent American film and one of the key traits differentiating the silent from the sound movie." For an excellent analysis of changes in sound practice between the silent and sound eras, see Carol Hamand, "Sound and Image," *Wide Angle* 6, 2 (1985): 24–33.

27. Sinn, *MPW* 8, 6 (11 February 1911): 293; W. Stephen Bush, "When 'Effects' Are Unnecessary Noises," *MPW* 9, 9 (9 September 1911): 690. See also Luz, *MPN* 6, 17 (16 October 1912): 29, and 8, 8 (23 August 1913): 29; *DM*, 1 September 1917, 12; Rapee, *Encyclopedia of Music for Pictures* 15–16; and Ahern, *What and How to Play for Pictures* 54.

28. Luz, *MPN* 7, 3 (18 January 1913): 20. See also Ahern, *What and How to Play for Pictures* 27–28.

29. Lang and West, *Musical Accompaniment of Moving Pictures* 57. See also Rapee, *Encyclopedia of Music for Pictures* 17; Ahern, *What and How to Play for Pictures* 53–56; and Reginald Foorte, *The Cinema Organ* (London: Pitman, 1932; repr. Vestal Press, 1970), 34–49.

30. Beynon, *Musical Presentation of Motion Pictures* 52.

31. James C. Bradford, cue sheet, *Beau Geste*, Cue Sheet Collection, Theatre Arts, UCLA.

32. Beynon, *Musical Presentation of Motion Pictures* 98.

33. *DM*, 21 July 1917, 11.

34. Beynon, *Musical Presentation of Motion Pictures* 137.

35. Lang and West, *Musical Accompaniment of Moving Pictures* 3.

36. Erno Rapee, *Motion Picture Moods for Pianists and Organists* (New York: Schirmer, 1924; repr. Arno Press, 1974), iii.

37. Lang and West, *Musical Accompaniment of Moving Pictures* 4. Somewhat more prosaic is the description which appeared in *MPN*: the accompanist's "fingers should be so much in sympathy with the film that appropriate music should pour out of his hands by musical gravitation." Vipond, *MPN* 3, 11 (12 March 1910): 6. See also *DM*, 8 September 1917, 13; Sinn, *MPW* 7, 22 (26 November 1910): 1227; and Tootell, *How to Play the Cinema Organ* 53–54.

38. "The Loew Music System," *American Organist* 7, 6 (1924): 332, 334, quoted in Anderson, "Presentation of Silent Films" 273; Potamkin, "Music and the Movies" 290.

39. Tootell, *How to Play the Cinema Organ* 85.

40. *DM*, 27 October 1917, 11. See also *DM*, 8 September 1917, 13; Beynon, *Musical Presentation of Motion Pictures* 16, 111, 144; Lang and West, *Musical Accompaniment of Moving Pictures* 62; and Rapee, *Encyclopedia of Music for Pictures* 24–25.

41. For a discussion of the relationship between Wagnerian opera and silent film accompaniment see Charles Merrell Berg, *An Investigation of the Motives and Realization of Music to Accompany the American Silent Film, 1896–1927* (New York: Arno, 1976), 70–83.

42. Richard Wagner, *The Music of the Future*, trans. Edward Dannreuther (London: Schott, 1873), 22.

43. Richard Wagner, *Opera and Drama*, trans. Edwin Evans (London: William Reeves, 1913), 2: 634.

44. Bush, *MPW* 9, 5 (12 August 1911): 354, and 6, 8 (2 September 1911): 608.

45. Rapee, *Encyclopedia of Music for Pictures* 7.

46. Vipond, *MPN* 3, 12 (19 March 1910): 7.

47. Lang and West, *Musical Accompaniment of Moving Pictures* 8.

Chapter 4: The Classical Hollywood Film Score

1. There are three short scenes, or portions of scenes, left unscored in the film. None lasts longer than thirty seconds.

2. Jolson actually played a dummy piano. Studio records indicate that Bert Fiske was the pianist on the set that day who played offscreen for Jolson.

3. Max Steiner, "Scoring the Film," in *We Make the Movies*, ed. Nancy Naumberg (New York: Norton, 1937), 219.

4. Max Steiner, "The Music Director," in *The Real Tinsel*, ed. Bernard Rosenberg and Harry Silverstein (London: Macmillan, 1970), 392.

5. Steiner, "Music Director" 392.

6. See *Los Angeles Times*, 28 December 1930; *Evening Express*, 21 February 1931; and *Hollywood Reporter*, 25 February 1931. All citations come from Max Steiner's personal scrapbook now on deposit at the Max Steiner Archive, Brigham Young University, Provo, Utah (hereafter referred to as Steiner Archive). I was able to use this material as well as the sketches for *The Informer* when they were in the possession of the late Mrs. Max Steiner, who graciously allowed me to use them. I would here like to thank Fred Steiner for making this possible.

7. Steiner, "Max Steiner on Film Music," in *Film Score: The View from the Podium*, ed. Tony Thomas (South Brunswick and New York: A. S. Barnes, 1979),

76. For a more thorough history of Steiner's participation in the making of *King Kong*, see Orville Goldner and George E. Turner, *The Making of King Kong: The Story behind a Film Classic* (New York: Ballantine, 1975), 188–91. Claudia Gorbman offers an insightful analysis of this score in *Unheard Melodies: Narrative Film Music* (Bloomington: Indiana University Press, 1987), 74–90.

8. For an interesting personal recollection of team scoring see David Raksin, "Holding a Nineteenth Century Pedal at Twentieth Century-Fox," in *Film Music I*, ed. Clifford McCarty (New York: Garland, 1989), 167–81. See also David Raksin, interview with Irene K. Atkins, 6 December 1977–15 February 1978, transcript, Yale Oral History Project, Yale University Library, New Haven, 120–28.

9. Max Steiner, pencil sketches, *The Informer*, Steiner Archive.

10. Steiner, "Music Director" 390.

11. Hugo Friedhofer, "Hugo Friedhofer: Arranging and Composing Film Music," interview with Irene Kahn Atkins, 13 March–19 April 1974, transcript, Louis B. Mayer Oral History Collection, Louis B. Mayer Library, American Film Institute, Los Angeles. Friedhofer was the principal orchestrator for *Captain Blood*, but Milton Roder also worked on it.

12. Ernst Klapholz, quoted in "Interview with Arthur Lange and Ernst Klapholz," *Cue Sheet* 7, 4 (December 1990), 159.

13. Rudy Behlmer, "Tumult, Battle, and Blaze: Looking Back on the 1920s— and Since—with Gaylord Carter, the Dean of Theater Organists," in *Film Music I* 27–28.

14. For examples of typical anecdotes concerning producers see Tony Thomas, *Music for the Movies* (South Brunswick and New York: A. S. Barnes, 1973), 72, 118; Irwin Bazelon, *Knowing the Score: Notes on Film Music* (New York: Van Nostrand Reinhold, 1975), 53; and Mark Evans, *Soundtrack: The Music of the Movies* (New York: Hopkinson and Blake, 1975; repr. Da Capo, 1979), 244. Maurice Jarre's anecdote appears in Fred Karlin and Rayburn Wright, *On the Track: A Guide to Contemporary Film Scoring* (New York: Schirmer Books, 1990), 16.

15. David Raksin, "David Raksin on Film Music," in *Film Score: The View from the Podium* 42–43.

16. Steiner, "Max Steiner on Film Music" 68.

17. Claudia Gorbman in *Unheard Melodies: Narrative Film Music* offers a paradigm for the classical film score. Her analysis of its conventions on 70–109 has been important in helping me to frame my own model. There are several points of confluence between us: the ideology of "inaudibility"; the importance of music to narrative and structural continuity; the centrality of music in creating

emotional response in the spectator; the privileging of dialogue over music; the function of the leitmotif; and the flexibility of these conventions. Gorbman makes the excellent point that the sound-collecting apparatus, the technology which permits nondiegetic music, must not be visible to the spectator. My model makes a distinction between implicit and explicit content as a determinant on the composer and places more emphasis on the classical score's symphonic medium and romantic idiom as determining characteristics. For Gorbman's discussion of music's unifying functions, see "Formal and rhythmic continuity" and "Unity" (89–91); music and narrative action, see "Narrative cueing" (82–89); music and emotion, see "Emotion" (79–82); music and subjectivity, see 83–84; music and mood, see 85; music and dialogue, see 77–78; music and spectacle, 68; the placement of music, 78; the leitmotif, 26–29. An analysis of Steiner's score for *Mildred Pierce* is on 91–98.

18. Robert Nathan, quoted in Marlin Skiles, *Music Scoring for TV and Motion Pictures* (Blue Ridge Summit, PA: Tab Books, 1976), 38.

19. Virgil Thomson, "A Little about Movie Music," *Modern Music* 10, 4 (1933): 188.

20. Skiles, *Music Scoring for TV and Motion Pictures* 94.

21. All of the musical examples in this chapter originated as my transcriptions. I was able to compare these against the full score in the Warner Brothers Archive/University of Southern California Cinema-Television Library (hereafter referred to as Warners). All future references to Korngold's score will be quoted from this copy. My analysis is based on the restored 119-minute original version of the film, not the 99-minute edited version that is in general distribution.

22. Director William Friedkin, in describing the unusual effects he wanted in the score for *The Exorcist* (1973), said, "I wanted the music to come and go at strange places and dissolve in and out. No music behind big scenes. No music ever behind dialogue. . . . Only music in the montage sequences. . . ." Quoted in Randall Larson, *Musique Fantastique: A Survey of Film Music in the Fantastic Cinema* (Metuchen, NJ: Scarecrow, 1985), 312.

23. Friedhofer, quoted in Skiles, *Music Scoring for TV and Motion Pictures* 234.

24. Erich Wolfgang Korngold to Hal B. Wallis, 11 February 1938, Warners. Rudy Behlmer suggests Korngold changed his mind when he heard of the meeting between Chancellor Schuschnigg of Austria and Hitler, effectively preventing him from returning to Austria to pursue his career. See Behlmer, *America's Favorite Movies* (New York: Ungar, 1982), 84–85.

25. Steiner, "Scoring the Film," 223.

26. Skiles, *Music Scoring for TV and Motion Pictures* 94.

27. Frank Skinner, *Underscore* (New York: Criterion Music, 1960), 191.

28. Samuel Chell, "Music and Emotion in the Classic Hollywood Film: The Case of *The Best Years of Our Lives*," *Film Criticism* 8, 2 (Winter 1984): 38.

29. Steiner, "Music Director," 396.

30. Elmer Bernstein, quoted in Thomas, *Music for the Movies* 193, quoted in Simon Frith, "Mood Music: An Inquiry into Narrative Film Music," *Screen* 25, 3 (1984): 84. For a discussion of the concept of emotional realism in narrative film scoring, see Frith 83–84.

31. Skinner, *Underscore* 191.

32. Karlin and Wright, *On the Track* 497.

33. Leonid Sabaneev, *Music for the Films*, trans. S. W. Pring (London: Pitman and Sons, 1935; repr. Arno, 1978), 20.

34. Karlin and Wright, *On the Track* 132.

35. Cutting notes, Hal B. Wallis, 10 December 1935, Warners.

36. Ibid.

37. Verney Arvey, "Composing for the Pictures by Erich Korngold: An Interview," *Etude* 55, 1 (January 1937), 15.

38. Erich Wolfgang Korngold, "Some Experiences in Film Music," in *Music and Dance in California*, ed. Jose Rodriguez (Hollywood: Bureau of Musical Research, 1940), 137.

39. Korngold's son, Ernst W. Korngold, told me his father didn't use a click track, but he did remember punches and streamers from his father's recording sessions. Their use was rare, however, and they were employed not to establish the rhythm of a scene but as a kind of insurance for specific musical cues that Korngold was largely able to synch by ear and eye.

40. Thomas, *Music for the Movies* 131.

41. Cutting notes, Hal B. Wallis, 10 December 1935, Warners.

42. Steiner, "Music Director" 393. See also *Film Music Notes* 2, 4 (January 1943), where he claims that "the great problem of composing for the films [is]—to give the score continuity, to keep the audience unconscious of any break. . . ."

43. Herbert Stothart, "Film Music," in *Behind the Screen*, ed. Stephen Watts (London: Barker, 1939), 143–44.

44. Karlin and Wright, *On the Track* 49.

45. John Williams, quoted in Tony Thomas, "A Conversation with John Williams," *Cue Sheet: The Journal of the Society for the Preservation of Film Music* 8, 1 (March 1991): 12.

46. Carol Flinn, "The Most Romantic Art of All: Music in the Classical Hollywood Cinema," *Cinema Journal* 29, 4 (Summer 1990): 47.

47. Evans (*Soundtrack*), Thomas (*Music for the Movies*), and Goldner and Turner (*Making of King Kong*) erroneously report the size of the orchestra as eighty players. Fred Steiner, who conducted the rerecording in 1976, established the original size through research on the score. See Fred Steiner, liner notes, *King Kong*, sound recording, Entr-acte ERS 6504, 1976.

48. Archive, American Federation of Musicians, Local 47, Los Angeles.

49. Korngold borrowed selections from two symphonic poems by Franz Liszt: *Prometheus* and *Mazeppa*. *Prometheus* is used briefly during the Spanish conquest of Port Royal and is quoted at length during the duel between Blood and Levasseur. *Mazeppa* is used during the final sea battle and briefly during the Spanish conquest of Port Royal. Because Korngold did not compose all of the cues for the film, he insisted on the credit "Musical Arrangements" in the main title.

50. Skiles, *Music Scoring for TV and Motion Pictures* 123.

51. Karlin and Wright, *On the Track* 176.

52. Wilfrid Mellers, "Film Music: The Musical Problem," in *Grove's Dictionary of Music and Musicians*, ed. Eric Blom, 5th ed. (London: Macmillan, 1954), 3:105.

53. See Aaron Copland, *Our New Music: Leading Composers in Europe and America* (New York: McGraw-Hill, 1941), 266–67.

54. Hanns Eisler and Theodor W. Adorno (uncredited), *Composing for the Films* (New York: Oxford University Press, 1947), 5.

55. Gerard Carbonara, "*Leit-motif* in Film Scoring," in *Music and Dance in California* 133.

56. "Music in the Cinema," *New York Times*, 29 September 1935, 4.

57. Steven D. Wescott, "Miklós Rózsa's *Ben-Hur*: The Musical-Dramatic Function of the Hollywood *Leitmotiv*," in *Film Music 1* 191.

58. I would like here to thank Fred Steiner, the principal composer of the original *Star Trek* television series, for relating this anecdote to me.

Chapter 5: *The Informer*

1. To put this figure in some context it is important to realize that it was the practice in the Hollywood studios before about 1936 to credit the head of the music department, usually entitled the musical director, for a film's music. As musical director of RKO from 1929 to 1935 Steiner retains screen credit for all RKO films which include music during those years. On many of these films his scoring may have been minimal, perhaps a few bridge sequences. Other

films were completely scored by him. For the sake of comparison, consider these statistics: Erich Wolfgang Korngold scored sixteen films in Hollywood; another contemporary, Alfred Newman, scored 171.

2. Peter Bogdanovich, *John Ford* (Berkeley: University of California Press, 1968), 61.

3. RKO General Pictures Archive, Financial Records and Shooting Schedule, *The Informer*. All other RKO material is taken from this archive unless otherwise noted. For further information on the production history of *The Informer*, see Emanuel Eisenberg, "John Ford: Fighting Irish," in *New Theatre*, April 1936, 42, and Andrew Sinclair, *John Ford* (New York: Dial Press, 1979), 64.

4. Max Steiner, "The Music Director," in *The Real Tinsel*, ed. Bernard Rosenberg and Harry Silverstein (London: Macmillan, 1970), 392.

5. RKO Correspondence, Steiner to Hendee, 23 January, 9 February, 14 February, 18 February 1935.

6. All of the musical examples in this chapter originated as my own transcriptions. I was able to compare these against two versions of the score: the full score at the RKO Archives, and the pencil sketches now in the Max Steiner Archive, Brigham Young University, Provo, Utah. All future references to Steiner's score will be quoted from Steiner's sketches unless noted otherwise.

7. For a discussion of female sexuality and the Hollywood film score see my "Musical Stereotyping in Hollywood Films," *Film Reader* 5 (1982): 76–82.

8. Max Steiner, full score, *The Informer*, RKO.

9. Max Steiner, "Max Steiner on Film Music," in *Film Score: The View from the Podium*, ed. Tony Thomas (South Brunswick and New York: A. S. Barnes, 1979), 78.

10. See for instance, *Los Angeles Herald Tribune*, 1 September 1935, and *Musical America*, August 1935, 9.

11. I am indebted to Charles Shattuck for pointing this out to me.

12. Review of *The Informer*, *Literary Digest*, 25 May 1935, 26.

13. "Mephisto's Musings," *Musical America*, August 1935, 9.

14. Richard Watts, Jr., "Sight and Sound," *Los Angeles Herald Tribune*, 1 September 1935.

15. Review of *The Informer*, *Hollywood Citizen News*, 30 April 1935.

Chapter 6: *The Magnificent Ambersons*

1. Bernard Herrmann, "Bernard Herrmann, Composer," in *Sound and the Cinema: The Coming of Sound to American Film*, ed. Evan Cameron (Pleasantville, NY: Redgrave, 1980), 121.

2. The prologue has been called "lyrical," cadence has been used to describe its narrative structure, and varying "tone" has been ascribed to Welles's voice. See, for instance, Stephen Farber, "*The Magnificent Ambersons,*" in *Focus on Orson Welles,* ed. Ron Gottesman (Englewood Cliffs, NJ: Prentice-Hall, 1976), 26, and Joseph McBride, *Orson Welles* (New York: Harcourt Brace Jovanovich, 1977), 35.

An awareness of Herrmann's work is growing within the discipline. Two extremely useful articles are Royal S. Brown, "Hitchcock, Herrmann, and the Music of the Irrational," in *Cinema Journal* 21, 2 (Spring 1982): 14–49, and Fred Steiner, "Herrmann's 'Black and White' Music for Hitchcock's *Psycho,*" in *Film-music Notebook* 1, 1 (Fall 1974): 28–36 (Part 1); 1, 2 (Winter 1974–75): 26–46 (Part 2). Graham Bruce's book is an attempt to redress the issue. Bruce argues: "The existing writing on Herrmann, then, not only constitutes a very incomplete investigation of his work, but also fails, for the most part, to give precise and detailed consideration to how a Herrmann score functions within a film." Graham Bruce, *Bernard Herrmann: Film Music and Narrative* (Ann Arbor: UMI Research Press, 1985), 3. Bruce offers extended analyses of *Vertigo* and *Psycho* as well as shorter analyses of *Citizen Kane, Obsession* (1976), and *Taxi Driver* (1976). Material on *The Magnificent Ambersons* is included on 38–42. See also Claudia Gorbman, *Unheard Melodies: Narrative Film Music* (Bloomington: Indiana University Press, 1987), 151–61, on Herrmann's score for *Hangover Square,* and Robert L. Carringer, *The Making of Citizen Kane* (Berkeley: University of California Press, 1985), 106–9, on Herrmann's contribution to *Citizen Kane.*

3. Quoted in "Bernard Herrmann," in Irwin Bazelon, *Knowing the Score: Notes on Film Music* (New York: Van Nostrand Reinhold, 1975), 234.

4. The broadcast of 29 October 1939 featured Walter Huston, his wife Nan Sunderland, and Welles both as narrator and George Amberson Minafer.

5. RKO General Pictures Archive, *The Magnificent Ambersons,* Legal files, Herrmann contract, 27 February 1942, Mercury Theatre Collection. Two sets of production records exist for *The Magnificent Ambersons*: Mercury Theatre records, which contain all the preproduction work done by Welles and his staff, and RKO records, which contain production material beginning with the start of shooting (October 1941) and continuing through the release (July 1942). Some material overlaps these periods and is duplicated in both files. Material in the Mercury Theatre Collection at Lilly Library, Indiana University, will be designated Mercury. Material exclusively in RKO General Pictures Archive will be designated RKO.

6. The piece, "At a Georgia Camp Meeting" by Kerry Mills, was recorded for use in the Christmas ball sequence.

7. Orson Welles, radio play, *The Magnificent Ambersons*, 29 October 1939, audio tape, my transcription.

8. "Toujours ou jamais" originated as my own transcription. I was able to compare it against the full score at RKO and Herrmann's autograph full score at the Bernard Herrmann Archive, University of California at Santa Barbara. The full score at RKO consists of the music which was used in the final release version and thus includes music by both Herrmann and Webb. Herrmann's autograph copy contains much though unfortunately not all that was cut from the final release print. Herrmann's music appears in similar, though not identical, form in both versions. All future references to Herrmann's score will be quoted from the autograph copy unless noted otherwise.

9. Eric Blom writes that Waldteufel was "less gifted, less versatile, less inventive than Strauss; a good example of Waldteufel is little inferior to one of Strauss's below his very best, though Strauss can be poetical, which Waldteufel never is." Andrew Lamb concurs: "His waltzes possess a distinctive poetic charm, though they lack the rhythmic and melodic variety of the best Strauss works." See Eric Blom, "Emile Waldteufel," *Grove's Dictionary of Music and Musicians*, ed. Eric Blom, 5th ed. (London: Macmillan, 1954), 9:132; and Andrew Lamb, "Emile Waldteufel," *The New Grove Dictionary of Music and Musicians*, ed. Stanley Sadie, 6th ed. (London: Macmillan, 1980), 20:159.

10. RKO Correspondence, Bakaleinikoff to Welles, 23 January 1942, Mercury. Usually the head of the music department had the power to make his authority felt, even in something as simple as the selection of musical background. Many composers worked around this problem by simply assuming the title of music department head themselves (Max Steiner and Alfred Newman for example). Herrmann's refusal to take Bakaleinikoff's prerogative into account was possible because of the force of his own personality and Welles's continued backing.

11. RKO Correspondence, Moss to Bakaleinikoff, 28 January 1942, Mercury.

12. The piano solo "The Snow Is Dancing" by Claude Debussy (1862–1918) is characterized by a combination of these same elements. Herrmann undoubtedly would have known the piece (Debussy was his favorite composer), and it is not improbable that it influenced Herrmann's choice of orchestration, rhythm, and structure.

13. For a more detailed history of the film's rocky postproduction see Carringer, *Making of Citizen Kane* 121–34.

14. Rui Nogueira, "Robert Wise at RKO," *Focus on Film* no. 12 (Winter 1972): 44. In fact many of the audience preview cards I saw were enthusiastic. But those in the negative were particularly venomous: "Who cares about that

junk. Out of date for these times"; "Too morose"; "Too much gloom"; "the G—— D—— thing stunk. Only Orson Welles could think up a thing like that." Preview comment cards, 18, 21, 24 March 1942, RKO.

15. Quoted in Nogueira, "Robert Wise at RKO" 44.

16. For Welles's complex contractual history with RKO see Carringer, *Making of Citizen Kane* 1–3, 26, 123.

17. In December 1942 the studio was running short of negative storage cans. On December 10, Charles Koerner, West Coast production chief, gave the go-ahead to "junk all positive and negative trims and out-takes which you have been holding on . . . *The Magnificent Ambersons*." RKO Correspondence, Memo, 10 December 1942, RKO.

18. Quoted in Charles Higham, *Hollywood Cameramen: Sources of Light* (Bloomington: Indiana University Press, 1970), 108.

19. *Variety*, "Await Welles Return from Brazil for Second Episode of RKO Battle," 8 July 1941, 7.

20. The pieces selected by Roy Webb for the Christmas ball were "Flower Song" by Gustav Lange and "Minuet" by Boccherini.

21. Thanks to Robert Carringer for providing valuable information to me regarding this cue.

22. Roy Webb, full score, Selections from *The Magnificent Ambersons*, RKO.

23. RKO Publicity Release, Mercury.

24. Originally Herrmann was to have been given a visual and aural credit for *Citizen Kane*. A piece of sheet music would be seen on the screen as Welles read Herrmann's name.

25. RKO Correspondence, Youngman to Hastings, 22 June 1942, Mercury.

26. RKO Correspondence, Youngman to Hastings, 23 June 1942, Mercury.

27. RKO Legal, Herrmann contract, 27 February 1942, Mercury.

28. Herrmann's contract explicitly states, "after we advise him that he has completed all of his services, if Herrmann is not in the vicinity of the place where we want such additional services rendered, he is not required to perform the same." RKO Legal, Herrmann contract, 27 February 1942, Mercury.

29. Richard Wilson Collection, Special Collections, UCLA, audio tape, my transcription.

30. Bazelon, *Knowing the Score* 234.

Chapter 7: *Laura*

1. David Raksin, quoted in Elmer Bernstein, "A Conversation with David Raksin, Part II," *Filmmusic Notebook* 2, 3 (1976):11.

2. Ibid.

3. Fred Steiner and Martin Marks, "Film Music," *The New Grove Dictionary of American Music,* ed. H. Wiley Hitchcock and Stanley Sadie (London: Macmillan, 1986), 2:121.

4. See, for instance, E. Ann Kaplan, *Women in Film Noir* (London: British Film Institute, 1976), especially Janey Place, "Women in Film Noir" (35–67), and Christine Gledhill, "*Klute*: Part 1: A Contemporary Film Noir and Feminist Criticism" (6–21).

5. For Caspary's version of production difficulties, see Vera Caspary, "My 'Laura' and Otto's," *Saturday Review,* 26 June 1971, 36–37.

6. Ibid. 37.

7. Ibid.

8. Vera Caspary, *Laura* (Boston: Houghton Mifflin, 1943), 17.

9. Caspary, "My 'Laura' and Otto's" 37.

10. According to Raksin, quoted in Bernstein, "Conversation with David Raksin" 12.

11. Darryl F. Zanuck, quoted in Rudy Behlmer, *America's Favorite Movies: Behind the Scenes* (New York: Ungar, 1982), 182–83. Behlmer offers an extended production history of *Laura* on 177–99.

12. This is according to Behlmer, ibid. 194.

13. Other ambiguous references include Waldo's preoccupation with McPherson's physique and "fiercely virile temperament"; Waldo's confession to the reader that he offered McPherson his "charm," and followed his career "with breathless excitement"; McPherson's description of Waldo as an old woman; and Laura's description of her relationship to Waldo in which she confesses that "there had been a certain delicacy in our avoiding any implication that the wooing might have purpose beyond its charm."

14. According to Preminger, "Zanuck was negative when I suggested Webb. The head of the casting department . . . took his cue from the boss's attitude and said that he had seen a test Webb made for MGM. He said the man was impossible. 'He doesn't walk, he flies.' " Otto Preminger, *Otto Preminger: An Autobiography* (Garden City, NY: Doubleday, 1977), 73. See also Preminger quoted in Gerald Pratley, *The Cinema of Otto Preminger* (New York: A. S. Barnes, 1971), 56.

15. Jay Dratler, with revisions by Ring Lardner, Jr., Samuel Hoffenstein, and Betty Reinhardt, *Laura,* Shooting Final, 18 April 1944, 1.

16. Richard Dyer, "Homosexuality in Film Noir," *Jump Cut* no. 16 (November 1977), 20.

17. Mel Gussow, *Don't Say Yes until I Finish Talking* (Garden City, NY: Double-

day, 1971), 137. See also Behlmer, *America's Favorite Movies* 196–97; Pratley, *Cinema of Otto Preminger* 60–61; and Preminger, *Otto Preminger* 77–78.

18. Kristin Thompson, "Closure within a Dream: Point-of-View in *Laura*" *Film Reader* no. 3 (1978), 90.

19. For various versions of Mamoulian's replacement, see Behlmer, *America's Favorite Movies* 184–92; Pratley, *Cinema of Otto Preminger* 58–60; and Preminger, *Otto Preminger* 74–75.

20. David Raksin, interview with the author, August 1980. For a detailed account of the score's composition, see David Raksin, interview with Irene K. Atkins, 6 December 1976–15 February 1977, transcript, Yale Oral History Project, Yale University Library, New Haven, 168–88.

21. Raksin, interview with the author.

22. Raksin, quoted in Bernstein, "Conversation with David Raksin" 12.

23. All of the musical examples in this chapter originated as my own transcriptions. I was able to compare these against Raksin's full score at Twentieth Century-Fox. Also at Fox are selections from the conductor part. All future references to Raksin's score will be quoted from the full score.

24. Raksin, quoted in Joe Collura, "dialogue in l.a. with david raksin," *Classic Images* no. 68 (24 March 1980), 24.

25. David Raksin, "*Carrie*," *Film Music Notes* 12, 1 (September–October 1952): 14.

26. Collura, "dialogue in l.a. with david raksin" 24.

27. David Raksin, liner notes, *Laura, The Bad and the Beautiful, Forever Amber*, sound recording, RCA Red Seal ARL 1-1490, 1976.

28. Raksin, interview with Irene K. Atkins 180. For a more detailed explanation of the process Raksin used, see 178–81.

29. "*Laura*," *Film Music Notes* 4, 2 (November 1944).

30. For an in-depth historical study of music as a marketing technique in films, see Alexander Doty, "Music Sells Movies: (Re) New (ed) Conservatism in Film Marketing," *Wide Angle* 10, 2 (1988): 70–79.

Chapter 8: John Williams and "The Empire"

1. Elmer Bernstein, "What Ever Happened to Great Movie Music?" *High Fidelity*, July 1972, 55.

2. Ibid. 58.

3. Irwin Bazelon, *Knowing the Score: Notes on Film Music* (New York: Van Nostrand Reinhold, 1975), 170; Jerry Goldsmith, quoted in Bazelon 190.

4. Goldsmith, quoted in ibid. 190.

5. David Raksin, quoted in ibid. 241.

6. Bernstein quoted in Joseph Curley, "Elmer Bernstein: How Rock Has Rolled over Film Scoring," *Millimeter*, August 1980, 134.

7. Giorgio Moroder, quoted in Terry Atkinson, "Scoring with Synthesizers," *American Film* 17, 10 (September 1982): 71.

8. Glenn Morley, "The Synthesizer: The Mockingbird of Instruments," *Cinema Canada* nos. 60–61 (December 1979/January 1980), 46.

9. John Williams, quoted in Bazelon, *Knowing the Score* 193.

10. John Williams, quoted in Derek Elley, "[An Interview with] John Williams," Part II, *Films and Filming* 24, 11 (August 1978): 31.

11. Ibid 32.

12. Ibid.

13. John Williams, quoted in Thomas Maremaa, "The Sound of Movie Music," *New York Times Magazine*, 28 March 1976, 45.

14. Max Steiner, "The Music Director," in *The Real Tinsel*, ed. Bernard Rosenberg and Harry Silverstein (London: Macmillan, 1970), 392; Elley, ["An Interview with] John Williams," Part I, *Films and Filming* 24, 10 (July 1978): 23.

15. Ibid. 24.

16. Ibid. The other three orchestrators are Arthur Morton, Angela Morley, and Al Woodbury.

17. Irvin Kershner, quoted in Alan Arnold, *Once upon a Galaxy: A Journal of the Making of The Empire Strikes Back* (New York: Ballantine Books, Del Rey Books, 1980), 249.

18. Williams, quoted in Tony Thomas, "A Conversation with John Williams," *Cue Sheet: The Journal of the Society for the Preservation of Film Music* 8, 1 (March 1991): 12.

19. Williams, quoted in Arnold, *Once upon a Galaxy* 265.

20. Greg Oatis, "John Williams Strikes Back, Unfortunately," *Cinemafantastique* 10, 2 (Fall 1980): 8.

Conclusion

1. Miklós Rózsa, quoted in *Film Score: The View from the Podium*, ed. Tony Thomas (South Brunswick and New York: A. S. Barnes, 1979), 35.

Any illustrations not credited are from the author's collection.

Page 18: *Vertigo* copyright 1958 Famous Music Corporation; courtesy Bernard Herrmann Archive, University of California at Santa Barbara, and Famous Music Corporation

Pages 42, 54: courtesy Museum of Modern Art

Page 46: courtesy David L. Junchen

Page 52: *Beau Geste* copyright 1926 Paramount Pictures; courtesy UCLA Theatre Arts Library, and Paramount Pictures Corporation

Page 57: *The Black Pirate* copyright 1926 Mortimer Wilson; courtesy Mortimer Wilson Collection, UCLA Music Library, and Mortimer Wilson, Jr.

Page 62: copyright 1927 Sam Fox Publishing Company; courtesy Academy of Motion Picture Arts and Sciences

Page 74: *King Kong* copyright 1933 Bourne Music; courtesy RKO Collection, UCLA Theatre Arts Library

Page 77: *Captain Blood* copyright 1935 Warner Brothers: courtesy USC Cinema-Television Library

Page 89: *Captain Blood* (Erich Wolfgang Korngold) copyright 1935 Warner Brothers, Inc. (Renewed). All rights reserved. Used by permission. Courtesy Warner Brothers Archive, USC Cinema-Television Library, and Warner/ Chappell Music, Inc.

Pages 91, 92, 103: *Captain Blood* copyright 1935 Warner Brothers

Pages 102, 138, 199, 201: courtesy Photofest

Page 110: courtesy Ernst W. Korngold

Page 119: *The Informer* copyright 1935 RKO Radio Pictures

Page 121: *The Informer* copyright 1935 RKO Radio Pictures; courtesy Academy of Motion Picture Arts and Sciences

Page 133: *The Informer* copyright 1935 RKO Radio Pictures; courtesy RKO Collection, UCLA Theatre Arts Library

Pages 147, 154, 156: *The Magnificent Ambersons* copyright 1942 Bourne Music; courtesy Bernard Herrmann Archive, University of California at Santa Barbara

Page 153: *The Magnificent Ambersons* copyright 1942 RKO Radio Pictures; courtesy National Film Archive, London

Pages 164, 165: *Laura* copyright 1944 Twentieth Century-Fox Film Corporation. All rights reserved. Courtesy UCLA Theatre Arts Library, and Twentieth Century-Fox Film Corporation

Pages 180–81: *Laura* copyright 1944 Robbins Music Corporation; courtesy David Raksin

Page 182: copyright 1944 Robbins Music corporation; courtesy UCLA Archive of Popular American Music

Page 196: *The Empire Strikes Back* copyright 1980 Twentieth Century-Fox Film Corporation

BIBLIOGRAPHY

General Works on Music and Music Theory

Adorno, Theodor W. *Introduction to the Sociology of Music*. Trans. E. B. Ashton. New York: Seabury Press, 1976.

Adorno, Theodor W. "On the Fetish-Character in Music and the Regression of Listening." In *The Essential Frankfurt Reader*, ed. Andrew Arato and Eike Gebhardt, 270–99. New York: Continuum, 1982.

Ballantine, Christopher. *Music and Its Social Meanings*. New York: Gordon and Breach Science Publishers, 1984.

Jackendoff, Ray. *Consciousness and the Computational Mind*. Cambridge: MIT Press, 1987.

Jackendoff, Ray, and Fred Lerdahl. "A Grammatical Parallel between Music and Language." In *Music, Mind, and Brain: The Neuropsychology of Music*, ed. Manfred Clynes, 83–117. New York: Plenum Press, 1982.

Leppert, Richard, and Susan McClary, eds. *Music and Society: The Politics of Composition, Performance and Reception*. Cambridge: Cambridge University Press, 1989.

Lerdahl, Fred, and Ray Jackendoff. *A Generative Theory of Tonal Music*. Cambridge: MIT Press, 1983.

Meyer, Leonard B. *Emotion and Meaning in Music*. Chicago: University of Chicago Press, 1956.

Nattiez, Jean-Jacques. *Music and Discourse: Toward a Semiology of Music*. Trans. Carolyn Abbate. Princeton: Princeton University Press, 1991.

Randel, Don Michael, compiler. *Harvard Concise Dictionary of Music*. Cambridge: Harvard University Press, Belknap Press, 1978.

Serafine, Mary Louise. *Music as Cognition*. New York: Columbia University Press, 1988.

Shepherd, John; Phil Virden; Graham Vulliamy; and Trevor Wishart. *Whose Music? A Sociology of Musical Languages*. London: Latimer, 1977. Repr. Transaction, 1980.

Sloboda, John A. *The Musical Mind: The Cognitive Psychology of Music*. Oxford: Clarendon Press, 1985.

233

Film Music Theory

Anzieu, Didier. "L'enveloppe sonore du soi." *Nouvelle revue de psychanalyse* 13 (Spring 1976): 161–79.

Avron, Dominique. "Notes pour introduire une métapsychologie de la musique." *Musique en jeu* 9 (November 1972): 102–10.

Blanchard, Gérard. *Images de la musique de cinéma.* Paris: Edilig, 1984.

Chion, Michel. *Le son au cinéma.* Paris: Cahiers du cinéma/Editions de l'Etoile, 1985.

Doane, Mary Anne. "The Voice in the Cinema: The Articulation of Body and Space." *Yale French Studies* no. 60 (1980): 33–50.

Eisler, Hanns, and Theodor W. Adorno (uncredited). *Composing for the Films.* New York: Oxford University Press, 1947.

Flinn, Carol. "Film Music and Hollywood's Promise of Utopia in Film Noir and the Woman's Film." Ph.D. diss., University of Iowa, 1988.

Flinn, Carol. "The 'Problem' of Femininity in Theories of Film Music." *Screen* 27, 6 (November–December 1986): 56–72.

Gallez, Douglas. "Theories of Film Music." *Cinema Journal* 9, 2 (Spring 1970): 40–47.

Gorbman, Claudia. *Unheard Melodies: Narrative Film Music.* Bloomington: Indiana University Press, 1987.

Hofstein, Francis. "Drogue et musique." *Musique en jeu* 9 (November 1972): 11–15.

Kassabian, Anahid. "Unconscious Workings, Emotional Appeals: Gender, Film Music, and Theory." Paper presented at the annual meeting of the Society for Cinema Studies, Iowa City, 1989.

Kracauer, Siegfried. *Theory of Film: The Redemption of Physical Reality.* New York: Oxford University Press, 1965.

Rosen, Philip. "Adorno and Film Music: Theoretical Notes on *Composing for the Films.*" *Yale French Studies* no. 60 (1980): 157–82.

Rosolato, Guy. "La voix: entre corps et langage." *Revue française de psychanalyse* 38, 1 (January 1974): 75–94.

The Silent Film Score

Ahern, Eugene. *What and How to Play for Pictures.* Twin Falls, Idaho: News Print, 1913.

Anderson, Gillian. "The Presentation of Silent Films, or, Music as Anaesthesia." *Journal of Musicology* 5, 2 (Spring 1987): 257–95. Repr. with additions as "A Warming Flame: The Musical Presentation of Silent Films," in *Music for Silent Films: 1894–1929, A Guide*, xiii–xliv. Washington, DC: Library of Congress, 1988.

Behlmer, Rudy. " 'Tumult, Battle, and Blaze': Looking Back on the 1920s—and Since—with Gaylord Carter, Dean of Theater Organists." In *Film Music I*, ed. Clifford McCarty, 19–59. New York: Garland, 1989.

Berg, Charles Merrell. *An Investigation of the Motives and Realization of Music to Accompany the American Silent Film, 1896–1927*. New York: Arno, 1976.

Beynon, George. *Musical Presentation of Motion Pictures*. New York: Schirmer, 1921.

Dramatic Mirror. 4 (1917)–. "Preparing Programs for Photoplay Accompaniments."

Foorte, Reginald. *The Cinema Organ*. London: Pitman, 1932. Repr. Vestal Press, 1970.

Hamand, Carol. "Sound and Image." *Wide Angle* 6, 2 (1985): 24–33.

Hofmann, Charles. *Sounds for Silents*. New York: Drama Book Specialists, 1970.

Junchen, David L. *Encyclopedia of the American Theatre Organ*. Vol. 1. Pasadena: Showcase Publications, 1985.

Landon, John W. *Behold the Mighty Wurlitzer: The History of the Theatre Pipe Organ*. Westport, CT: Greenwood Press, 1983.

Lang, Edith, and George West. *Musical Accompaniment of Moving Pictures*. Boston: Boston Music, 1920.

London, Kurt. *Film Music: A Summary of the Characteristic Features of Its History, Aesthetics, Techniques, and Possible Developments*. Trans. Eric S. Bensinger. London: Faber and Faber, 1936. Repr. New York: Arno, 1970.

Marks, Martin. "Film Music of the Silent Period, 1895–1924." Ph.D. diss., Harvard University, 1989.

Moving Picture News. 3 (1910)–. Variously titled "The Art of Playing to Pictures," "Picture Music," "The Musician and the Picture."

Moving Picture World. 7 (1910)–. "Music for the Picture."

Rapee, Erno. *Encyclopedia of Music for Pictures*. New York: Belwin, 1925. Repr. Arno, 1970.

Rapee, Erno. *Motion Picture Moods for Pianists and Organists*. New York: Schirmer, 1924. Repr. Arno, 1974.

Shirley, Wayne D. " 'A Bugle Call to Arms for National Defense!': Victor Herbert and His Score for *The Fall of a Nation*." In *Wonderful Inventions: Motion Pictures, Broadcasting, and Recorded Sound at the Library of Congress*, ed. Jon Newsom, 173–85. Washington, DC: Library of Congress, 1985.

Tootell, George. *How to Play the Cinema Organ.* London: Paxton, n.d.

Winkler, Max. *A Penny from Heaven.* New York: Appleton-Century-Crofts, 1951.

The Classical Film Score

Antheil, George. "New Tendencies in Composing for Motion Pictures." In *Film and the Liberal Arts*, ed. T. J. Ross, 238–42. New York: Holt, Rinehart and Winston, 1970.

Bartush, Jay. "*Citizen Kane*: The Music." *Film Reader* 1 (1975): 50–54.

Bazelon, Irwin. *Knowing the Score: Notes on Film Music.* New York: Van Nostrand Reinhold, 1975.

Brown, Royal S. "Herrmann, Hitchcock, and the Music of the Irrational." *Cinema Journal* 21, 2 (Spring 1982): 14–49. Repr. with revisions in *Film Theory and Criticism*, 3d ed., ed. Gerald Mast and Marshall Cohen, 615–49. New York: Oxford University Press, 1985.

Bruce, Graham. *Bernard Herrmann: Film Music and Narrative.* Ann Arbor: UMI Research Press, 1985.

Chell, Samuel L. "Music and Emotion in the Classic Hollywood Film: The Case of *The Best Years of Our Lives.*" *Film Criticism* 8, 2 (Winter 1984): 27–38.

Cue Sheet: The Journal of the Society for the Preservation of Film Music. 1 (January 1984)–.

Darby, William, and Jack Du Bois. *American Film Music: Major Composers, Techniques, Trends, 1915–1990.* Jefferson, NC: McFarland, 1990.

Evans, Mark. *Soundtrack: The Music of the Movies.* New York: Hopkinson and Blake, 1975. Repr. Da Capo, 1979.

Film and TV Music. 1 (October 1941)–. Various titles: *Film Music Notes* 1941–51; *Film Music* 1951–56; *Film and TV Music*, 1956–58.

Filmmusic Notebook. 1–4 (1974–78).

Films: A Quarterly of Discussion and Analysis 1 (Winter 1940). Repr. as *Music in Films: A Symposium of Composers.* New York: Arno, 1968.

Flinn, Carol. "The Most Romantic Art of All: Music in the Classical Hollywood Cinema." *Cinema Journal* 29, 4 (Summer 1990): 35–50.

Friedhofer, Hugo, "Hugo Friedhofer: Arranging and Composing Film Music." Interview by Irene Kahn Atkins, 13 March–19 April 1974, transcript. Louis B. Mayer Oral History Collection, Louis B. Mayer Library, American Film Institute, Los Angeles.

Frith, Simon. "Mood Music: An Inquiry into Narrative Film Music." *Screen* 25, 3 (1984): 78–87.

Gorbman, Claudia. *Unheard Melodies: Narrative Film Music.* Bloomington: Indiana University Press, 1987.

Hagen, Earl. *Scoring for Films.* New York: E. D. J. Music, 1971.

Herrmann, Bernard. "Bernard Herrmann, Composer." In *Sound and the Cinema: The Coming of Sound to American Film*, ed. Evan Cameron, 117–35. Pleasantville, NY: Redgrave, 1980.

Jaubert, Maurice. "Music on the Screen." In *Footnotes to the Film*, ed. Charles Davy, 101–15. New York: Oxford University Press, 1937.

Kalinak, Kathryn. "Musical Stereotyping in Hollywood Films." *Film Reader* 5 (1982): 76–82.

Karlin, Fred, and Rayburn Wright. *On the Track: A Guide to Contemporary Film Scoring.* New York: Schirmer Books, 1990.

Korngold, Erich Wolfgang. "Some Experiences in Film Music." In *Music and Dance in California*, ed. Jose Rodriguez, 137–39. Hollywood: Bureau of Musical Research, 1940.

Larson, Randall. *Musique Fantastique: A Survey of Film Music in the Fantastic Cinema.* Metuchen, NJ: Scarecrow, 1985.

London, Kurt. *Film Music: A Summary of the Characteristic Features of Its History, Aesthetics, Techniques, and Possible Developments.* Trans. Eric S. Bensinger. London: Faber and Faber, 1936. Repr. New York: Arno, 1970.

Mancini, Henry. *Sounds and Scores: A Practical Guide to Professional Orchestration.* Northridge Music, 1967.

Manvell, Roger, and John Huntley. *The Technique of Film Music.* London: Hastings House, 1957.

Newsom, Jon. "David Raksin: A Composer in Hollywood." *Quarterly Journal of the Library of Congress* 35 (1978): 142–72. Repr. in *Wonderful Inventions: Motion Pictures, Broadcasting, and Recorded Sound at the Library of Congress*, ed. Jon Newsom, 117–57. Washington, DC: Library of Congress, 1985.

Palmer, Christopher. *The Composer in Hollywood.* London: Marion Boyers, 1990.

Prendergast, Roy. *Film Music: A Neglected Art.* New York: Norton, 1977.

Raksin, David. "Holding a Nineteenth Century Pedal at Twentieth Century-Fox." In *Film Music I*, ed. Clifford McCarty, 167–81. New York: Garland, 1989.

Raksin, David. Interview with Irene K. Atkins, 6 December 1977–15 February 1978, transcript. Yale Oral History Project, Yale University, New Haven.

Rosar, William. "Music for the Monsters." *Quarterly Journal of the Library of Congress* 40, 4 (Fall 1983): 390–421.

Rosar, William. "Stravinsky and MGM." In *Film Music I*, ed. Clifford McCarty, 109–22. New York: Garland, 1989.

Sabaneev, Leonid. *Music for the Films*. Trans. S. W. Pring. London: Pitman and Sons, 1935. Repr. New York: Arno, 1978.

Skiles, Marlin. *Music Scoring for TV and Motion Pictures*. Blue Ridge Summit, PA: Tab Books, 1976.

Skinner, Frank. *Underscore*. New York: Criterion Music, 1960.

Steiner, Fred. "Herrmann's 'Black and White' Music for Hitchcock's *Psycho*." *Filmmusic Notebook* I, I (Fall 1974): 28–36 (Part I); I, 2 (Winter 1974–75): 26–46 (Part II).

Steiner, Fred. "The Making of an American Film Composer: A Study of Alfred Newman's Music in the First Decade of the Sound Era." Ph.D. diss., University of Southern California, 1981.

Steiner, Fred. "What Were Musicians Saying about Movie Music during the First Decade of Sound? A Symposium of Selected Writings." In *Film Music I*, ed. Clifford McCarty, 81–107. New York: Garland, 1989.

Steiner, Fred, and Martin Marks. "Film Music." In *The New Grove Dictionary of American Music*, ed. H. Wiley Hitchcock and Stanley Sadie, 2:118–25. London: Macmillan, 1986.

Steiner, Max. "The Music Director." In *The Real Tinsel*, ed. Bernard Rosenberg and Harry Silverstein, 387–98. London: Macmillan, 1970.

Steiner, Max. "Scoring the Film." In *We Make the Movies*, ed. Nancy Naumberg, 216–38. New York: Norton, 1937.

Stothart, Herbert. "Film Music." In *Behind the Screen*, ed. Stephen Watts, 139–44. London: Barker, 1939.

Thomas, Tony. *Music for the Movies*. South Brunswick and New York: A. S. Barnes, 1973.

Thomas, Tony, ed. *Film Score: The View from the Podium*. South Brunswick and New York: A. S. Barnes, 1979.

Tiomkin, Dimitri. "Composing for Films." In *Film and the Liberal Arts*, ed. T. J. Ross, 230–36. New York: Holt, Rinehart and Winston, 1970.

Ulrich, Allan. *The Art of Film Music: A Tribute to California's Film Composers*. Oakland: Oakland Art Museum, 1976.

Wescott, Steven D. "Miklós Rózsa's *Ben-Hur*: The Musical-Dramatic Function of the Hollywood *Leitmotiv*." In *Film Music I*, ed. Clifford McCarty, 183–207. New York: Garland, 1989.

Bibliography and General Reference on Film Music

Anderson, Gillian. *Silent Film Music, 1894–1929: A Guide.* Washington, DC: Library of Congress, 1988.

Krummel, D. W., et al. *Resources of American Music History: A Directory of Source Materials from Colonial Times to the Present.* Urbana: University of Illinois Press, 1981.

Limbacher, James L. *Film Music: From Violins to Video.* Metuchen, NJ: Scarecrow Press, 1974.

Limbacher, James L. *Keeping Score: Film Music, 1972–1979.* Metuchen, NJ: Scarecrow Press, 1981.

Marks, Martin. "Film Music: The Material, Literature, and Present State of Research." *Notes* 36, 2 (December 1979): 282–325. Repr. with additions in *Journal of the University Film and Video Association* 34, 1 (Winter 1982): 3–40.

McCarty, Clifford. "Introduction: The Literature of Film Music." In *Film Music I*, ed. Clifford McCarty, ix–xv. New York: Garland, 1989.

McCarty, Clifford. "The Score of the Scores." In Tony Thomas, *Music for the Movies*, 236–64. South Brunswick and New York: A. S. Barnes, 1973.

McCarty, Clifford, ed. *Film Composers in America: A Checklist.* New York: Da Capo, 1972.

Mehr, Linda Harris. *Motion Pictures, Television, and Radio: A Union Catalogue of Manuscript and Special Collections in the Western United States.* Boston: G. K. Hall, 1977.

Wescott, Steven D. *A Comprehensive Bibliography of Music for Films and Television.* Detroit: Detroit Studies in Music Bibliography, 1985.

Wright, H. Stephen. "The Materials of Film Music: Their Nature and Accessibility." In *Film Music I*, ed. Clifford McCarty, 3–17. New York: Garland, 1989.

INDEX

241